KEY IDEAS in ECONOMICS

Rob Dransfield   Don Dransfield

D0415226

Text © Rob Dransfield and Don Dransfield 2003
Original illustrations © Nelson Thornes Ltd 2003

The right of Rob Dransfield and Don Dransfield to be identified as authors of this work
has been asserted by them in accordance with the Copyright, Designs and Patents Act
1988.

All rights reserved. No part of this publication may be reproduced or transmitted in any
form or by any means, electronic or mechanical, including photocopy, recording or
any information storage and retrieval system, without permission in writing from the
publisher or under licence from the Copyright Licensing Agency Limited, of 90
Tottenham Court Road, London W1T 4LP.

Any person who commits any unauthorised act in relation to this publication may be
liable to criminal prosecution and civil claims for damages.

Published in 2003 by:
Nelson Thornes Ltd
Delta Place
27 Bath Road
CHELTENHAM
GL53 7TH
United Kingdom

03 04 05 06 07 / 10 9 8 7 6 5 4 3 2 1

A catalogue record for this book is available from the British Library

ISBN 0 7487 7081 X

Page make-up by Florence Production Ltd

Printed and bound in Spain by GraphyCems

PORTSMOUTH CITY COUNCIL LIBRARY SERVICE	
330	C800081789

PORTSMOUTH
CENTRAL LIBRARY
TEL: 023 9281 9311

Contents

Introduction

A biographical approach to economics

This book examines some of the key ideas of people who have made major contributions to our knowledge and understanding of how the economy functions, and their recommendations about the sorts of decisions that may need to be taken to enable the economy to work 'better'. Most of these individuals have gone beyond the world of ideas to involve themselves in practical actions, for example, by serving as advisors to governments and inter-governmental groups, and taking direct action against powerful interest groups in some cases.

We feel strongly that one of the best approaches to studying economics is to explore the ideas and beliefs of influential thinkers, rather than simply taking a topic by topic approach to the subject. While the main problems of modern capitalism (poverty, environmental degradation, unemployment, and inflation) must be studied as problems, and cannot be wrapped up in the thought of a single personage, it is helpful to identify contrasting systems of thought as represented by the output of significant individual writers.

There are many viewpoints and perspectives about the nature and purpose of economic activity. Studying the contrasting thought systems of key thinkers provides us with an important insight into different ways of viewing economic relationships. Taking a critical view of different value systems and approaches helps us to develop a better understanding of our own values and beliefs and how they are different (or similar) to those of other thinkers.

Biography

The ideas of these key thinkers are examined against a background of a biographical perspective in order to identify how their thinking has been shaped by the societies of which they were a part, including family influences, teachers, cultural background, formative influences, and the conventional wisdom of the period in which they lived as well as key events in the economies in which they grew up. Many of the key ideas of economists are shaped by the prevalent concerns of the time they were brought up in, and the concerns of their contemporaries as well as the conventional wisdom that pervaded thinking at the time. Having reviewed the evidence, it did not surprise us that Adam Smith, the proponent of the free market, should grow up in a society (Britain) and time (eighteenth century) in which the market economy was expanding both at a national and international level, or that Karl Marx, the believer in communist revolution, was writing at a time in which large numbers of people lived in poverty. John Maynard Keynes, who advocated government intervention in the economy to smooth out fluctuations in the market, was writing against a backcloth of a failure of the capitalist system to employ resources adequately in the 1920s and 30s. Harrod and Domar, writing in the 40s and 50s developed theories (of growth) based on turbulence rather than order, a legacy of their experiences of the 30s. Friedrich Hayek's (the Austrian economist) critique of the state and its interference in the economy stemmed from a reaction to the centralisation with which he was all too familiar in the Nazi era.

More recently, writers like David Pearce, Rachael Carson and José Bové, who have been brought up in an era of environmental degradation and the commodification of nature (i.e. the treatment of nature as a commodity that can be bought and sold) have sought to develop new agendas for environmental economics and direct action for the human economy. Amartya Sen witnessed the Bengal famine of the early 1940s, and this helped to shape his thinking about famines and poverty.

Parental influences have played a major part in shaping the thinking of the writers examined here: John Stuart Mill's father instilled in him the principles of utilitarianism; Boulding's parents introduced their son to non-conformist religious values; and Rachael Carson's mother passed on to her daughter a reverence and love for nature. The influence of wives, husbands and other companions has also been of major importance, for example the husband and wife teams of Milton and Rose Friedman (both free marketers and monetarists), Kenneth and Elise Marie Boulding (both pacifist Quakers, and environmentalists).

Teachers have been the other major key influence – Keynes was taught by Alfred Marshall and Arthur Pigou, Amartya Sen by Joan Robinson, Paul Samuelson by Alvin Hansen, and so on. And, of course, the development of ideas was not just a one-way process. Many of the teachers learnt and developed ideas from their pupils; for example, Richard Kahn, one of Keynes' pupils, helped him to develop the multiplier effect that appeared in the General Theory.

Autobiographical notes written by the subjects of this book testify time and time again to the way in which formative experiences (personal circumstances, religious views, the influence of a teacher, and so forth) have shaped their worldview and hence their economics, or as Boulding (1992) puts it: *'Perhaps the most general principle of the universe is that "everything is what it is because it got that way" or, more elegantly, "every structure is the result of past processes".'*

Methodology

Researching this book has involved drawing together a number of sources of evidence to develop a focused picture of the relationship between personal biography and economic thought.

Sources of evidence used include:

1. Personal interview
2. E-mail and telephone interview
3. Use of autobiographical sources
4. Use of biographical sources
5. Use of published writing by authors in which they have set out their key ideas
6. Use of secondary sources based on authors' ideas, e.g. general texts.

Methods 1 and 2 have been used with a number of writers still living. Methods 3–6 have been used with all writers. It is hoped that by a process of 'triangulation' (throwing light on an idea by examining it from a number of angles) of these various sources of evidence that we have been able to establish clear links between biography and economic thought.

Acknowledgements

We would like to thank the library staff at Nottingham Trent University and Trinity College Cambridge for helping to provide research materials. Brian Yeomans for helping with the research for Keynes, and Malcolm Plant for sharing some of his concerns for the environment. Also Pete Lloyd for some of his important critical comments relating to the field of development economics. We would also like to thank Jane Cotter and Clare Wheelwright of Nelson Thornes for their brilliant support.

This work arose from a discussion on what we felt were the key areas for young economists to study. In particular, it focuses on pressing areas of social and economic concern. In our view, learning about economics comes as much from talking to people who work hard to earn a living in often harsh conditions, as it does from rigorous academic study. We would therefore like to thank our mentors in this endeavour: Claire, Elspeth, Colin, Ken and Jean Dransfield, Daniel and Louisa Martins, Bernard Ladet and Hubert Panafieu, as well as some of our excellent teachers.

In addition, we would particularly like to thank Shaun Best for contributing the chapters on Karl Marx, Margaret Thatcher and Anthony Giddens. We greatly value Shaun's enthusiasm for new ideas.

Photos courtesy of:

Bettmann/Corbis (p.61, p.122, p.165)

Corel 654 (NT) (p.143)

Corel 725 (NT) (p.27)

Duke University, North Carolina (p.156)

Hulton-Deutsch Collection/Corbis (p.80)

Hulton Getty (p.53)

Isopress Senepart/REX Features (p.214)

Karl Schoendorfer/REX Features (p.196)

Kings College Cambridge (p.88)

London School of Economics (p.205)

National Portrait Gallery, London (p.1)

National Portrait Gallery, London (p.11)

National Portrait Gallery, London (p.18)

National Portrait Gallery, London (p.67)

Nubar Alexanian/Corbis (p.104)

Roger Ressmeyer/Corbis (p.131)

Thoemmes Press, Bristol (p.41)

Universal Pictorial Press (p.115)

University College of London (p.183)

Washington University, St. Louis (p.174)

Rob Dransfield lectures in Business and Economics at The Nottingham Trent University. Don Dransfield is studying Economics at Trinity College Cambridge. Shaun Best lectures in Politics and Sociology at Manchester University.

Adam Smith
(1723–1790)

A STUDY OF THE IDEAS OF ADAM SMITH, THE FOUNDING FATHER OF ECONOMICS, IS essential reading for anyone wishing to gain a good picture of the development of economics. Although approaches to studying economics have changed enormously since Smith's day, the range of concerns remains broadly the same.

Smith was a firm believer in making writing accessible to the reader and that intellectual pursuit should be bounded by 'common sense'. Smith's disdain for intellectual posturing is nicely captured in his criticism of another writer of the time when he states that *'it is plain this author had it greatly in view to go out of the common road in his writings and to dignify his stile by never using common phrases or even names for things, and we see hardly an expression in his works but what would appear absurd in common conversation'*.

Most (if not all) of the important ideas that have shaped future thinking are the product of the age in which they are written. 'New' ideas stem from the biographical experience of the thinkers that 'create' and 'develop' these ideas.

The American sociologist Max Lerner described Smith's work as *'the outpouring not only of a great mind, but of a whole epoch'*.

Smith was writing at a time when industrialisation was beginning to take hold in Britain, when the international economy was becoming increasingly important, and when privileged individuals like Smith were able to benefit from the advantages of foreign travel, extensive reading and exposure to new ideas and ways of thinking within Europe.

Smith was able to write his most celebrated book *An Inquiry into the Nature and Cause of the Wealth of Nations* because he had had the opportunity to read about, observe and discuss the things that he was writing about – for example, 'the operation of paper money', 'produce of land and labour, the source of all revenue', 'the different returns of home and foreign trade', 'roads, good, the public advantage of', 'pinmaking, the extraordinary advantage of a division of labour in this art', etc.

Smith was fortunate in that he came into personal contact with other great thinkers including fellow Scots Francis Hutcheson and David Hume, and leading French thinkers including Voltaire and Diderot.

Smith is most widely known for his support for free markets, which he believed to be a central part of the natural order of things.

Methodology

THE METHODOLOGY SMITH USED FOR HIS STUDY OF ECONOMIC SOCIETY WAS TO DRAW on a range of available evidence – information from books, precise observation and widespread experience, to carry out his investigations and to draw out broad conclusions which are of relevance in understanding relationships in economic society. Smith drew widely on both historical evidence (based on his wide research and conversations with others) and acute observation and study of changes that were taking place in early industrial Britain.

Biography

ADAM SMITH WAS A SCOTSMAN WHOSE IDEAS WERE FIRMLY ROOTED IN THE excitement of the Scottish Enlightenment, a period of intense intellectual discussion and open-minded thinking about real issues. He was born in the small fishing village of Kirkcaldy in 1723 to a family of considerable means for the time. Smith's father had been a Judge Advocate and Comptroller of Customs at Kirkcaldy, and his mother came from a land-owning family. However, his father died a few months before Adam was born and thus he was brought up in a single parent family. Studies have shown that a significant number of geniuses have been brought up in similar circumstances. Smith was to benefit enormously from the attention and support provided by his mother which enabled him to enjoy the most privileged education available. His mother continually championed his cause enabling his ideas to become well known.

At the age of 14 Smith was privileged to attend Glasgow University, which although it was only little more than a secondary school possessed some very fine teachers in a city that was undergoing an intellectual revolution.

In particular, Smith was influenced at this time by one of his teachers, the philosopher Francis Hutcheson, whose ideas were to underpin Smith's moral philosophy.

Hutcheson believed that we are all born with an inner moral sense (similar to our other senses, e.g. touch, sight, hearing etc.). This moral sense restrains us from purely indulging in self-gratification. Hutcheson believed that this natural order is superior to any artificially created order resulting from man. Social organisation, if it is to be successful therefore, should seek to be as close as possible to the natural order of things. Hutcheson coined the phrase 'the greatest happiness of the greatest number' which was to become the guiding principle for utilitarianism (see page 19).

In 1740 Smith won a scholarship to Balliol College, Oxford. However, he was to be disappointed by the teaching in Oxford where Smith reported 'the professors have, for these many years, given up altogether even the pretense of teaching'. He was also to encounter a vein of 'anti-Scotch' prejudice, on the part of fellow students and the college authorities. These sentiments resulted in some measure from a dislike of the Jacobites, the supporters of the exiled branch of the house of Stuart who wished to restore James II and his descendants to the throne. In 1745 they advanced as far as Derby under the command of Bonnie Prince Charlie. It was at this time that the National Anthem was written and performed. At the time it contained the infamous fifth verse:

Lord grant that Marshal Wade,
May be the mighty aid,
Victory bring.
May he sedition hush,
And like a torrent rush,
Rebellious Scots to crush,
God save the King.

(Marshall Wade was one of the senior officers in the English army sent from London to meet the Scottish advance.)

At Oxford, Smith was able to take advantage of the extensive library facilities available to educate himself. Anti-Scottish prejudice only served to make him more determined and to take an interest in a range of non-standard ideas. At one stage he was almost expelled for reading David Hume's *Treatise on Human Nature*.

Hume (a fellow Scot) was a key influence on the ideas of Smith and the two corresponded for many years. At the heart of Hume's ideas was the belief that 'all true knowledge comes from experience'. This is why Smith was to rely so much on personal observation and experience in formulating his ideas and his works.

Hume took the empirical view that ideas and theories should be based on observation and experiment, that is, a scientific approach.

In addition, Smith's ideas were firmly rooted in the Scottish tradition of 'common sense'. The notion of 'common sense' was central to Scottish philosophy giving priority to practical reason over theoretical reason. The Scottish method set out to provide a wide ranging and balanced critical picture of social reality through investigating actual facts and events and exploring social institutions within a historical context.

Sheila Dow (1987) has described this tradition in the following way: '*Political econo-mists . . . start with policy issues rather than theoretical curiosa, they consider the histor-ical background to these issues, they study institutional arrangements and they study the history of economic thought in order both to understand theory and to adapt it for appli-cation to particular contexts.*'

To Smith, common sense is a fundamental inheritance of all mankind, being closely connected by 'the reality of which we have daily experience'. As a result it makes no sense to try and enforce ideas or social institutions on people which do not fit with their common sense understanding.

During his time at Oxford he suffered from poor health complaining to his mother in letters of '*an inveterate scurvy and shaking in the head*'. This 'shaking in the head' was to burden Smith for the remainder of his life.

In 1746 he returned to Scotland, to seek work. His mother arranged for him to give a series of public lectures at Edinburgh. His lectures were wide ranging, covering the broad fields that interested Smith – philosophy, politics and the law. Smith was a great believer in the inter-related nature of knowledge and enjoyed weaving together the threads of seemingly different subjects. At 27 he was appointed professor of logic at Glasgow University and later professor of moral philosophy. Like many academics Smith had a reputation for absent-mindedness. He was an extremely hard worker often rising early to give a lecture at 7.30 in the morning and spending his afternoon in study. His thirst for knowledge was fired by a passionate belief that progress and enlightenment involved seeking to understand how society worked and that we have a moral duty to seek this understanding. He believed that this understanding rested in studying reality – real events, real relationships etc. give an understanding of society and philosophy.

Key works

Adam Smith produced two key works:

Theory of Moral Sentiments (1759)

An Enquiry into the Nature and Cause of the Wealth of Nations (1776).

Key Ideas

SMITH'S FIRST WORK, *THEORY OF MORAL SENTIMENTS* (1759) WAS AN EXAMINATION OF individual human nature and is primarily concerned with seeking the answers to two questions: (1) *'wherein does virtue consist?'*; (2) *'by what means does it come to pass, that the mind prefers one tenour of conduct to another?'*.

The way that Smith tackled these questions was to argue that within each individual there is an 'inner man' who acts as an 'impartial spectator' to all our actions. Smith's 'inner man' is similar to what Freud was to later refer to as the 'superego', that is, an inner conscience or guilt feelings which censures individuals and often stops them from resorting to their baser impulses.

Smith identified six key motivations which drive human actions. These are self-love, sympathy for others, the desire to be free, a sense of propriety, a habit of labour, and the desire to exchange one thing for another. Everyone is a judge of their own self-interest so they will weigh up the relative merits of these sometimes competing motivations. Allowing individuals to choose between these motivations leads to the greatest individual benefit as well as to the greatest common good.

Just because individuals are pursuing their own interest doesn't mean that they are riding roughshod over others. Sympathy for others is an important natural motive which helps to drive society towards the greater good. It was at this point that Smith introduced one of the ideas which is widely regarded to be important in underpinning his thinking – that an individual in pursuing self-interest is *'led by an invisible hand to promote an end which was no part of his intention'*.

Smith (1759) shows that individual selfishness and greed, in spite of its focus on the individual benefits the whole society: *'the proud and unfeeling landlord views his extensive fields, and without a thought for the wants of his brethren, in imagination consumes himself the whole harvest that grows upon them . . . The capacity of his stomach bears no proportion to the immensity of his desires, and will receive no more than that of the meanest peasant. The rest he is obliged to distribute among those who prepare, in the nicest manner, that little which he himself makes use of . . . the rich only select from the heap what is most precious and agreeable. They consume little more than the poor, and in spite of their natural selfishness and rapacity, though they mean only their own conveniency, though the sole end they propose from the labours of all the thousands whom they employ, be the gratification of their own vain and insatiable desires, they divide with the poor the produce of all their improvements. They are led by an invisible hand to make nearly the same distribution of the necessaries of life, which would have been made, had the earth been divided into equal portions among all its inhabitants, and thus without intending it, without knowing it, advance the interests of society.'*

This notion underpins Smith's belief in what the French refer to as *laissez-faire* – that is, leaving society to find its own natural order. Smith argued that man's interference with this natural order will have a negative impact: *'I have never known much good done by those who affected to trade for the public good'*. Smith's assertion that government can rarely be more effective than when it stays out of things was to become a central pillar of what is referred to as 'classical economic theory'. He believed that government intervention is generally harmful because it interferes with natural law which, as we have seen, leads to the common good.

Theory of Moral Sentiments was an overnight bestseller. It was read by Charles Townshend who was to become Chancellor of the Exchequer. Townshend asked Smith to become the tutor of his stepson, the young Duke of Buccleuth, and to travel in Europe with his charge for what in those days was a princely sum of £300 per year, followed by a pension of £300 a year for life. These were exceptionally good terms and Smith leapt at the opportunity.

Smith was thus able to travel and meet many of the eminent European thinkers of the time associated with the Enlightenment. In particular, he was able to share ideas with Voltaire, and some of the emerging group of economic thinkers in France, including Quesnay whose *droit naturel* (natural law) was closely akin to ideas that Smith was developing.

Of equal importance was Smith's meetings with the scientist d'Alembert and the philosopher Diderot who were responsible for the *Encyclopedie*, a publication designed to bring together all of the branches of knowledge. This approach struck a chord with Smith who, in his lectures at Edinburgh and Glasgow, had sought to weave together the threads of vast fields of human knowledge.

Smith started to write his new book, which was to be his major work during this period, and the extensive references to French ideas which appear in the book is a testimony to how much this experience influenced his thinking.

In 1776 the Duke of Buccleuth's younger brother caught a fever and died in Paris while under the charge of Smith and he hurriedly returned across the Channel.

52

So, at 42 Smith returned to Kirkcaldy to live off his pension and the returns from *An Inquiry into the Nature and Cause of the Wealth of Nations*, which was published in 1776, just before the Declaration of American Independence.

An Inquiry into the Nature and Cause of the Wealth of Nations

Smith's most famous work was wide ranging, drawing on evidence from Smith's studies of history, society and the development of industrialisation in Britain. The title of the work represents Smith's concern with one of the key economic questions – that is, what factors lead to the growth and development of economic systems? Smith used the term 'political economy' to mean the inquiry into 'the nature and causes of the wealth of nations'.

Wealth of nations/economic growth

Drawing on the evidence that he had researched Smith arrived at the following explanation. Wealth is production – what we today refer to as national product (GNP). Smith examined the reasons why national product is large or small, and whether it is growing, as well as the causes of growth. He concluded that national product/wealth is large when large numbers of factors of production (labour, land, capital and enterprise) are employed, and where these factors are used with high efficiency. This involves using more efficient labour and capital in the production process. Because he was writing at a time in which production was increasingly taking place in factories he was able to draw on evidence based on current examples to show how changes in production could lead to improvements in the wealth of nations.

Productivity

Productivity is the relationship between the quantity and quality of inputs that go into the production process and the quantity of output that they produce. Smith explained that wealth is increased by '*the skill, dexterity, and judgement with which labour is applied in any nation*' and also by '*the proportion of those who are employed in useful labour, and that of those who are not so employed*', that is, economic growth is promoted by economic productivity.

Division of labour

The division of labour involves separating the work carried out by labour into separate specialist tasks and activities. Smith (1776) used the classic example of division of labour in a pin factory to show how division of labour increases productive efficiency: '*To take an example from a very trifling manufacture . . . the trade of pinmaker. An inexperienced workman, unfamiliar with this business, could scarce, with his utmost effort make one pin in an entire day. But in the way in which this business is now organized, not only is the whole work in a particular trade, but it is divided into a number of individual branches, each of which can be considered as a particular trade of its own. One man draws out the wire, another straightens it, a third cuts it, a fourth points it, a fifth grinds it at the top in preparation for the head; to make the head requires two or three distinct operations; to put it on is a peculiar business; to whiten the pins is another; it is even a trade by itself to put them into the paper; and the important business of making a pin is, in this manner divided into about eighteen distinct operations, which in some manufactories, are all undertaken by separate people.'* (It is likely that in setting out this example Smith was drawing on his French studies – an article about the division of labour in pinmaking having been printed in the *Encyclopedie* in 1755).

Having given a clear and graphic example of the advantages of specialisation in the use of factors of production Smith went on to generalise (although he recognised that pinmaking provided an 'ideal example': *'In every other art and manufacture, the effects of the division of labour are similar to what they are in this very trifling one; though, in many of them, the labour can neither be so so much subdivided, nor reduced to so great a simplicity of operation.'*

Extent of the market and the division of labour

Smith (1776) explained that the division of labour, or any form of specialisation depended on the extent of the market. If the market is small, there is little scope for specialisation so that, for example, in a rural area like the Highlands of Scotland *'every farmer must be butcher, baker and brewer for his own family. In such situations we can scarce expect to find even a smith, a carpenter, or a mason, within less than twenty miles of another of the same trade.'* The larger the market the greater the scope for speciali-sation, so that, for example, in the Britain of Smith's day *'the woolen coat . . . which covers the day labourer is the joint produce of a great multitude of workmen. The shepherd, the sorter of the wool, the wool-comber or carder, the dryer, the scribbler, the spinner, the weaver, the fuller, the dresser, with many others, must all join their different arts in order to complete even this homely production.'*

Economic development

Smith (1776) went on to show that the development of human societies had progressed through a number of stages of economic development, each involving increasing sophistication of economic relations.

The first stage is the *'lowest and rudest such as we find it among the native tribes of North America; and in England before the invasion of Julius Caesar'*. Here societies consisted of small tribal groups where *'every man is a warrior as well as a hunter'*. In this state of development *'there is scarce any property, which means disputes are rare . . . and this encourages self reliance and personal liberty'*.

Smith's second stage consisted of *'nations of shepherds . . . such as we find among the Tartars and Arabs'*. These people were nomadic moving on from one place to another. Sometimes the effect was terrifying as when nomadic hordes such as those of Genghis Khan were on the move. Smith wrote that *'Nothing can be more dreadful than a tartar invasion'*. However, these nomadic societies introduced the notion of private property. In effect the law worked in favour of the strong – the rich and powerful to protect their property. Smith describes this in the following way: *'Civil government, so far as it is instituted for the security of property, is in reality instituted for the defence of the rich against the poor, or of those who have some property against those who have none at all.'*

The third stage was that of the settled agricultural society typified by Greece, Rome feudalism in Britain and France. Feudal society was based on settled farmers supplying produce and paying taxes to a central state based in the cities. In order to make this society work it was necessary to have large armies to secure the peace.

The market economy and self-interest

The final stage was that of the market place, with which Smith was familiar from his everyday experience. For Smith the driving force behind historical change was human nature, which is motivated by self-interest.

In the final stage of development the market becomes the controlling force in society. In describing how this society worked Smith (1776) drew on the idea of the 'invisible hand' first mentioned in *Theory of Moral Sentiments*. Although individuals seek their own personal ends this leads to the greatest wellbeing of everyone.

'. . . *It is not from the benevolence of the butcher, the brewer, or the baker, that we expect our dinner, but from their regard to their own self-interest. We address ourselves, not to their humanity but to their self-love.*'

'. . . *As every individual, therefore, endeavours as much as he can both to employ his capital in the support of domestick industry, and so to direct that industry . . . in such a manner as its produce may be of the greatest value, he intends only his own gain, and he is in this, as in many other cases, led by an invisible hand to promote an end which was no part of his intentional.*'

Self-interest is '*a desire that comes with us from the womb, and never leaves us until we go into the grave*'.

'The great society'/market economy

Smith believed that the market economy was a product of the natural order of things. In this market place prices acted as signals guiding human endeavour. High prices would encourage more enterprise and other factors to be channelled into a particular line of activity. Price signals served the enormous field of the 'great society' that 'no human wisdom and knowledge could ever be sufficient' to survey. In this statement Smith was effectively placing the powers of the market to order human society above individual endeavours.

Role of government

However, it would be a mistake to assume that Smith believed that the government should have nothing to do with economic affairs. In particular, Smith argued that the government should ensure that the market worked smoothly.

He noted that '*People of the same trade seldom meet together, even for merriment and diversion, but the conversation ends in a conspiracy against the public, or in some contrivance to raise prices*' (Smith 1776). Hence the need for the government to stop such conspiracies from harming the market system. In addition, Smith argued that the building and maintenance of public institutions and public works was a function of the state surpassed in importance only by the provision for the common defence and administration of justice. The government thus had a role at the heart of society, although not as a meddler in economic affairs.

The importance of free trade

Adam Smith's support of free trade was a natural extension of his belief in the free market. Smith saw that in the same way that it is wasteful for individuals to use up resources in doing those things that they are not particularly good at, it was pointless for nations to waste effort on things that could be bought cheaply from elsewhere. *'It is the maxim of every prudent master of a family, never to attempt to make at home what it will cost him more to make than to buy . . . What is prudence in the conduct of every private family, can scarce be folly in that of a great kingdom'*. Smith therefore became a champion of free trade based on his 'common sense' observation.

Indeed, a major part of his work is an attack on mercantilism – the notion that a strong protective state would lead to a wealthy nation. Smith was particularly opposed to the notion that protection of a country's domestic industries through import taxes was beneficial to a nation. In contrast, Smith argued that the preservation of competition in all areas was the responsibility of the state. This view helps in part to explain Smith's popularity because in his support of liberalisation he spoke with the voice of traders and industrialists who were anxious to sweep away all restrictions on the market and on the supply of labour. Previously earning a living through commerce and trade had been looked down on by the land-owning gentry. The new commercial classes of the towns sought to dispel this idea and thus Smith became their champion.

Use value and exchange value

Another area of discussion on which Smith was able to throw some light was that of the nature of 'value'. Although Smith did not fully understand the nature of value he was able to draw out an important contradiction between the use value of an item and the exchange value. He explained how diamonds, *'the greatest of superfluities'*, had scarcely any value in use but could be exchanged for a huge amount, whereas water which is one of the most valuable commodities in use has very little exchange value. It was left to later economists to be able to more effectively explain the nature of value.

Conclusion

Smith's work in the field of developing economics in this country was without equal. Later economists have made major contributions but it was Smith who established the field of study. Clearly, many of his ideas were derived from other thinkers, but the greatness in Smith's contribution was in his ability to pull together these ideas and to create a coherent approach to studying the economy. He will always be associated with the early development of a market ideology based on conceptions of natural law. However, it is important to remember that Smith attributed to human beings a range of motivations including that of 'sympathy for others' so that the Smithian economic actor is not solely concerned with self-interest. Smith believed in the fallibility of human beings and the inability of human institutions to provide better solutions than those that could be achieved by the natural co-ordinating force of the market place. Every British economist who has followed has owed a debt to Smith, and the 'common sense' empirical basis of his approach has had many followers.

Further Reading

BARTLEY, W.W. (1991) (ed.) *The trend of economic thinking: essays on politics, economics and economic history. (The collected works of F.A. Hayek, Vol 3)*.

COMIM, F. (2002) The Scottish tradition in economics and the role of common sense in Adam Smith's thought. *Review of Political Economy* 14(1), 91–114.

DOW, S.C. (1987) The Scottish political economy tradition. *Scottish Journal of Political Economy* 34, 335–348.

GALBRAITH, J.K. (1976) *Economics, peace and laughter*. Penguin Books, ch. 9.

ROLL, E. (1992) *A history of economic thought*. Faber & Faber, (fifth edition), ch. 4.

ROSS, I.S. (1995) *The life of Adam Smith*. Oxford University Press.

ROTHSCHILD, E. (2001) *Economic sentiments: Adam Smith, condorcet and the enlightenment*. Harvard University Press.

SMITH, A. (1975) An enquiry into the nature and cause of the wealth of nations. *Works and correspondence of Adam Smith*. Oxford University Press.

SMITH, A. (1984) Theory of moral sentiments. *Works and correspondence of Adam Smith*. Glasgow, Liberty Fund.

SMITH, A. (1994 edition) *An enquiry into the nature and cause of the wealth of nations*. Random House.

STRATHERN, P. (2001) *Dr Strangelove's game: a brief history of economic genius*. Hamish Hamilton, ch. 4.

David Ricardo

(1772–1823)

DAVID RICARDO WAS THE SECOND MAJOR FIGURE IN CLASSICAL ECONOMICS. HIS interest in writing about economics stemmed from reading Smith's *Wealth of Nations* while visiting Bath for the sake of his wife's health. Ricardo was 27 at the time. He was greatly interested in what Smith had to say and realised that based on his own experience and thinking he could add new ideas to the developing field of political economy. It is interesting to note that Ricardo's first words in his major work on political economy are *'It has been observed by Adam Smith'*.

Ricardo's major contributions to the development of economics are the product of his experience of working in the City of London which was at the heart of the world trading and financial systems, and from operating in the market for land as a buyer and seller of substantial estates. Ricardo developed an unparalleled understanding of the way in which the economy of his day functioned. As a theorist he was then able to make deductions about key economic relationships. Whereas Smith's work was largely based on the gathering of observations and evidence, Ricardo's approach was to develop theories based on sets of defining premises.

Methodology

RICARDO DEVELOPED A THEORETICAL APPROACH TO BUILDING UP NEW IDEAS, WHICH may have been based on his interest in scientific method. His approach involved making a number of limiting assumptions and then seeking to reason out a conclusion based on these assumptions. This approach is today known as 'model building' and is a method which requires extreme caution to avoid jumping to false conclusions. Indeed Joseph Schumpeter refers to this tendency as the 'Ricardian vice' (the 'Ricardian vice' rests in taking hypothetical premises, deducing conclusions from these premises, and making no attempt to verify the results). However, this approach proved to be influential and is still widely used today.

Biography

DAVID RICARDO WAS THE SON OF A STOCK EXCHANGE DEALER, ABRAHAM ISRAEL Ricardo. Abraham was from a Portuguese Jewish family that had settled in the Netherlands. While visiting London on business Abraham was so captivated by the feel of the place that he decided to move there.

David Ricardo was born into a large Jewish family that placed a strong emphasis on education and learning. When he was young he was sent to Holland, not only to learn business, but also that he might be placed at a school of which his father entertained a very high opinion. This school was the Talmud Tora school which was attached to the Portuguese Synagogue. The curriculum included the Bible and the Talmud, as well as Hebrew literature and rhetoric. Although David Ricardo only spent a few years studying in Holland he developed a thirst for knowledge and learning which was to stay with him throughout his life.

Returning to London he started to work alongside his father at the Stock Exchange from the age of 14. At that time only a dozen 'Jew brokers' were allowed to trade in the Exchange, and were restricted to a part of the floor known as 'Jews' Walk'.

It seems likely that during his life Ricardo experienced a certain amount of prejudice against him because he was Jewish – alluded to in a memoir of him written by his brother which recorded that '*as has been more than insinuated that Mr. Ricardo was of very low origin, and that he had been wholly denied the advantages of education; a reflection upon his father which he by no means deserved*'. Like Adam Smith before him, Ricardo had to prove himself against this inherent racial prejudice which was later to be reflected in an address by the English economist Alfred Marshall who described Ricardo as that 'masterful genius', though adding that he '*was not an Englishman . . . the faults and virtues of Ricardo's mind are traceable to his Semitic origin, no English economist has had a mind similar to his*'.

The Ricardos were well respected in the City of London, which was a clear requirement for individuals whose work is based on honour, trust and integrity – the famous motto of the Stock Exchange being 'My word is my bond'.

While it is clear that his father was a great influence in his early formation it is also evident that Ricardo developed an independent streak in opposition to his father's conformity.

In a *Memoir of David Ricardo*, his brother Moses wrote that '*His father was a man of good intellect, but uncultivated. His prejudices were exceedingly strong; and they induced him to take the opinions of his forefathers in points of religion, politics, education . . . upon faith, and without investigation . . . When young, Mr Ricardo showed a taste for abstract and general reasoning; and though he was without any inducement to its culti-vation, or rather lay under positive discouragement, yet at the age of nineteen and twenty, works of that description which occasionally occupied his attention afforded him amuse-ment and cause for reflection*' (Ricardo 1824).

At 21 David Ricardo had a major fall out with his family when he fell in love with a girl from a Quaker family. His mother would not accept the marriage, so he was forced to leave home and to leave his father's business. It seems likely that the Ricardo attachment to the Jewish faith was only lukewarm so his marriage to Priscilla Wilkinson was simply an extension of his growing independence.

David Ricardo seems to have weathered the storm of the rift from his family remarkably well and was quickly able to establish himself in business on his own account, being able to borrow £800 from friends to set up trading on his own account. This was a considerable sum of money, as in those days £1000 was enough to buy a country estate.

Ricardo's understanding of how the economy worked was based on his interest in theory which he developed at an early age, coupled with his extensive experience of working on the Stock Exchange, and later as a buyer and seller of land and estates. Ricardo spent most of his life working in the City of London which helped him to develop a clear understanding or money, banking, finance, trade, and other key ingredients of the economy.

His brother Moses was to write of Ricardo in a short memoir that *'The talent for obtaining wealth is not held in much estimation, but perhaps in nothing did Mr. Ricardo more evince his extraordinary powers than he did in his business. His complete knowledge of all its intricacies; his surprising quickness at figures and calculation; his capability of getting through without any apparent exertion, the immense transaction in which he was concerned; his coolness and judgment, combined certainly with (for him) a fortunate tissue of public events, enabled him to leave all his contemporaries at the Stock Exchange far behind, and to raise himself infinitely higher not only in fortune, but in general character and estimation, than any man had ever done before in that house.'*

Ricardo played a major part as a contractor for government loans during the Napoleonic War helping the government to raise funds to finance the war. At the time contractors competed to make loans to the government on an annual basis. Ricardo and his syndicate of fellow contractors, Barnes and Steers, won the contract in 1807, and later from 1811 to 1815. While Ricardo was only able to make relatively modest profits from these government loans in the early years he made a massive profit in 1815 on the news of British victory, with the premium reaching 13 per cent on 27 June 1815. At the highest premium Ricardo wrote *'I have all my money invested in Stock, and this is as great an advantage as ever I expect or wish to make by a rise'*. It is possible that at this period he might have doubled his money within a fortnight. In a letter to Malthus he wrote *'Perhaps no loan was ever more generally profitable to the Stock Exchange'*. Ricardo was able to use this profit to retire from business.

A key influence on the ideas of Ricardo was his intellectual sparring partner Thomas Malthus. The two regularly corresponded and disagreed on a great many issues. However, Ricardo valued Malthus highly and left him a substantial bequest in his will when he died.

Thomas Malthus is best known for his *Essay on the principle of population as it affects the future improvement of society* (1798). According to Malthus, given the *'passion between the sexes'*, the need for food, the fact that population increases when the means of subsistence increases, and the declining yield of the soil, a point must be reached when the increase of population overtakes the increase in the supply of food.

Malthus acquired for economics the term 'the dismal science' because his predictions were so pessimistic. He argued that because food supplies would only increase in an arithmetic way, while population would increase at a geometric rate this would lead to disasters such as war, famine and disease. Malthus's ideas were based on his observations of increases in population at the time coupled with what he saw as logical reasoning based on, for example, his reading of Adam Smith's notion of diminishing returns to factors of production. In recent years we have seen neo-Malthusian thinkers arguing that our planet is very close to the limits to growth resulting from using resources up too quickly. In contrast, Ricardo provides a more optimistic view of the use of scarce resources.

In his later years Ricardo transferred his profits from the Stock Exchange to the purchase of extensive estates, and at one time was the proud owner of Gatcomb Park. Ricardo realised the value of holding and improving land. He saw that the progressive improvement of valuable estates enabled the owner to be able to demand increasing levels of rent from the tenant.

Ricardo was socially active in economic and political circles, and in 1819 he became a Member of Parliament. His parliamentary influence on economic affairs was considerable. In 1822 he toured the continent, recording his impressions in a Journal, and his sudden death at Gatcomb from an ear infection in 1823 cut short a brilliant career.

Key works

The High Price of Bullion (1810)

The Principles of Political Economy and Taxation (1817)

Key Ideas

IN 1809 RICARDO WROTE A LETTER TO THE *MORNING CHRONICLE* SETTING OUT HIS ideas as to why bank notes had been falling in value. He then worked these ideas into a pamphlet entitled *The High Price of Bullion, a Proof of the Depreciation of Bank Notes*.

From 1797 bank notes in this country were no longer convertible into gold, putting an end to the promise that still exists on notes today: 'I promise to pay the bearer the sum of.' Once this connection between gold and bank notes was removed there was a real danger of the monetary authorities printing too much money. If the monetary authorities increased the number of notes in circulation this would lead to price rises and hence to a fall in the value of the pound. Ricardo's letter set out to make this connection at a time when the Bank of England were stating that the connection did not exist. Ricardo argued that printing too much money was having a negative effect on the foreign exchange rate.

Of course, Ricardo was not arguing that the economy should return to gold coins as a means of exchange rather than paper money. Rather he argued the case for combining the advantage of a paper currency with the security of money based on gold. He argued that paper money is useful because the amount of it in circulation can be altered in accordance with the volume of commerce and trade. Ricardo argued that should the value of money decrease there will be an increase in demand for redemption of money into gold at an agreed rate, thus taking money out of circulation and raising its value. This pamphlet was written primarily for other political economists.

Ricardo's major work was entitled *Principles of Political Economy and Taxation*. This book elaborated on the work of Smith and added a number of new insights, most notable of which were Ricardo's account of the law of comparative advantage as the basis for trade, his theory of economic rent, and his account of relative scarcity as an alternative to Malthus's gloomy predictions.

The law of comparative advantage

Ricardo's explanation of the law of comparative advantage outlines the modern theory of international trade. He showed that trading between countries enables them both to be better off provided exchange takes place at mutually beneficial rates. In simple terms Ricardo (1817) showed that if by the purchase of English goods to the amount of £1000, a merchant can obtain a quantity of foreign goods, which he can sell in the English market for £1200, he will obtain 20 per cent profit by such an employment of his capital.

'*Under a system of perfectly free commerce, each country naturally devotes its capital and labour to such employments as are most beneficial to each . . . It is this principle which determines that wine shall be made in France and Portugal, that corn shall be grown in America and Poland, and that hardware and other goods shall be manufactured in England.*'

'*If Portugal had no commercial connexion with other countries, instead of employing a great part of her capital and industry in the production of wines, with which she purchases for her own use the cloth and hardware of other countries, she would be obliged to devote a part of that capital to the manufacture of those commodities, which she would thus obtain probably inferior in quality as well as quantity.*'

In providing this example of how Portugal would benefit from concentrating on what it did best (i.e. those things in which it had the greatest comparative advantage), Ricardo was essentially drawing on a deductive method of reasoning. Ricardo's illustrations are generally hypothetical whereas for Smith they were historical. However, it is clear that many of Ricardo's ideas were strongly based on his own experience of his world.

Today, the law of comparative advantage is used to justify international specialisation. Rich countries which are well endowed with resources concentrate on their best lines, and less well-endowed nations make their way in the trading world by concentrating on their best or least worst lines.

Economic rent

Ricardo (1817) set out to explain how the wealth of a nation should be shared out. He stated that '*there are three classes in the community . . . and the purpose of political economy is to determine the laws which regulate this distribution is the principal problem* in *Political Economy*'. He therefore set out to explain the distribution of income between rent, profit and wages.

In terms of the focus of interest for political economy he argued that rather than the study of creation of wealth '*it should rather be called an inquiry into the laws which determine the division of the produce of industry amongst the classes who concur in its formation.*'

Ricardo's work (1817) on distribution implies antagonism between different factors of production '. . . *The interest of the landlord is always opposed to that of the consumer and manufacture*'. It is to '*the interest of the landlord that the cost attending the production of corn should be increased. This, however, is not the interest of the consumer . . . neither is the interest of the manufacturer . . . All classes, therefore, except the landlord will be injured by the increase in the price of corn.*'

Ricardo (1817) introduced the theory of economic rent with which we are familiar today. In his initial analysis his theory of rent was developed in relation to land. He used the term 'economic rent' to describe the surplus achieved by a piece of land relative to what it could earn in its next best use. He argued that '*If all land had the same properties, if it were unlimited in quantity, and uniform in quality, no charge could be made for its use*' – in other words there would be no economic rent.

However, the reality is that '*land is not unlimited in quantity and uniform in quality, and because in the progress of population, land of an inferior quality, or less advantageously situated, is called into cultivation, that rent is ever paid for the use of it. When in the progress of society, land of the second degree of fertility is taken into cultivation, rent immediately commences on that of the first quality, and the amount of that rent will depend on the difference in the quality of these two portions of land*' (Ricardo 1817). Rent is thus earned for the use of land which is more desirable than on land which is not so desirable.

This theory is today applied to all factors of production. For example, professional footballers earn economic rent which is what they earn over and above what they could earn in their next best lines of activity. Today, therefore, we think of rent as any surplus earned by factors of a superior quality.

Iron law of wages

Ricardo also proposed a theory of the law of wages which has long since been abandoned. He suggested *laissez-faire* conditions would tend to promote a 'natural' wage rate for labour and – as a consequence – full employment. If wages increased beyond this level the inference was that fewer workers would be employed. Consequently, Ricardo specifically counselled against state interference in the setting of wage levels. He referred to this as the 'Iron Law of Wages' suggesting that any attempt to better the lot of workers was futile.

Relative scarcity

Another important contribution made by Ricardo to political economy was in relation to the debate about absolute and relative scarcity. Whereas Malthus had painted a picture of a society increasingly experiencing diminishing returns in terms of productivity and running out of scarce resources, Ricardo showed how relative scarcity would lead society to adjust its patterns of behaviour. Ricardian analysis shows that as resources become more scarce their prices rise. Rising prices lead to a reduction in the exploitation of these scarce resources as society seeks to develop alternative resources. In recent years we have seen an increasing emphasis on Ricardian logic. For example, as non-renewable resources, such as energy supplies, run out, increasing emphasis is being placed on developing alternative fuel sources, e.g. wind farms. The Ricardian view of scarcity is thus much more optimistic than the Malthusian one.

Conclusion

David Ricardo built on the classical tradition of Adam Smith and introduced some new ideas that are still with us today. His dialogue with Malthus regarding the potential crisis facing the planet, is echoed today in discussions in which one side takes the view that we are already living beyond our means, while others take a more optimistic Ricardian view that relative scarcity will force up prices leading to a better use of scarce resources. Ricardo shaped thinking about economic rent and we still examine surpluses to factors of production over and above their supply price using a neo-Ricardian approach. The contrast between Smith's use of historical examples and evidence in contrast to Ricardo's theorising still provides a major division in economics between inductive and deductive approaches to economic enquiry.

 Further Reading

O'BRIEN, D.P. (1975) *The classical economists*. Clarendon Press, ch. 2.

RICARDO, D. (1810) *The High Price of Bullion*.

RICARDO, D. (1817) *Principles of political economy and taxation*. Reprinted in 1971. Pelican Classics.

RICARDO, M. (1824) A Memoir of David Ricardo, The Annual Biography and Obituary, Vol VIII. London.

ROLL, E. (1992) *A history of economic thought*. Faber & Faber, ch. 4.

SRAFFA, P. (1955) *The works and correspondence of David Ricardo*. Vol. X, *Bibliographical miscellany*. Cambridge University Press, The Royal Economic Society.

STRATHERN, P. (2001) *Dr Strangelove's game: A brief history of economic genius*. Hamish Hamilton.

John Stuart Mill

(1806–1873)

JOHN STUART MILL WAS THE FINAL MAJOR FIGURE IN THE CLASSICAL SCHOOL OF economics. His work marks a transition period between the earlier classical economists who sought to provide a justification and explanation of the market place and the coming socialist ideas set out by Karl Marx and others. The conflict in Mill's thinking between support and opposition to unfettered capitalism is representative of the turmoil in his own personal life as he began to challenge some of the ideas of his father who had been one of the prime forces in the utilitarian school of thinking.

John Stuart Mill is as widely known for his political as for his economic ideas although the economics textbook (*Principles of Political Economy*, 1848) that he authored was to become the standard work on the subject for many years.

Whereas Smith and Ricardo had been optimistic about the benefits of the capitalist economy, Mill had greater reservations. By the mid-nineteenth century the contradictions of the capitalist system revealed all too starkly the problems of poverty for large numbers of working people. Mill rejected some of the ideals of free market capitalism.

He wrote (1844), '*I confess I am not charmed with the ideal of life held out by those who think that the normal state of human beings is that of struggling to get on; that the trampling, crushing, elbowing and treading on each other's heels, which form the existing type of social life, are the most desirable lot of human kind, or any but the disagreeable symptoms of one of the phases of industrial progress*'.

However, he only gave a limited amount of support to the new socialism of the nineteenth century.

Methodology

THE METHODOLOGY EMPLOYED BY JOHN STUART MILL WAS TO COMBINE THE theoretical deductive approach of Ricardo with the gathering of evidence as used by Adam Smith. While Mill defended the theoretical approach used by Ricardo and others, if we look at what he actually 'did', as represented by his *Principles of Economics*, we find that Mill gathered a substantial amount of historical evidence to support his work. Mill's aim was to update the *Wealth of Nations* both in terms of the theory involved and in the facts. Schumpeter calculated that Mill's principles were made up of about one-sixth of factual information (far less than Smith's *Wealth of Nations* but substantially more than Ricardo's *Principles* which contained hardly any facts at all).

MILL WAS EDUCATED BY HIS FATHER, THE SCOTSMAN JAMES MILL, AS IF HE WERE AN adult. At three he was learning ancient Greek, by seven he had read most of Plato. He was later unable to shake off some of the ideas that his father introduced to him, particularly in relation to the ideas of the classical economists. At the age of 13 his father had given him an exposition on political economy together with the works of Smith and Ricardo to read.

He was to retain many of the ideas of Malthus, Smith and Ricardo in his thinking about how the economy functions – for example, the idea that population would outstrip production, and that there was only a limited fund available for paying wages so that wages could not rise.

He was also introduced to the ideas of utilitarianism as set out by James Mill (1773–1836) and Jeremy Bentham (1748–1832). The roots of utilitarianism go back to Frances Hutcheson who coined the phrase 'the greatest happiness of the greatest number'. Utilitarianism identified happiness or utility with 'that property in any object, whereby it tends to produce benefit, advantage, pleasure, good, or happiness' or which prevents 'mischief, pain, evil, or unhappiness'. Jeremy Bentham invented a 'felicific calculus' designed to identify ways of calculating and thus improving happiness. Bentham's concept of utilitarianism could be applied to all sorts of projects designed to improve the welfare of society; for example, to prison and welfare reform. The key test was to increase pleasure relative to pain. The utilitarians believed that by definition people are motivated by the pursuit of pleasure and avoidance of pain, so any action, however benevolent in appearance, must be undertaken for the pleasure it gave or the avoidance of (psychological) pain which would be associated with an alternative course of action. In the view of the utilitarians it followed that the maximisation of happiness could and indeed did come from the maximisation of the production of goods, the product of the new industrial era. Industrialisation was thus seen as desirable because of its potential to lead to the greatest happiness of the greatest number.

John Stuart Mill was typical of those infant prodigies that we read too often about today. He was put under too much pressure too young and was not allowed to develop through the typical stages of childhood. In his *Autobiography* Mill was to write '*I was never a boy*' and that he grew up '*in the absence of love and in the presence of fear*'. At 19 he edited Bentham's work *On Evidence* which was a particularly exacting task involving piecing together thousands of pieces of handwritten material. As a result he was to experience a nervous breakdown in his early 1920s. In his *Autobiography* he wrote that what brought on his breakdown was considering whether the schemes and plans of the utilitarians would make him happy – when he realised that his considered answer was 'No' then he felt miserable. In this period of breakdown he reacted against the continual work ethic by reading the Romantic Poets, in particular Coleridge and Wordsworth. This contact with Romanticism was to have a profound effect on his thinking and he reacted against the narrow calculating approach of utilitarianism and began to take an interest in socialist ideas. In his essay on Bentham (written in 1838) Mill rejected Bentham's view of human nature that human beings are motivated purely by '*either self-love or love or hatred towards other sentient beings*'. He criticised Bentham for ignoring other motives which involve the search for perfection, honour and other ends entirely for their own sake. However, much of his thinking was still rooted in utilitarian ideas and classical economics. He never fully recovered from his nervous breakdown and inevitably he was emotionally scarred by his early 'hothousing'. Harriet Taylor, who became his wife in 1851 (after the death of her husband), was also an important influence on his ideas and she persuaded him to the idea, which was radical for the time, that women should be enfranchised. Mill described Harriet as the '*inspirer of my best thoughts*'. Harriet was passionate about new ideas. After her death in 1858 Mill was looked after by his step-daughter Helen Taylor and spent half of each year in Avignon to be near Harriet's grave.

The other major influence on Mill was Auguste Comte who developed the idea of positivism and the science of society. Comte introduced Mill to the idea that through scientific study of society it is possible to identify future patterns. Mill borrowed the idea of statics and dynamics from Comte. Statics relates to non-evolutionary forces that lead to equilibrium states. In contrast dynamics is concerned with evolutionary phenomena in society. Mill sought to explain economic growth and change in terms of these dynamic forces. Although Mill had accepted from Auguste Comte the idea of the historical evolution of human society, he did not believe that socialism would necessarily follow on from capitalist society and from struggles between the classes in society.

A major difficulty facing Mill was that he was writing in a period of transition. While some of his ideas looked to the future others were still rooted in past thinking. By the middle of the nineteenth century, the ideas of economic and political liberalism that Mill had been brought up on were already outdated. The contradictions of the capitalist economy, illustrated by the poverty of large numbers of people, the emerging class struggle of the proletariat, and the critique of capitalist society by socialist thinkers, had already undermined faith in the market system as the path to prosperity for all, and the notion of 'one nation' based on a consensus of interests.

At 16 Mill joined his father working for the East India Company which was as important at the time as the government of India. He worked for the company until 1858 when the British government took over the government of India. Most of the time that Mill spent at the East India Company was in organising the Political Department's dealings with the individual states of India although he never actually visited the subcontinent. Finally Mill ended up with his father's position of 'Examiner of India Correspondence', the senior position in the government of India. Mill's chief influence was in encouraging self-government in India and the reduction of state bureaucracy.

In 1865 Mill was appointed MP for Westminster and made a number of important contributions in Parliament. He lost his seat in 1868.

Key works

Liberty (1859)

Essays on Unsettled Questions (1844)

Principles of Political Economy (1848)

Liberty

Like his father, John Stuart Mill was a believer in representative democracy. James Mill had argued the case for representative democracy in the following way. He stated that individuals tend to try and 'get one over' other members of society in order to increase their own pleasure at the expense of others. What is needed, therefore, is a representative government to protect society and hence individual members of society from the harmful acts of others. Representative government is elected by the members of society to represent their interests. John Stuart Mill echoed these ideas in his famous political work *Liberty* in which he set out to establish the basic rules for a democratic society. He was a firm believer in individual liberty. In *Liberty* he sets out and defends the principle that '*the sole end for which mankind are warranted, individually or collectively, in interfering with the liberty of action of any of their number, is self-protection. That the only purpose for which power can be rightly exercised over any member of a civilized community, against his will, is to prevent harm to others. His own good, either physical or moral, is not a sufficient warrant.*' The notion of individual liberty is the one that Mill is most strongly associated with in the political sphere. He believed strongly in the unfettered liberty of individuals to make their own decisions provided this did no harm to others. This idea provides the underpinning for modern liberal thinking.

Mill believed that although in England people were moving towards political freedom they did not enjoy social freedom. Too many people were worried about social disapproval and this constrained their actions. Mill was opposed to this conformism with two principles: (1) That we must coerce other people only in self-defence and not to force them to think like us; (2) That we must see that individuality is the distinguishing mark of humanity and that we are only free when are lives are our own.

Competition

The legacy of classical economics that remained with Mill and his belief in liberty influenced him to support the idea of competition. He stated (1848) that '*every restriction of competition is an evil*' and '*every extension of it is always an ultimate good*'.

However, his support of competition like his support of the free market seems at times to be based on his belief that it was the best available system: '*Competition may not be the best conceivable stimulus, but it is at present a necessary one, and no one can foresee the time when it will not be indispensable to progress.*'

In contrast Mill (1848) saw that co-operation provided a more noble ideal for the organisation of society: 'Co-operation is the noblest ideal' and it 'transforms human life from a conflict of classes struggling for opposite interests to a friendly rivalry in the pursuit of a good common to all'.

Demand and supply

Mill's understanding of how prices are determined in the market was far more sophisticated than that of previous economists. Mill recognised that there were schedules of demand and supply, that is, quantities that consumers and suppliers would be willing to buy and sell at different prices. He showed that although changes in demand and supply would alter price, changes in price would also affect quantities demanded and supplied.

Mill (1848) showed that equilibrium is created in the market where quantity demanded matches the quantity supplied in the market: 'The rise or the fall continues until the demand and supply are again equal to one another; and the value which a commodity will bring in any market is no other than the value which in that market gives a demand just sufficient to carry off the existing or expected supply.'

Importantly, Mill was able to apply the law of supply and demand in an international context when examining the relative price of internationally traded goods. He argued that the prices of goods was not determined by cost, as had been assumed by Ricardo, but to 'a principle antecedent to that of cost of production, and from which that law holds as a consequence – the principle of demand and supply . . . We require to find the causes that enable a country like England to obtain a greater or a lesser quantity of wine in exchange for her coal. In other words, the law of international values no longer involves a comparison of costs of production, but is simply the law of demand and supply.'

Rejection of full employment as a natural state of affairs

Until Mill, the classical economists had always assumed that natural laws ensured a smooth running economy leading to full employment. Classical economists lent heavily on a principle known as 'Say's Law' named after Jean-Baptiste Say, the French economist (1767–1832). Say had been heavily influenced by Adam Smith's view of the 'invisible hand'. Say's Law states that 'a product is no sooner created than it, from that instant, affords a market for other products to the full extent of its own value'. This has been simplified to the statement 'supply creates its own demand'. As a result the total supply of goods in the economy should always be equal to the total demand – hence leading to full employment.

It was not until the work of Keynes became the conventional wisdom after the Second World War that this idea was to be rejected.

However, a careful read of Mill's work indicates that he was already thinking along Keynesian lines.

Mill (1848) stated that: 'Of the capital of a country there is at all times a very large proportion lying idle. The annual produce of a country is never anything approaching in magnitude to what it might be if all the resources devoted to reproduction, if all the capital, in short, of a country, were in full employment.'

Mill (1848) showed that in a money-based economy supply did not always instantly create a demand for goods. *'Interchange by means of money is . . . ultimately nothing but barter. But there is the difference – that in the case of barter, the selling and the buying are simultaneously confounded in one operation . . . The effect of the employment of money, and even the utility of it, is that it enables this one act of interchange to be divided into two separate acts or operations . . . Although he who sells really sells only to buy, he needs not buy at the same moment when he sells; and he does not therefore necessarily add to the immediate demand for one commodity when he adds to the supply of the other.'*

The implications of what Mill was saying here are profound in that it seems that he understood why it was that the market economy did not always clear. If this is the case then there is a clear justification for at least some government intervention in economic management.

A role for government intervention in the economy

Although Mill was the great advocate of individual liberty he also set out a framework for government interference in the economy which went beyond that of the earlier classical economists. In particular, he emphasised the role of government as a 'civilizer' – in providing educational facilities, parks, museums etc. He felt that this was important in improving the lot of the working class. He also felt that the state could play an important role in taxing the surplus funds of wealthy individuals who might have speculated the funds rashly, and channelled these taxes into government spending on socially useful projects leading to more desirable social outcomes.

Mill (1859) provided a set of rules for the limitation of state interference:

1. When the action is likely to be better done by private persons than by the government;

2. When, though private persons usually do it less well than the officers of government, it is still desirable that they should do it as a means to their own education; and

3. Whenever there is a danger of adding unnecessarily to the government's power.

Mill (1859) also argues against the dangers of bureaucracy: *'For the governors are as much slaves of their organization and discipline as the governed are of the governors.'*

The possibility of improving the conditions of working people

Classical economists before Mill had believed that the 'invisible hand' created a natural state of affairs in which working people were doomed to subsistence wages, with any surpluses being gained by landlords and capitalists.

Mill rejected this notion although his analysis was still flawed. Mill agreed with the classical economists that the laws of production were determined by nature (an assumption that is rejected today). However, he felt that the laws of distribution (i.e. who gets what share of the national cake) were not pre-ordained (an assumption that is regarded to be true today). He therefore was optimistic about the possibility of working people improving their conditions should society reorganise to create a fairer distribution of rewards and incomes.

In drawing out this division between production and distribution Mill (1848) wrote: 'The laws and conditions of the Production of wealth partake of the character of physical truths, There is nothing optional or arbitrary in them . . . It is not so with the Distribution of wealth. That is a matter of human institution solely. The things once there, mankind individually or collectively can do with them as they like. They can place them at the disposal of whomsoever they please, and on whatever terms. Within production eternal and inexorable natural laws dominate; within distribution what dominates is the free will of human beings, who can distribute their produce as they see fit and carry out any social reforms.'

Growing support for socialist ideals

As Mill grew older he increasingly began to see the benefits of socialism although he never set out a detailed outline of what socialism would involve. In any case his view of socialism was based more on co-operative arrangements and social partnerships between employers and employees rather than wide-scale state control.

He believed that the capitalist system was brutally unfair but that over time it could improve and that capitalists would become less greedy.

The fruits of the industrial capitalist system that was flourishing in Mill's day did not appeal to his sensitivities. This is made clear in his comments that 'Hitherto it is questionable if all the mechanical inventions yet made have lightened the day's toil of any human being. They have enabled a greater population to live the same life of drudgery and imprisonment, and an increased number of manufacturers and others to make fortunes.'

On moral and social ground, therefore, he was led to state that 'If, therefore, the choice were to be made between Communism with all its chances, and the present state of society with all its sufferings and injustices, if the institution of private property necessarily carried with it as a consequence, that the produce of labour should be apportioned as we now see it, almost in an inverse ratio to the labour – the largest portions to those who have never worked at all, the next largest to those whose work is almost nominal, and so in a descending scale, the remuneration dwindling as the work grows harder and more disagreeable, until the most fatiguing and exhausting bodily labour cannot count with certainty on being able to earn even the necessaries of life; if this or Communism were the alternative, all the difficulties, great or small, of Communism would be but as dust in the balance' (Mill 1844).

Communism is certainly better, he says, than 'the regime of individual property as it is', but whether or not it would be preferable to 'private property as it might be made' if submitted to thoroughgoing social reforms, we still do not know. 'We are too ignorant either of what individual agency in its best form, or Socialism in its best form, can accomplish to be qualified to decide which of the two will be the ultimate form of human society.'

As a result much of Mill's work (1844) focused on revising and improving the capitalist system, calling for land reform in India, encouraging greater autonomy for regional government in India, suggesting ways of making the tax system fairer, encouraging government involvement in education etc., rather than the radical communism of Karl Marx which was to follow.

Mill was thus essentially a liberal reformer seeking to improve capitalist society to become more humane. In his *Autobiography* he wrote 'While we repudiated with the *greatest energy that tyranny of society over the individual which most Socialist systems are supposed to involve, we yet looked forward to a time when society will no longer be divided into the idle and the industrious; when the rule that they who do not work shall not eat, will be applied not to paupers only, but impartially to all; when the division of the produce of labour, instead of depending, as in so great a degree it now does, on the accident of birth, will be made by concert on an acknowledged principle of justice; and when it will no longer either be, or be thought to be impossible for human beings to exert themselves strenuously in procuring benefits which are not to be exclusively their own but to be shared with the society they belong to.'*

Tax theory

Mill made an important contribution to the theory of taxation. He showed that as people became better off the marginal utility of their income fell. He argued that taxation systems should force people to make equal sacrifices, suggesting that higher incomes should be taxed at higher rates.

Conclusion

Mill's life and work provides a fascinating study of British economics at the crossroads between the free market and socialism. He lived in a society of increasingly apparent inequalities and obvious poverty living side by side with conspicuous wealth. Mill's early training had been in classical economics coupled with utilitarian reformist ideas. He was thus not able to break away from the economic tenets of the society he had been brought up in although his sensitivities and his developing intellectual awareness informed him of the need for radical change. Mill's greatest contributions to economics therefore rested in clarifying and adjusting existing thinking while at the same time providing a rationale for an enhanced role for government in a more humane society.

 **Further Reading**

BARBER, W. (1987) *A history of economic thought*. Pelican, ch. 4.

BLAUG, M. (1973) *Economic theory in retrospect*. Heinemann Educational, ch. 6.

GALBRAITH, J.K. (1991) *A history of economics*. Penguin Books, ch. 10.

GIDE, C. AND RIST, C. (1915) *A history of economic doctrines*. George G. Harrap and Co. Ltd, bk 3, ch. 1.

MILL, J.S. (1869) *Liberty*. Longman, Roberts and Green.

MILL, J.S. (1899) *Principles of political economy*. Colonial Press.

MILL, J.S. (1948) *Essays on some unsettled questions of political economy*. John W. Parker.

PLAMENATZ, J. (1966) *The English utilitarians*. Basil Blackwell, ch. 8.

RUBIN, I.I. (1979) *A history of economic thought.* Ink Links, ch. 39.

RYAN, A. (1989) (ed.) *The invisible hand.* Macmillan Reference.

SPIEGEL, H.W. (1971) *The growth of economic thought.* Prentice-Hall, ch. 16.

STRATHERN, P. (2001) *Dr Strangelove's game: a brief history of economic genius.* Hamish Hamilton, ch. 7.

Karl Marx

(1818–1883)

CLASSICAL MARXISM IS BASED UPON THE NINETEENTH-CENTURY WRITINGS OF KARL Marx and Friedrich Engels. Marx and Engels constructed a philosophy of history which singled out class divisions as the motor of history – the ingredient which pushed history forwards – which is commonly known as 'dialectical materialism'. The Marxist analysis is a class-based analysis in which the forces and relations of production are the determining factors in bringing about social change. From the Marxian perspective, if a group owns the means of production they not only have economic power; they also have political power. The state is viewed as an institution that helps to organise capitalist society in the best interests of the bourgeoisie. Making working class people victims of a false consciousness maintains the legitimacy of the system. In other words, working class people are said to hold values, ideas and beliefs about the nature of inequality, which are not in their own economic interests to hold. Working class people have their ideas manipulated – by the media, schools and religion for example – and may regard economic inequality as fair and just.

Methodology

MARX MADE A SIGNIFICANT CONTRIBUTION TO METHODOLOGY BY DEVELOPING THE method of the *materialist dialectic*, a form of 'scientific philosophy' that emphasised contradiction and resolution. In a letter to Maurice Lachatre (18 May 1872) Marx argued that no one before him had attempted to apply dialectical arguments to the study of economics and that it was this methodology that made his work distinctive. This was in contrast to Hegel, who argued that *ideas* were the key element in the process of social change. Underpinning this methodology is the assumption that all parts of the economy and society, including the resources from nature, raw materials and labour power, are interconnected within the mode of production. In addition, the mode of production changes because of general laws of motion that Marx was attempting to identify. As Ernest Mandel explains in his introduction to *Capital* Volume I: *'The method of investigation must differ from the method of exposition. Empirical facts have to be gathered first, the given state of knowledge has to be fully grasped. Only when this is achieved can a dialectical reorganisation of the material be undertaken in order to understand the given totality. If this is successful, the result is a "reproduction" in man's thought of this material totality: the capitalist mode of production'* (Mandel 1976).

In other words, for Marx there is a distinction between 'appearance' and 'reality' and we must look at the given state of knowledge in an area and compare this with our own experience in order to break down the layers of 'appearance' and successfully discover the 'reality', the laws of motion, that explain how history moves forward. For Marx, then, scientific activity and the findings of scientific investigation were not 'ideological' in nature. Similarly the findings of Royal Commissions were also untainted by ideology and could be used in this dialectical fashion.

KARL MARX WAS BORN IN THE PRUSSIAN TOWN OF TRIER TO A JEWISH FAMILY THAT converted to Christianity when Marx was a child. In the 1830s he initially studied law at the University of Bonn but quickly transferred to philosophy. During this time Marx became interested in the work of the idealist philosopher Hegel. Marx was still a 'young Hegelian' at the time of his first job as the editor-in-chief of the radical newspaper *Rheinishe Zeitung* in 1842. The paper was forced to close by the authorities in 1843 because of the radical views it expressed. Marx married his childhood sweetheart Jenny von Westphalen, the daughter of a Prussian aristocrat and moved to Paris in 1844 where he wrote his *Economic and Philosophical Manuscripts,* but again Marx fell foul of the authorities because of his radical views and was expelled from Paris and moved to Brussels. By this time Marx and Engels had become friends and started writing together within the Communist Correspondence Committee and in 1848 they wrote *The Communist Manifesto* together. In 1848 Marx was expelled from Brussels and returned to Paris where he was again expelled in 1849. This time Marx moved to London – the years in England were a period of great poverty in which Marx worked on his book *Capital* and made a little money from occasional journalism. During these years he was under constant surveillance from the Prussian spies. It was only after Engels had given Marx a £350 annuity that Marx could live in some comfort, and employ a maid. In 1883 Marx died in London but was never granted British citizenship.

Friedrich Engels (1820–1891) was born in Bremen in Germany, his father was a capitalist, a textile manufacturer, who sent his son to Manchester in 1842 to manage the partnership of Ermen and Engels. The company had a mill in Pendleton and offices in Deansgate, central Manchester. Engels met Marx while in England working for his father's company. The two men struck up a close and lasting friendship, which included Engels providing Marx with an allowance of £350, although Marx's wife was said to have openly shown her disapproval of Engels living with two women, Lizzie and Mary Burns, in a form of common-law marriage. In Manchester, Engels became politically active within the Chartist Movement, and developed an interest in the social reforms of Robert Owen.

It was these two young Irish working-class women who worked at the Ermen & Engels Mill who introduced Engels to the living and working conditions of the poor in Manchester and provided him with the inspiration to write *The Conditions of the*

Working Class in England (1844). Later Mary, Lizzie and Engels moved to London where they continued to live together as a common-law threesome until Mary's death in 1863. Lizzie and Engels lived together for a further 15 years until Lizzie died. In what many people might consider to be a strange act, Engels married Lizzie as she lay on her deathbed.

Since the collapse of communism in Eastern Europe few social scientists believe that Marx has anything valid to say about the current state of either the economy or the wider society. However, it would be wrong to dismiss the Marxian analysis totally. Although the great bulk of Marx and Engels' writing were highly critical of capitalism – which they regarded as robbery – they did recognise how capitalism had allowed people to control the forces of nature for profit. Marx and Engels also recognised the inventiveness that flourished under capitalism: the railway, the electric telegraph, the application of chemistry to both industry and agriculture and steam navigation were all discussed by Marx and Engels in positive terms. However, capitalism brings with it inequality, exploitation and alienation. The bourgeoisie – the capitalist class who own the means of production – can only make a profit if they do not pay their workers (the proletariat) the true value of their labour power. It was upon this premise that Marx developed the 'labour theory of value'. In addition, for Marx and Engels individual people are essentially creative beings, to make things is the key element of our *species being*, Marx and Engels argued. However, within capitalism work is dull, boring and monotonous and does not give people opportunity to express their creativeness. This inability to express creativity is what Marx and Engels termed *alienation* – within capitalism workers are made to feel that they are merely part of the machine.

In addition, a number of Marxists have argued that what Marx had to say is still relevant today. Alex Callinicos in *The Revenge of History: Marxism and the East European Revolutions* (1991) attempts to outline what he sees as the implications for socialism of the collapse of Stalinism. Stalinism was a doctrine named after the Soviet dictator Joseph Stalin who maintained the enforcement of his own rule by ability to 'liquidate' people who were seen as a threat to his domination. Callinicos's argument is that the collapse of Stalinism cannot be used to justify the argument that Marxism is irrelevant in explaining the modern world. In addition, Callinicos points out that as long ago as 1947 socialists such as Tony Cliff had argued that the working classes would bring down Stalinist regimes such as the Soviet Union. Hence Callinicos argues: '*The East European revolutions and the turmoil in the USSR itself are thus the vindication, rather than the refutation, of the classical Marxist tradition*' (Callinicos 1991).

Key works

Das Kapital: A Critique of Political Economy (1867)

Communist Manifesto (1848)

Key Ideas

THE MARXIAN ANALYSIS REVOLVES AROUND THE CONCEPT OF CLASS. IN *CAPITAL* MARX outlines his *abstract* model of class, which is essentially a two-class model. There are other classes in capitalist society but they are disappearing and in any case are largely irrelevant to the essential dynamic of capitalist society. The key distinction between people is ownership and non-ownership of the means of production; for Marx, it is this division that separates the classes. The bourgeoisie own the means of production and the proletariat do not own the means of production. The relationship between the bourgeoisie and the proletariat is an exploitative one; the bourgeoisie exploit the proletariat.

The exploitative relationship between the bourgeoisie and the proletariat is explained by the *labour theory of value*, which Marx derived from David Ricardo. Marx begins *Capital* with a discussion of the commodity. A commodity is anything that is manufactured, has a value and can be sold. There are two forms of value for Marx: first, there is *use value,* which reflects the intrinsic value or personal value that a person gets from having or consuming a commodity. Marx has little interest in the value, desire or pleasure that you or I can enjoy from consumption. Marx is interested in the second type of value, which he terms *exchange value,* the value in monetary terms that a commodity can fetch in the market place. For Marx the exchange value of a commodity reflects the amount of labour power that went into the production of a commodity.

What is labour power? Each worker has muscles, limbs and brains that they can use to make things. In other words, each person carries with them a potential stock or fund of labour – each person has a potential capacity to make products. Although each person has different skills, abilities and levels of intelligence, Marx argues that such differences can be subsumed under the abstract concept of a unit of labour power. It is the number of such abstract units present within a commodity that determine its exchange value. However, Marx also argues that *labour power* is also a commodity, and the value of labour power reflects the amount of labour power that went into the reproduction of labour power itself.

Marx argues that workers have to be paid enough to feed themselves, clothe themselves and also be paid a little bit extra to reproduce labour power; to bring a new generation of children into the world who will become the next proletariat. In terms of the length of the working day, Marx argues that the first part of the working day is *socially necessary labour time* in which the workers are paid the full value of their labour power. However, any time that the workers work beyond *socially necessary labour time* is what Marx terms *surplus value labour time* in which the workers are not paid for the value of their labour power, but are rather creating *surplus value* for the bourgeoisie. People working for the bourgeoisie after they have completed *socially necessary labour time* is what Marx regards as exploitation. In addition, there is pressure on the bourgeoisie to extend *surplus value labour time* and pay workers only enough to reproduce their own labour power and little else. It is only by the bourgeoisie behaving in this exploitative manner that the profitability of individual capitalistic enterprises can be maintained. Hence Marx argues that workers will go through a period of getting poorer (*Verelendung)*, a process of *immiserisation.*

Marx viewed society as a *mode of production,* and history is the change from one mode of production to the next. Initially people lived in a form of society that he termed 'primitive communism' a mode of production in which there was no private ownership, no class system, no family and no incest taboo. With the development of private ownership came the institution, such as the state and the family that have a central role to play in modern capitalism.

The mode of production is made up of two parts: first, the *economic base*, which contains the *forces of production* and the *relations of production*. The forces of production are all the things that we need to produce commodities such as raw materials and technology. The relations of production are the class relations; in capitalism this would be the relationship between the bourgeoisie and the proletariat.

Above the economic base there is the *superstructure* – this is the realm of culture, politics, ideas and ideology. In the Marxian analysis, the economic base determines culture and ideas within a society.

Marx on globalisation

In the 1990s the notion of globalisation became a central concept across all of the social sciences. What underpinned the notion of globalisation was the idea that the world was becoming a single place, in that barriers of an economic, cultural and political nature were breaking down. However, as far back as the 1870s Marx and Engels gave globalisation a central role in their theorising. It is worth quoting at length from *The Communist Manifesto* what Marx and Engels had to say:

'The bourgeoisie cannot exist without constantly revolutionizing the instruments of production, and thereby the relations of production and with them the whole relations of society. Conservation of the old modes of production in unaltered form was on the contrary, the first condition of existence for all earlier industrial classes. Constant revolutionizing of production, uninterrupted disturbance of all social conditions, everlasting uncertainty and agitation distinguish the bourgeois epoch from all earlier ones. All fixed, fast-frozen relations, with their train of ancient and venerable prejudices and opinions, are swept away, all new-formed ones become antiquated before they can ossify. All that is solid melts into air, all that is holy is profaned, and man is at last compelled to face with sober senses, his real conditions of life, and his relations with his kind.*

The need of a constantly expanding market for its products chases the bourgeoisie over the whole surface of the globe. It must nestle everywhere, settle everywhere, and establish connexions everywhere.

The bourgeoisie has through its exploitation of the world-market given a cosmopolitan character to production and consumption in every country. To the great chagrin of Reactionists, it has drawn from under the feet of industry the national ground on which it stood. All old-established national industries have been destroyed or are daily being destroyed. They are dislodged by new industries, whose introduction becomes a life and death question for all civilized nations, by industries that no longer work up indigenous raw material, but raw material drawn from the remotest zones; industries whose products are consumed, not only at home, but in every quarter of the globe. In place of the old wants, satisfied by the productions of the country, we find new wants, requiring for their satisfaction the products of distant lands and climes. In place of the old local and national seclusion and self-sufficiency, we have intercourse in every direction, universal interdependence of nations. And as in material, so also in intellectual production. The intellectual creations of individual nations become common property. National one-sidedness and narrow-mindedness become more and more impossible, and from the numerous national and local literatures, there arises a world literature' (Marx and Engels 1872).

What is significant about this quote is how much of the theorising on both economic and cultural globalisation was anticipated by Marx and Engels. For example, Arjun

Appadurai (1989) explains that the notion of political/cultural globalisation is brought about by a number of flows:

- Ethnoscapes – the flow of people, tourists, immigrants, refugees, exiles and guest workers;
- Technoscapes – the movement of technology;
- Finanscapes – the rapid movement of money via money markets and stock exchanges;
- Mediascapes – information and images generated and distributed by film, television, newspapers and magazines;
- Ideoscapes – the movement of political ideas and ideologies.

All of these points are contained in the above quote. Since Lenin in 1916, Marxist writers in particular have discussed the economic consequences of globalisation as forms of colonialism or imperialism. Marxists have argued that the development of capitalism has been dependent upon the economic exploitation of the labour and natural resources of the third world. In addition, the third world is used as a market place.

rule by one country over many others

The Marxian argument should not be used to suggest that the age of independent nation states has come to an end. Nation states are still performing their economic role and service foreign capital on the same basis as domestic capital. However, nation states have lost many of their powers over economic activity because of the high level of activity by foreign capital that is highly politically opportunist.

Robert Cox (1987) built upon Lenin's argument that the state provided 'indispensable functions' for capitalists. For Cox, the new world order – which we now have a clearer view of after the collapse of communism in Eastern Europe – has led directly to a transformation but not a diminution of the activities of the state. Cox argues that there has been an *internationalisation* of the state built upon an international consensus and visible in international agreements. There is a common ideological framework, common goals, and common criteria for judging economic events and a common assumption that an open world market needs common solutions by states. This *internationalisation* of the state is supported by various international agencies such as: the World Trade Organisation; the World Bank; the International Monetary Fund; the Trilateral Commission; the Club of Rome; the Bilderberg conferences and the Organisation for Economic Cooperation and Development. Together these international organisations and agreements have produced a global centralisation of influence over policy. The end result has been the creation of what Cox terms the 'Thatcher–Reagan hyperliberal state form'; in other words, all states are forced into supporting liberal capitalist policies that maintain capital.

'There is a transnational process of consensus formation among the official caretakers of the global economy. This process generates consensual guidelines, underpinned by the ideology of globalisation, that are transmitted into the policy-making channels of national governments and big corporation . . . The structural impact on national governments of this centralisation of influence over policy can be called the internationalisation of the state. Its common feature is to convert the state into an agency for adjusting national economic practices and policies to the national economy, where therefore it had acted as the bulwark defending domestic welfare from external disturbances. Power within the state becomes concentrated in those agencies in closest touch with the global economy –

the offices of presidents and prime ministers, treasurers, central banks. The agencies that are more closely tied with domestic clients – ministries of industries, labour ministries, etc. – become subordinated. This phenomenon, which has become so salient since the crisis of the post-war order, needs much more study' (Robert Cox cited in Panitch 1994).

One of the clearest Marxian world system approaches, which discards the idea of the unified nation state as an important factor in a global system, is that of Immanuel Wallerstein. Wallerstein (1979) argues that capitalism is always global in nature and never confined by national boundaries. Wallerstein makes a distinction between two types of world system:

- World empires – these empires colonised areas of the world by military means and imposed a ridged bureaucracy on the population to extract taxes. These empires were displaced by world economies that are much more flexible.

- World economies – these are market based and capitalistic in nature and based upon capital accumulation. The world economy is neocolonial in nature, and is largely free from any influence of nation states.

In Wallerstein's view the modern world system is *'a single division of labour comprising multiple cultural systems, multiple political entities and even different modes of surplus appropriation'* (Wallerstein 1980) divided into three components:

- The core – in the beginning Northern Europe and North America, the places of origin of the first transnational corporations (TNCs) which dominated the global market and exploited the world's population for profit.

- The semi-periphery – in the first instance Mediterranean and Eastern Europe, these countries did face exploitation from the TNCs but did have some capital which was not directly under the control of TNCs.

- The periphery – the colonised and former colonised countries which are now visibly within neocolonial economic relationships.

The relationship between the core and the periphery is an exploitative one in the Marxian sense. The core–periphery relationship should be based upon the transfer of surplus value from the periphery to the core – the value can be extracted from workers in two different ways, either political or economic.

Ankie Hoogvelt (1982) describes the political/economic arrangements within the world system in the following way: *'. . . the global distribution of wealth and poverty is seen as a result of market forces reinforcing an accident of history which gave a head start to the European nations. But there is also political interference in the market. While the single world market rewards some activities and penalises others, the actors can and do interfere with the operation of the world market by appealing to their nation-states to interfere on their behalf. And once we get a difference in strength of the state machinery's [sic], we get the operation of unequal exchange imposed by strong states on weak ones in peripheral areas – by core areas on peripheral areas. In this way capitalism involves not only appropriation of the surplus value by an owner from a labourer but an appropriation of the whole world economy by core areas.'*

In other words, the capitalist economy has built a division of labour that is neocolonial and global in nature. Power and wealth is shifted to the core, while the periphery and semi-periphery are left comparatively poor and powerless.

Wallerstein also assumes that states have no other sources of power to draw upon other than economic power. This means that Wallerstein had difficulty dealing with the former Soviet Union; the Soviet Union had to operate with a global economy dominated by capitalistic institutions yet it was militarily a super power, which clearly meant that it was in a position to manipulate the world system. In general, it would be wrong to assume that nations outside of the core are powerless, simply because of the lack of economic development; as was seen in the events leading up to the Gulf War, economically less developed nations can make a significance difference in the world.

It is a great shame that Marx did not write in English – this might have prevented people from presenting his work as a set of meaningless slogans. Marx himself invented none of Marx's key concepts: class, socialism, the labour theory of value, dialectic, base-superstructure, ideology, alienation etc. What Marx did while he was sat in the British Museum reading room picking his boils and living off the surplus value extracted from Engel's employees, was to bring these ideas and concepts together and produce a coherent theory, very different than the sum of its parts. A nineteenth-century political economy Fat Boy Slim!

These are interesting times if you are a Marxist. When Corus, Motorolla, Dunlop, Goodyear, Viyella, Ford and Vauxhall announced mass job losses in 2001, the 'value' of these companies rose on the stock market. We live in a brutal and brutalising global capitalist system in which it appears that global companies have developed the ability to generate value without the need to extract surplus value from labour. Moreover, it is the *lumpenproletariats* that suffer most in the context of global capitalism. Should we continue to share Marx's contempt for these people? What is the nature of exploitation now?

The dominant ideology

For Marxists the dominant ideas of any historical period are the ideas of the ruling class, the bourgeoisie. The notion of a 'dominant ideology' refers to a system of thought that is manipulated by the bourgeoisie and imposed upon the proletariat in support of capitalism. The Marxian conception of ideology is based upon a humanistic notion that consent should be based upon an authentic consciousness free from any distortion. For Marxists, the term ideology suggests that the bourgeoisie do something to the way in which working class people think about the world. The bourgeoisie create a 'world-view' for the proletariat; which is shaped via the mass media, the education system and organised religion, together with other institutions that are concerned with ideas. Class interests shape ideas and the bourgeoisie distort the ideas of the proletariat by imposing 'false consciousnesses' upon them. Television manipulating the ideas of individual people is an often-considered example. Working class people make use of their false consciousness to justify their own subordination within the capitalist system.

However, the Marxian analysis undervalues the role of the human agent. Marxists assume that forces that are outside their control push about people. This deterministic assumption, shared by all Marxists, may not be correct. In addition, Marxists have a very simplistic notion of 'representation' contained within the notion of ideology. As we have suggested, in the Marxian analysis, working class people have their ideas and worldview manipulated. The bourgeoisie are said to be capable of taking any object or idea and giving it a new representation or meaning in the minds of the working class. This new representation is supportive of capitalism, justifies the position of the bourgeoisie and legitimises the exploitation of the working class in their own minds. The problem here is that Marxists do not explain how this happens. What goes on, at a cognitive level, inside the mind of a working class person for them to reject their own economic interests so fully and totally? How can the 'agency' – the ability to make decisions in our own interests for our own reasons – of working class people be so completely destroyed without their revolutionary potential not also being destroyed?

The term 'dominant ideology' could mean at least two very different things. On the one hand, the term suggests that there is one ideology that all people accept because it is imposed upon everybody. In contrast, the term could equally mean that there is one dominant ideology and any number of non-dominant ideologies. The suggestion here is that any group of like-minded people could construct a set of ideas and beliefs in opposition to the dominant belief system. The construction of new ideologies is one of the key activities of New Social Movements.

Marx in textbooks

'Lego Marxism' (Marxism as presented in introductory textbooks), is a Marxism in which the labour theory of value has been removed. The labour theory of value is the foundation of the Marxian analysis; it provides the theory of exploitation, the foundation for the theory of power, the basis for the Marxian conception of class. Without an understanding of this theory you will be unable to understand what Marxism is about. However, the labour theory of value is the Achilles' heel of Marxism; it is also seriously flawed.

Our textbook authors need to answer this question: Why do you not include a critical evaluation of the central plank of the Marxian analysis in your textbook?

Marxism without the labour theory of value is either:

- a form of deception – 'keep it secret from the students or we'll be dead in the water'
- a form of moralising – 'Don't be bad to the working class – be excellent to each other'.

Alternatively, Marxism without the labour theory of value is post-Marxism in the same vein as Jameson (1991) – a position one textbook author, Paul Manning (1996), has shown some sympathy for.

Jameson also redefines the relationships contained within the 'labour theory of value' into a 'linguistic account'. In contrast to the traditional Marxist analysis of the labour theory of value, Jameson's view is that 'value' emerges as something independent of the labour power that went into making it. This 'value' is an 'abstraction' or 'concept' and the market place becomes a place of the 'symbolic exchange' of value.

In other words, 'value' is said by Jameson to be independent of the labour power that produced it. 'Value' is a concept, it is an idea, and must be explained in cultural terms. Jameson's concepts are free of the traditional Marxist meaning. The significance of this is that Jameson has collapsed the economic base into the superstructure, and suggested that we can only make sense of the world in cultural terms. The economic base, including the relations of production, is irrelevant in the postmodern condition. The economic base is no longer the force that moves history forward; it is culture and ideas that generate future social change.

It can be noted, then, that although Jameson does not reject the labour theory of value, he rejects its traditional form, and redefines it as a cultural or superstructural thing. A similar postmodern critique is developed by Jean Baudrillard who argues that 'reality' is a human creation made by media products and our feedback of these products. Our values are brought about by consumer demand that is itself influenced by an endless rotation of interpretations, reflections and advertising codes, in which there is no clear division, or objective criteria that can be used to distinguish between what is true and what is ideological. Jean Baudrillard has argued that imagery has evolved through a number of stages, over the course of history:

- initially, any sign once stood for a truth, for example a pain in the chest may be a sign of heart disease;

- in the nineteenth century with the development of Marxism, signs began to be seen as concealing or deliberately distorting the truth, the Marxian conception of ideology;

- as we move in to the twentieth century, signs then became seen as masking the absence of the truth, this is the idea that style is used to make up for the lack of substance;

- finally, in the contemporary world, we believe that there is no link between an image and truth. In other words, in the postmodern condition there is no representation, what you see is what there is. The image is real.

For Baudrillard, reality is a human creation made by media products and our feedback of these products – for example, our feedback on what we may have seen on television. Our values are brought about by consumer demand that is itself influenced by an endless rotation of interpretations, reflections and advertising codes. There is no clear division, or objective criteria that can be used to distinguish between what is true and what is ideological. In other words, it is no longer possible to clearly state the difference between what is seen on television, and the world it is meant to represent.

In *The Mirror of Production* (1973) Baudrillard casts doubt upon the Marxian distinction we outlined above, between 'use value' and 'exchange value'. In Baudrillard's opinion, 'use value' is seen by Marxists as based upon genuine need, whereas 'exchange value' is brought about by capitalists distorting the consciousness of the population by ideology and alienation. By alienation, Marx means that individual people are essentially creative in nature; within capitalism, however, work is dull and boring to such a degree that we are unable to express our creativity. In contrast, in a socialist society people would work for the common good. Making use of the Marxian concepts we outlined above we could say a socialist society is based upon the principle of 'from each according to his ability, to each according to his needs'. In other words, solely taking care of our 'use values' would satisfy all our needs. For the Marxist, the concepts of 'value' and 'labour' are non-negotiable concepts, they cannot be questioned, and they are essential for any analysis of the world.

In contrast, for Baudrillard, genuine need is impossible to identify, without taking into account how our needs are manipulated, explained and even created by the mass media. It is at this point that Baudrillard introduces us to his concept of 'simulacra', which is explained by David Ashley (1997) as follows: '*In the same year [1992], the line between image and reality became so confused that TV viewers were able to watch a sitcom character ("Murphy Brown") pose as a real journalist criticising an allegedly real vice president (Dan Quayle) for condemning her fictional pregnancy. (The baby's TV shower was, of course, attended by "real" reporters.) Viewers were subsequently treated to the spectacle of Quayle discussing with "real" journalists Murphy Brown's criticism of him as if this attack had been launched by a real newswoman on a real news show. Needless to say, the vice president's increasingly bizarre behaviour – which included persistent attempts to send flowers to a character he seemed not to understand was fictional – was itself covered as a major news event about which the public needed to be kept fully informed.'*

Thus, people make use of the media, both fictional and news programmes, not only to make sense of the world but also to give their own views, beliefs and feelings, enhanced validity.

There are serious problems with Marxism that clearly need to be addressed. The terminology in Marx is unclear, even with fundamental concepts such as 'base' and 'superstructure'. Do 'base' and 'superstructure' refer to 'processes' or 'relations'? Is everything that we understand as 'social' either 'base' or 'superstructure'? Productive forces develop over time and condition the character of relations of production. A key element in this process is our knowledge of how to control and transform nature. However, what are these productive forces? Is what *enables* production a productive force or should we also include things that *stimulate* production, such as ideological factors? Science and knowledge produced by universities are classed by Marx as a mental productive force; but is such knowledge 'base' and/or 'superstructure'? Productive forces are made up of the means of production and labour power. What are the means of production for Marx? Should we include: space, premises, and fuel? Why is the means of subsistence for working animals – what working animals eat – classed by Marx as part of the means of production, while what working people eat is not classed as part of the means of production?

Most people who are sympathetic to the Marxian analysis make a distinction between Marxism and Stalinism. The problem with this argument is that Stalin wrote at great length about Marxism and for pro-Marxian argument to be convincing he really needs to explain to his reader what was wrong with Stalin's revision and explain why we should reject it. Ross Abbinnett's argument sounds very convincing when he explains that *'The labour camps of the former Soviet Union did not exist as "transitional" institutions; rather, they attested to the economy of domination-resistance produced by the administration of "proletarian democracy"'* (Abbinnett 1998).

However, the fundamental difficulty with both Lego Marxism and *real* Marxism is reification and the consequent loss of subjectivity. Nothing is attributed to individual people, who are classed as merely supports of the *'places and functions determined by the mode of production'* (Althusser 1971). How is it possible for individual people to act independently when the world they live in is externally determined? How is it possible for Marx to sustain the notion of an autonomous individual? The notion of a 'species being' – which is the essence of what it means to be a person for Marx – is limited and stated in purely functional terms. The autonomy of the individual is reduced to an instrumental function of economic life. Why do Marxists place such a strong emphasis upon functional interdependence?

What type of society did Marx and his supporters want to achieve? In *The Critique of the Gotha Programme* Marx said he wanted to build a society based upon the principle of *'from each according to his ability, to each according to his needs'*. However, in *The*

Communist Manifesto Marx was very specific in terms of how such a society could be brought about:

- Confiscation of landed property – this was because in the eyes of Marx all private property was theft and should not be in private hands.
- All rent should be given not to private landlords but to public purposes.
- A heavily progressive income tax, in which the higher an income a person had the greater the proportion of their income they should give up in tax.
- Abolition of all rights to inheritance.
- Confiscation of property belonging to émigrés and people who rebelled against the movement towards a communist society.
- The creation of a centralised state band and the monopoly of credit in the hands of the state.
- Centralisation and state control of the means of communication – all newspapers, the postal service, and the telegraph should be owned and controlled by the state – today this would also include television, radio, cinema and the Internet.
- Centralisation and state control of transport.
- Centralisation and state control of all production, including agriculture, and production to be on the basis of a national plan.
- All people would have an obligation to work.
- The state would abolish the distinction between urban and rural areas.
- All children would be banned from working in factories and be given free entitlement to a publicly funded state education system.

Many commentators have cast doubt upon the validity of the labour theory of value. Marx rejected the analysis and conclusion of most classical economists because they refused to accept his assumption that labour power was the only productive agent capable of creating value within commodities. However, the choice of 'labour power' in the process of value creation is arbitrary. Labour cannot function without sufficient food; Marx therefore could have constructed a theory of value in which food units, rather than labour units were at the root of the creation of surplus value.

In addition, we can also cast doubt on Marx's decision to largely ignore 'use value' and place emphasis upon 'exchange value'. By doing this Marx displaces the central role of 'desire' in our decision to purchase. For Marx: *'The price then, is merely the money-name of the quantity of social labour realized in his commodity'* (Marx 1961). Clearly, many fashionable products from replica football shirts, to cars and houses are regarded as valuable irrespective of the labour power that went into making the commodity. If I live in an Edwardian house built in 1904 and currently valued at £200,000, this figure bears no relationship to the number of units of labour that went into its production. What gives commodities their value is the intensity of the desire for them; if there is no desire to enjoy one's personal use value of a commodity then it contains no value.

Marx argues that the value of a commodity reflects the labour power contained within that commodity. However, Marx also assumes that capital goods, machinery, raw materials that are also key elements in the production of a commodity, are bought from other capitalists at their *true* value. In other words, Marx assumes that capital goods, machinery, raw materials do not generate surplus value. In the real world however, if a factory becomes fully automated it can still generate a profit, suggesting that in contrast to the Marxian argument, it is possible to exploit capital goods, machinery, raw materials, etc. and generate surplus value. Moreover, in recent years a number of capitalists, such as farmers and manufacturers supplying supermarkets, have complained that they are having their profit margins squeezed by the need for supermarkets to maintain profit margins. What this suggests is that capitalists can exploit – that is, extract surplus value – from other capitalists, and that the value of a commodity has a number of possible sources and is not dependent upon labour power alone. Surprisingly, even though Marx was highly critical of classical economists, and argued that they were merely apologists for capitalism, Marx assumes conditions of perfect competition when discussing the labour theory of value. Whereas in the real economy, effective capitalists have devised a series of economic and non-economic measures and strategies to exploit other capitalists.

The relationship between man and environment

Marx outlined a relationship between man and nature which is today echoed in the writings of ecological economists. He appreciated that people live in a symbiotic relationship with nature. In his *Economic and Philosophical Manuscripts* he wrote that '*As plants, animals, minerals, air, light etc. in theory form part of human consciousness, partly as objects of a natural science, partly as objects of art . . . so they also form in practice a part of human life and activity . . . Nature is the inorganic body of man, that is, nature insofar as it is not the human body. Man lives by nature. This means that nature is his body with which he must remain in perpetual process in order not to die.*'

Marx recognised that man interacts with nature through technology, and that technological processes transform nature. In capitalist society nature has become commodified (treated as a commodity that can be bought and sold). Man needs to be aware of the transforming potential of technology, because in transforming nature we are transforming part of the reality that is part of our everyday existence, and that by doing this in a negative way we threaten our own destruction. In *Das Kapital*, Marx wrote that '*Technology discloses man's dealing with nature, the process of production by which he sustains his life, and thereby lays bare the mode of formation of his social relations, and the mental conceptions that flow from them.*'

This theme of the relationship between man, nature and technology has been picked up on and developed by more recent thinkers such as Rachel Carson, who outlined the impact of the production of chemical like DDT on the environment, and José Bové, who warns of the dangers of treating the natural world as a commodity.

Marx was arguably the most influential thinker of the twentieth century but his ideas have suffered because of their close association with the Stalinist dictatorship in the Soviet Union and because of the way in which his ideas were turned into a number of slogans: 'All property is theft', 'Dictatorship of the proletariat' etc. It is important to make a distinction between what Marxists have done and said with the economic analysis of Marx himself. As we have seen above Marx did not outline a blueprint on how to organise and run a communist society. Moreover, Marx assumed that capitalism contained within itself the seeds of its own destruction. We could argue that his predictions were wrong; however, some of his predictions were remarkably accurate: on increasing globalisation, on the concentration of ownership in the hands of a few capitalists, on the long-term tendency of the rate of profit to fall.

Further Reading

ABBINETT, R. (1998) *Truth and social science*. London, Sage.

ALTHUSSER, L. (1971) *Reading Capital*. London, Allen Lane.

APPADURAI, A. (1989) Disjunction and difference in the global cultural economy. *Theory Culture and Society* 7, 295–310.

ASHLEY, D. (1997) *History without a subject*. Boulder, Westview Press.

BEST, S. (2002) *Introduction to politics and society*. London, Sage.

BEST, S. (2003) *Beginners' guide to social theory*. London, Sage.

CALLINICOS, A. (1991) *The revenge of history: Marxism and East European revolutions*. Cambridge, Polity.

ENGELS, F. (1844) Letter to Bloch. *Karl Mark and Frederich Engels selected works in one volume*. London, Lawrence and Wishart.

HOOGVELT, A.A. (1982) *The Third World in global development*. London, Macmillan.

JAMESON, F. (1991) *Postmodernism: or the cultural logic of late capitalism*. London, Routledge.

MANDEL, E. (1976) Introduction. In Marx, K. *Capital: a critique of political economy*. Volume 1, Fowkes, B. (trans.). Harmondsworth, Penguin.

MANNING, P. (1996) Postmodernisms and the mass media: some further criticisms and teaching strategies. *Social Science Teacher* 25(3), 22–27.

MARX, K. (1844) Theses on Feuerbach. *Karl Mark and Frederich Engels selected works in one volume*. London, Lawrence and Wishart.

MARX, K. AND ENGELS, F. (1872) *The German ideology*. London, Lawrence and Wishart.

PANITCH, L. (1994) Globalisation and the state. In Miliband, R. and Panitch, L. *Between globalisation and nationalism*. London, The Merlin Press.

WALLERSTEIN, E. (1979) *The capitalist world economy*. Cambridge, Cambridge University Press.

WALLERSTEIN, E. (1980) *The modern world system II*. New York, Academic Press.

Alfred Marshall
(1842–1924)

ALFRED MARSHALL, THE CAMBRIDGE ECONOMIST, WALKED IN THE FOOTPRINTS OF THE giants of the classical school and like them was to make his own major imprint on the subject of economics. Not only were his ideas communicated through his published works but also through his students, for Marshall was a wonderful teacher. Marshall's famous text, *Principles of Economics*, was to become the standard work in economics. It was published in 1890 and ran through eight editions during Marshall's lifetime. If you manage to borrow a library copy of Marshall's *Principles* you will be in privileged company, for the book that you hold will have been valued by many students before you, and you can be sure that it will have helped them to understand how the economy works in a more informed way. Reading the text today you will be struck by how modern the treatment is, particularly in the field of micro-economics.

Marshall strongly believed that he was the recipient of an important inheritance from Smith, Ricardo, Bentham and Mill. He saw his work as being part of a process of continuity which he valued above radical change. His motto was *natura non facit saltum*, 'nature does not leap', which adorned the title page of his *Principles of Economics*. He wrote: *'The present treatise is an attempt to present a modern version of old doctrines with the aid of the new work, and with reference to the new problems, of our own age.'*

For Marshall, therefore, economics was seen as a constantly developing way of thinking that needed to be regularly updated to take account of changes in the real world. Whereas the earlier classical economists had been writing in an era in which agriculture and trade were only just starting to be replaced by industry as the driving force in the economy, Marshall was writing in an era in which industry had become well established so that his analysis of business activity was closely related to industrial as well as agricultural and trading situations.

Marshall was the most important British economist of the neoclassical school (a group which improved on the classical ideas of value by showing how value is determined by the twin forces of demand and supply). In 1885 he became the chair of economics at Cambridge, and the enthusiasm and influence that Marshall put into his work at Cambridge enabled the university to become a world centre of excellence in this field of study. Many famous economists studied under Marshall, including the best known of them all, John Maynard Keynes. These economists were able to take the subject forward partly because they had had such expert tuition.

While the work of a number of his contemporaries was essentially theoretical, Marshall was more concerned with producing work which could be applied to the real world. Marshall shared his ideas with his students and only published his work when he had finally honed the finished article. This enabled others to borrow some of his ideas and to publish first.

He was a firm believer that economics was of value in throwing light on practical problems rather than just an academic exercise. It was this pragmatic approach to economics that gave Marshall's interpretations the edge over rival theoretical inter-pretations of economics at the time.

Marshall strongly stated the case that economics is about everyday life: *'Political economy or economics is a study of mankind in the ordinary business of life; it examines that part of individual and social action which is most closely connected with the attain-ment and with the use of the material requisites of wellbeing.*

Thus it is on the one side a study of wealth; and on the other, and more important side, a study of man. For man's character has been moulded by his everyday work, and the material resources which he thereby procures, more than by any other influence unless it be that of his religious ideas; and the two great forming agencies of the world's history have been the religious and the economic.'

Methodology

MARSHALL STUDIED MATHEMATICS BEFORE HE MOVED ON TO ECONOMICS. AS AN expert mathematician with a first-class intellect he was very cautious about how mathematics should be used in economics. He saw economics as providing an engine of enquiry which when used by intelligent people would help them to understand better how society functions and to make contributions which would help to improve society.

Because he understood the limitations of mathematics he used it sparingly, and only when it helped to throw light on a subject. The approach he used in his *Principles* was to place the mathematical and graphical sections in the footnotes and appendices so as not to interfere with the clarity of his explanations. This is a practice that is unfor-tunately lacking in many modern economists, some of whom mask their inability to use the engine of enquiry in confusing mathematics.

In a letter of 27 February 1906 Marshall gave some very useful advice: *'a good mathematical theorem dealing with economic hypotheses was very unlikely to be good economics; and I went more and more on the rules –*

1. *Use mathematics as a shorthand language, rather than as an engine of inquiry.*
2. *Keep them till you have done.*
3. *Translate into English.*
4. *Then illustrate by examples that are important in real life.*

5. *Burn the mathematics.*

6. *If you can't succeed in 4 burn 3'* (Pigou 1925).

Instead of representing pure theory, an approach popular in the neoclassical economics of the time, Marshall's work harked back to the blend of empiricism and analysis which Smith used in *The Wealth of Nations.* *by experiment*

At the start of his *Principles* (1920) Marshall wrote: *'The study of theory must go hand in hand with that of facts; and for dealing with most modern problems it is modern facts that are of the greatest use. For the economic records of the distant past are in some respects slight and untrustworthy; and the economic conditions of early times are wholly unlike those of free enterprise; of general education, of true democracy, of steam, of the cheap press and the telegraph.'*

His emphasis was therefore on making economics useful: *'Economics has then as its purpose firstly to acquire knowledge for its own sake, and secondly to throw light on practical issues.'*

Marshall's approach to applying common sense in thinking through economic problems bears strong parallels with Adam Smith. Marshall (1920) stated that *'Economic science is but the working of common sense aided by appliances of organized analysis and general reasoning, which facilitate the task of collecting, arranging, and drawing inferences from particular facts. Though its scope is always limited, though its work without the aid of common sense is vain, yet it enables common sense to go further in difficult problems than would otherwise be possible.'*

Marshall realised the power of economics to set out general laws relating to human behaviour and actions, and that economics has as powerful a role to play in human understanding as do the natural sciences such as physics. However, as a social science it is often more difficult for the economist to set out clear and simple laws because of the complexity of human behaviour. He wrote that *'economic laws are statements with regard to the tendencies of man's action under certain conditions. They are hypothetical only in the same sense as are the laws of the physical sciences; for those laws also contain or imply conditions. But there is more difficulty in making the conditions clear, and more danger in any failure to do so, in economics than in physics. The laws of human action are not indeed as simple, as definite or as clearly ascertainable as the law of gravitation, but many of them may rank with the laws of those natural sciences which deal with complex subject matter.'*

Marshall saw that economics could play an important part in illuminating the relationship between cause and effect. However, he felt that the laws of economics were not the same as ethical principles, so economists alone could not provide the answers as to how society should make progress. He states that *'In accordance with English traditions, it is held that the function of the science is to collect, arrange and analyse economics facts, and to apply the knowledge gained by observation and experience, in determining what are likely to be the immediate and ultimate effects of various groups of causes; and it is held that the Laws of economics are statements of tendencies expressed in the indicative mood, and not ethical precepts in the imperative. Economic laws and reasonings in fact are merely a part of the material which Conscience and Common-sense have to turn to account in solving practical problems, and in laying down rules which may be a guide in life'* (Marshall 1961).

Marshall (1961) saw that the study of economics was particularly relevant to understanding business relationships. He set out the scope of economics in the following way: 'Economics is a study of men as they live and move and think in the ordinary business of life. But it concerns itself chiefly with those motives which affects, most powerfully and most steadily man's conduct in the business part of his life.'

Marshall's view of measuring incentives and motivations underpins much of mainstream modern economic thinking about the monetary measurement of the strength of motivation. The modern student can learn a lot from Marshall's (1920) statement that economics 'concerns itself chiefly with those desires, aspirations and other affections of human nature, the outward manifestations of which appear as incentives to action in such a form that the force or quantity of the incentives can be estimated and measured with some approach to accuracy; and which therefore are in some degree amenable to treatment by scientific machinery. An opening is made for the methods and the tests of science as soon as the force of a person's motives – not the motives themselves – can be approximately measured by the sum of money, which he will just give up in order to secure a desired satisfaction; or again by the sum which is just required to induce him to undergo a certain fatigue.'

Marshall saw this process of 'monetisation' of the strength of motives as giving an edge to economics over other social sciences. He stated (1920) that 'It is this definite and exact money measurement of the steadiest motives in business life, which has enabled economics far to outrun every other branch of the study of man . . . this economist's balance, rough and imperfect as it is, has made economics more exact than any other branch of social science . . . But of course economics cannot be compared with the exact physical sciences; for it deals with the ever changing and subtle forces of human nature.' Marshall's sense of realism made him view his economics not as complete and absolute but as tentative and provisional, a link in the endless quest for truth.

Marshall recognised that economists had little to say about the nature of motives in themselves – however, through rough money measurement it is able to pass comment and to measure the strength of their driving force. He expressed this in the following way (1920): 'We cannot indeed measure motives of any kind, whether high or low, as they are in themselves, we can measure only their moving force. Money is never a perfect measure of that force, and it is not even a tolerably good measure unless careful account is taken of the general conditions under which it works, and especially of the riches or poverty of whose action is under discussion. But with careful precautions money affords a fairly good measure of the moving force of a great part of the motives by which men's lives are fashioned.'

Another of Marshall's key methodological approaches was to use the ceteris paribus approach (other things remaining equal) to single out particular segments of economic interaction for scrutiny while holding other elements constant. This approach involves altering selected economic variables while holding others constant. This is essential because economic variables are so closely interconnected.

Biography

ALFRED MARSHALL WAS BORN IN 1842, THE SON OF A CLERK AT THE BANK OF ENGLAND and a butcher's daughter. His father was a tough task master often interrogating his son until eleven at night on the intricacies of Hebrew grammar. He was expected to study hard and to achieve academic excellence. Fortunately, he was able to escape from this hothousing during summer holidays on his uncle's farm. From an early age he showed exceptional promise and one of his schoolteachers said that he had a 'genius for mathematics'. However, his father was keen for his son to enter the church and with this vocation in mind he won a scholarship to Oxford to study Classics. During his time at Oxford he began to take an interest in the ideas of Smith, Ricardo and Mill. He is reported to have made this change in the course of a discussion with another student who criticised Marshall's ideas for social reform and had said to Marshall 'Ah! You would not talk in that way, if you knew anything about business, or even Political Economy.' This criticism had led Marshall to start reading the economists. As a result of this shift in his interests Marshall switched universities to Cambridge, receiving financial support from his uncle and from money earned by coaching other students in mathematics.

Keynes (1975) described this transition in the following way: '*No! he would not be buried at Oxford under dead languages; he would run away – to be a cabin boy at Cambridge and climb the rigging of geometry and spy out the heaven.*'

Marshall's contribution to economics was substantially determined by his beliefs. While studying at Cambridge he became a firm supporter of Christian values without ever being convinced about Christian beliefs. In particular he was concerned to find ways of alleviating poverty and in combining ethics with economics. In a biographical note he wrote '*In my vacations I visited the poorest quarters of several cities and walked through one street after another, looking at the faces of the poorest people.*' In the slums of London's East End he was particularly struck by the number of 'cringeing wretches'.

Marshall therefore committed his life to the pursuit of economics teaching and research as the means to finding ways to alleviate poverty. He lectured primarily at Cambridge University where he developed a reputation for clarity of explanation, and for making ideas relevant to real issues. In addition he played a prominent part in public life, acting as an advisor to governments and business alike so that his work had a major influence on the society of his day. He was confident that economics was capable of providing a way forward. He set out the positive contribution of economics as follows: '*The social and economic forces already at work are changing the distribution of wealth for the better: that they are persistent and increasing in strength; and that their influence is for the greater part cumulative; that the socio-economic organism is more delicate and complex than at first sight appears; and that large ill-considered changes might result in grave disaster*' (1920).

Because Marshall believed in gradual change he opposed radical proposals such as socialism which he criticised in the following way: '*The collective ownership of the means of production would deaden the energies of mankind, and arrest economic progress; unless before its introduction the whole people had acquired a power of unselfish devotion to the public good which is now relatively rare. And . . . it might probably destroy much that is most beautiful and joyful in the private and domestic relations of life. These are the main reasons which cause patient students of economics generally to anticipate little good and much evil from schemes for sudden and violent reorganization of the economic, social and political conditions of life*' (1920).

With Marshall economic analysis began to expand into the very nitty-gritty of commercial life and its processes. The majority of Marshall's students went on to play an important role in business life – and they were able to do so with a fuller understanding of economic relationships.

In addition to the classical economists, the two major influences on Marshall's development of economic theory were the French mathematical economist Antoine Cournot (1801–77), and the German mathematical economist Heinrich von Thünen. Cournot believed in working things out through reason rather than experience.

As a mathematician Marshall was able to appreciate the logic of Cournot's reasoning. However, whereas Cournot was a firm believer in explanation through mathematical symbols, Marshall preferred words. In the English edition of his *Recherches* (1897), Cournot wrote that *'every one has a vague idea of the effect of competition. Theory should have attempted to render the idea more precise, and yet, for lack of regarding the question from the proper point of view, and from want of recourse to symbols (of which the use in this connection becomes indispensable), economic writers have not the least improved on popular notions in this respect. These notions have remained as ill defined and ill-applied in their works as in popular language.'*

Cournot developed some key ideas in the area of competition theory introducing the notion of the marginal cost of production as the cost of the additional unit produced, and the marginal revenue as the sales receipt from this additional unit. He examined a number of different forms of competition in the market. In addition he developed the idea of demand and supply, showing that demand and supply could be set out as functions – relating physical quantities to prices and costs. For example, in his *Recherches* (1838) he set out the law of demand in the following way: *'Let us admit therefore that the sales or the annual demand D is, for each article a particular function F (p) of the price of such articles. To know the form of this function would be to know what we call the law of demand or of sales. It depends evidently on the kind of utility of the article, on the nature of the services it can render, or the enjoyment it can procure, or the habits and customs of the people, or the average wealth, and on the scale on which wealth is distributed.'*

From reading von Thünen Marshall was able to better understand the marginal principle in the theory of production. Von Thünen illustrated the impact of varying labour inputs while holding capital constant, and vice versa. He showed that the net revenue of the firm is maximised when the value of the marginal product (the last unit of output) is equal to the marginal factor cost to produce that unit. Not only did Marshall value the techniques employed by these economists but he also admired the philanthropic humanitarianism of von Thünen, which matched Marshall's own view of ethics.

Although he continually sought to avoid unnecessary mathematics in his work his insights and approaches prepared the ground for the rise of econometrics. Many of the techniques and ideas that he developed encouraged further empirical and statistical studies by other scholars, for example in statistical research into the creation of demand curves, and the analysis of elasticity of demand.

Key works

Although Marshall produced a range of important papers and books, his finest writing is to be found in his *Principles of Economics* which contemporaries identified as the defining work on the subject.

Building on 'common sense'

All of the great economists understood the importance of making their field of study applicable to the real world and to everyday problem solving. Marshall inherited the legacy of applying 'common sense' from Adam Smith. His work was all about communicating economic ideas in a clear and easy to understand way. However, he also emphasised the importance of developing a methodology involving the application of organised analysis and general reasoning. He set out in his *Principles* (1920) that *'Economic science is but the working of common sense aided by appliances of organized analysis and general reasoning, which facilitate the task of collecting, arranging, and drawing inferences from particular facts. Though its scope is always limited, though its work without the aid of common sense is vain, yet it enables common sense to go further in difficult problems than would otherwise be possible.'*

The Marshallian cross

The Marshallian cross is perhaps the best-known piece of economic analysis in wide use today – only paralleled in significance by the later Keynesian cross that is discussed in the chapter on Keynes.

In creating the cross Marshall brought together two central concepts in economics – demand and supply – to show how price is determined in the market place.

The supply curve is based on the classic notion of the costs of production. Suppliers require a higher price to supply more output to the market to compensate for rising costs. However, in order to understand how price and hence value is determined we also need to take account of the other blade of the scissors – demand. Price is determined by the interaction between supply and demand.

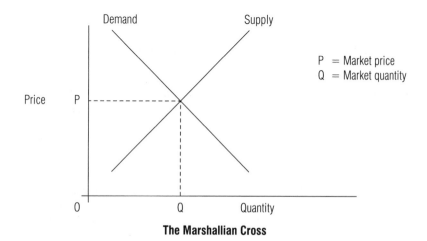

The Marshallian Cross

Equilibrium in the market place is created where the demand and supply curves intersect because at this point the requirements of suppliers and buyers are both realised.

Marshall drew on the writing of von Thünen and Cournot and to a lesser extent the English economist William Stanley Jevons in developing this analysis. These writers had shown that demand for a good is determined by its marginal utility – corresponding to the extra satisfaction gained from consuming additional units of a good.

Marshall was thus able to provide a clear exposition of the theory of price. We use this approach today.

The Marshallian demand curve

The Marshallian demand curve relates changes in the quantity demanded to changes in the demand price, and only to changes in the demand price.

Marshall (1920) explained the demand curve in the following way: *'To obtain complete knowledge of demand for anything, we should have to ascertain how much of it he would be willing to purchase at each of the prices at which it is likely to be offered; and the circumstance of his demand for, say, tea can be best expressed by a list of the prices which he is willing to pay; that is, by his several demand prices for different amount of it (This list may be called his demand schedule).'*

Marginal utility

Marshall was not the first to explain the concept of marginal utility, but he explained its importance more clearly than previous attempts. He was able to show that it was the marginal utility to be obtained from an item that determined its price – thus successfully explaining the paradox of value – helping us to understand, for example, why diamonds are sold for a high market price even though their total utility to society is less than water, which often does not command a price but in many places can be found in abundance. He described the way in which we make decisions based on marginal utility in the following way: *'if we find a man in doubt whether to spend a few pence on a cigar, or a cup of tea, or on riding home instead of walking home, then we may follow ordinary usage, and say that he expects from them equal pleasures'.*

Price elasticity of demand

In his *Principles* (1961) Marshall explained with considerable clarity the nature of elasticity of demand. He set this out in the form of a double fraction. Price elasticity measures the responsiveness or changes in quantity demanded to a price change. This is important in making business decisions. Raising the price of a good leads to a fall in demand. But how far will demand fall? Elasticity gives a measure of this change by showing:

$$\text{Price elasticity of demand} = \frac{\text{Proportionate change in quantity demanded}}{\text{Proportionate change in price}}$$

Today the concept of price elasticity is widely used in making pricing decisions. For example, in 2002 Notts County Football Club made substantial reductions in the price of their season tickets in the preseason period. They did this in the belief that price would be elastic, that is, the proportionate increase in quantity demanded would be much higher than the proportionate reduction in price. The government considers price elasticity in deciding whether it will pay to raise or lower taxes on cigarettes, spirits, wine etc.

Consumer and producer surplus

Another area that Marshall explained clearly in relation to demand and supply was that of consumer and producer surplus. He showed that at the market price many consumers gained a surplus because they would be prepared to pay more than the market price for the good. The consumer surplus is illustrated by the shaded area beneath the demand curve in the graph below.

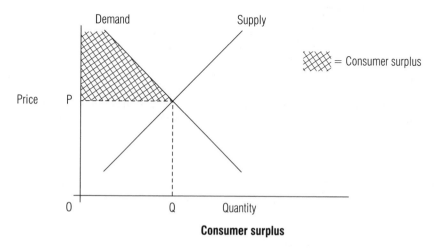

Consumer surplus

In the same way suppliers often receive a producer surplus. They would be prepared to supply some of the goods they supply to market at less than the market price. They therefore receive a surplus shown by the shaded area on the graph below. Monopolists typically receive a producer surplus. Because monopolists are able to restrict supply they are sometimes accused of profiteering at the expense of the consumer.

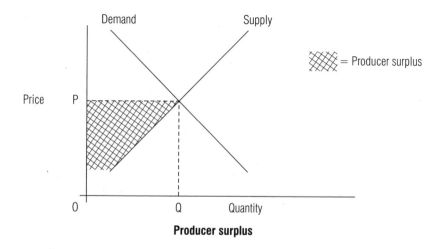

Producer surplus

Partial equilibrium analysis

Marshall was particularly interested in throwing light on the nature of business, industry and markets. Thus, while the focus of some economists like Jevons was on the micro-economic equilibrium of the individual consumer, and others were interested in the macro – total equilibrium analysis – Marshall was more interested in the particular equilibrium of the firm or industry, a focus that is referred to as partial equilibrium analysis. Marshall therefore opened up whole new areas of discussion and study into aspects such as the scale of operations of firms, the effects on output of changing quantities of factors of production employed etc.

The law of diminishing returns

Economists from the time of Smith onwards set out to explain the impacts of altering quantities of factors of production involved in producing outputs. While it is clear that combining increasing quantities of factors of production more effectively leads to more efficient production, there clearly comes a point when the use of additional quantities of a factor of production will start to have a negative effect. Marshall (1920) set out the law or statement of tendency to 'diminishing returns' in the following way: '*An increase in the capital and labour applied in the cultivation of land causes in general a less than proportionate increase in the amount of produce raised, unless it happens to coincide with an improvement in the arts of agriculture*'.

Marshall used historical observations to show that initially agriculturalists can benefit from applying more capital and labour to acres of land to benefit from increasing returns. However, an optimum point will be arrived at beyond which diminishing returns start to set in.

Marshall argued that rational behaviour involved weighing up the marginal return from using additional factors of production against the marginal cost of employing them. The entrepreneur should only employ additional factors of production up to the point at which the marginal cost of employing them is equal to the marginal revenue they produce.

Economies of scale

Marshall explained clearly the principle of economies of scale – that is, the cost advantages that firms are able to benefit from as a result of producing on a larger rather than a smaller scale. The principle of economies of scale has become an important part of development theory (the study of how economies can develop over time), as well as of business theory. Marshall divided economies of scale into internal economies resulting from the growth of an individual firm, and external economies resulting from development that benefited a range of firms in the same industry or locality.

A firm receives benefits from the internal economies which it is able to derive from even narrower specialisation, from the growing scale of its operations and from improved management. There are, in addition, external economies, benefits flowing to the firm considered as part of a larger industry. As examples of such benefits Marshall mentioned the availability of trade papers with technical and other information and the advantages that a firm derives from being located in a region with many firms of its kind, where it can draw on a pool of skilled labour and have on hand suppliers of highly specialised machinery and a host of subsidiary industries.

Time periods

Marshall introduced an approach to the application of time in economics which has proved invaluable to the present day particularly in the analysis of supply.

The Marshallian approach to time does not refer to clock time but to periods affecting changes in the output of products, that is, supply. Marshall identified three distinct time periods for the purpose of analysis.

1. The *market period*: this is the period in which there can be no adjustment in the supply of a product. In this period supply is perfectly inelastic – it is fixed whatever the price that a consumer is willing to pay for the product.

2. In the *short period* those inputs that are responsible for variable costs can be adjusted. For example, a firm may use more raw materials or variable labour costs. In the short period the firm can therefore increase supply. However, there is a limit to increases in supply resulting from the fact that certain factors cannot be altered, such as the size of the plant, fixed machinery and so on.

3. In the *long period* all of the inputs can be altered, including the plant. In the long period a business can build a new factory, buy in extra machines etc.

As a result, in the long period supply is relatively elastic. In the short period it is relatively inelastic, and in the market period it is perfectly inelastic.

The net result is that the effect of supply on market price is far greater in the longer period than in the short and market periods.

Quasi-rent

Marshall's understanding of the importance of time periods helped him to build on earlier research into economic rent to introduce the concept of quasi-rent. Earlier we saw that output restricting firms are able to benefit from producer surplus. However, they may not be able to hold on to this surplus indefinitely.

Quasi-rent is short period rent that is competed away in the course of time. Quasi-rent as an economic surplus can be earned by owners of equipment and land, and individuals with special skills and natural abilities. These resources are in fixed supply for short periods and thus yield surplus. For example, when the first ballpoint pens were developed they sold for what today would be regarded as ridiculously high prices. However, it was not too difficult for new firms to enter the ballpoint industry, and to compete away the abnormal profits earned by the firms that brought the idea most quickly to market.

In a similar way, in the early days of the dot.com revolution a number of entrepreneurs were able to earn very high salaries, or to earn large profits from setting up their own companies. However, within months many others copied these ideas so that earnings and profits were quickly reduced.

Quasi-rent therefore recognises that in the immediate period scarce factors are able to command high producer surpluses. However, quickly this rent may be squeezed. It is thus quasi (impermanent) rather than pure economic rent.

Conclusion

It seems likely that Marshall's *Principles* will always retain its position as the most influential economic text of its period. Today, new ideas about economics come from a range of sources and from a variety of texts. In contrast, the eight editions of Marshall's work represented the essentials of what was taught and learnt about economics in this country. However, today we have moved on from Marshall's work, and Marshall would be the first to recognise that over time new work must replace the old. For example, since Marshall's day far more emphasis is placed on macroeconomic and economy wide equilibrium. Over time new ideas have evolved from the old. However, what is striking about reading Marshall's work again is how much that you find in today's microeconomic textbooks still bears the imprint of Marshall. Unfortunately many modern writers lack the clarity of expression, and the practical application of ideas that was Marshall's trademark.

 **Further Reading**

BACKHOUSE, R. (2002) *The Penguin history of economics*. Penguin Classics, ch. 8.

BLAUG, M. (1968) *Economic theory in retrospect*, 2nd edn. Heinemann Educational, ch. 10.

COURNOT, A. (1897) *Researches into the mathematical principles of wealth* (trans. Bacon, N.T.). Macmillan.

MARSHALL, A. (1920) *Principles of economics, an introductory volume*, 8th edn. Reprinted 1961. Macmillan and Co Ltd.

KEYNES, M.M. (1975) Alfred Marshall 1842–1924 in Pigou, A.C. (ed.) *Memorial of Alfred Marshall*. Cambridge University Press.

PIGOU, A.C. (ed.) (1925) *Memorials of Alfred Marshall*. Macmillan and Co.

ROLL, E. (1954) *A history of economic thought*, 3rd edn. Faber & Faber, ch. 8.

SCHUMPETER, J.A. (1997) *Ten great economists*. Routledge.

SPIEGEL, H.W. (1971) *The growth of economic thought*. Prentice Hall, ch. 25.

Mahatma Gandhi

(1869–1948)

MOHANDAS K. GANDHI, OR MAHATMA GANDHI AS HE IS MORE WIDELY KNOWN, provided a radical critique of economics based on an ethical approach to human development with an abiding concern for the individual as 'the ultimate unit'.

He had no time for existing neoliberal growth models, or for an ideology based on capitalism. Gandhi's critique of existing Western ideas and value systems was expressed as much in his way of life and the role model that he set as in his published work. Much of his writing appeared in the press (*Young India*, in English, *Navajiban*, in Gujarati, and *Harijan*, in Hindi) where it was targeted at a wide audience. He outlined key development issues which faced the world of his day and the global economy of our day, for example in his statement that '*God forbid that India should ever take to industrialisation after the manner of the West. The economic imperialism of a single tiny island kingdom (England) is today keeping the world in chains. If an entire nation of 300 million took to similar economic exploitation, it would strip the world bare like locusts*' (*Young India*, 1925).

Gandhi's approach to economic decision-making was largely based on his religious and moral beliefs. He identified alternative approaches to organising the economy based on small scale, local initiatives, rather than on the economies of the larger market. He believed that decision-making should take place in small communities, and that well-being resides in a spiritual rather than a material dimension. Gandhi never set out to provide a coherent programme for the development of economic society, simply because he was opposed to the idea that individuals can impose their will on others. In his view individuals must develop their own perspectives and plans. An understanding of Gandhian economics is essential to everyone seeking to develop a true picture of the nature and purposes of society.

Gandhian economics provides a radical critique of the modern global economy based on the existing exploitation of resources and ecological irresponsibility.

J.C. Kumarappa (1948), one of Gandhi's 'disciples' (who has set out to formalise Gandhian economics in a series of texts), criticises the notion of globalisation and makes a plea for ecological responsibility by stating that '*If we produce everything we want from within a limited area, we are in a position to supervise the methods of production; while if we draw our requirements from the ends of the earth it becomes impossible for us to guarantee the conditions of production in such places*'.

Gandhi's ideas force traditional economists to question many of the assumptions on which they base their work, and possibly provide a more relevant framework for dealing with some of the key economic issues of the modern world, such as environmental degradation and widespread poverty.

In reality Gandhi's economic ideas had very little impact on economic policies in India following independence. The route chosen for development in India was one that was based on industrialisation and not on localisation. Gandhi admitted his failure to influence macroeconomic policy-making in India when he wrote to the press shortly after independence: *'Those who are in charge of the Government are my fellow-workers . . . If I have failed to convince them of the soundness and feasibility of (Gandhian) economics, how should I expect to convince others? They do not feel that they would be able to carry the people of India with them in the prosecution of what may be summed up as the "Khadi economics" and to renovate the villages of India through village industries.'*

In recent years, however, Gandhian economics has provided inspiration for the Chipko movement in India, and protest against the Narmada Dam project. The Chipko movement started in the Garwhal Himalaya in April 1973 and heralded the start of a wider movement of people to defend community rights to natural resources. The protest involved men, women and children 'hugging' forest trees rather than allowing them to be used for export. Typically these protests have been those of the poor against the rich, peasant against multinational, the local economy against the global economy. The Narmada protest movement was by the people of central India to prevent the development of a huge dam on the Narmada river taking away their rights to the natural resources of the area.

Gandhian economics provides an opportunity to reappraise the values of society in order to consider individual needs, and the relationship between man and nature. It is a challenge that conventional economists cannot ignore.

Methodology

GANDHI'S APPROACH TO ECONOMICS WAS BASED ON HIS OBSERVATION OF RELATIONS that existed in the world based on his own experience. He was able to draw on direct experience of apartheid in South Africa, colonialism in India, and the clash between Eastern and Western values. He was able to make comparisons between industrial consumer-based societies, and simple agrarian societies, and to compare the impact of the two models on the existing resource base. Given the evidence based on his own experience he liked to employ analytical reasoning to work out possible solutions to problems such as the most suitable approaches to 'grassroots development'. He experimented with a new model of economic relationships based on his own lifestyle. Although Gandhian economics is criticised for its 'idealism', Gandhi's approach was based directly on setting up economic relationships, and trying them out through experimentation, and in this respect was based on testing out reality, albeit on a local scale. Gandhi was opposed to collectivist solutions to problems, always placing a strong emphasis on individualism of thought. He valued tradition but saw that too much reliance of traditional thinking was harmful – *'It was good to swim in the waters of tradition but to sink in them was suicide'*.

Biography

MOHANDAS K. GANDHI WAS BORN IN A SMALL VILLAGE IN WESTERN INDIA CALLED Porbandar. He was brought up in a strict Hindu family, in which his mother emphasised the values of simplicity, and religious values, while his father, as the chief minister of the local town provided a strong role model in leadership and community values.

Gandhi was brought up to follow a branch of Hinduism called Vaisnavism, based on the worship of the god Vishnu. The family were also strict followers of Jainism. Jainism involves a number of ethical and practical principles which include vegetarianism, tolerance of other people and cultures, a frequent use of fasting for spiritual purposes, and the practice of *ahimsa* (i.e. non-injury to all living things). *Ahimsa* provides a strong ethical ideology because it is based on the assumption that all living things are to be valued. Followers of Jainism will seek to avoid treading on insects, and may place a cloth over their mouth to avoid breathing in living organisms. They are fervent believers in non-violence in human relationships.

Gandhi's school education was not systematic, being broken up, for example, by periods in which he took time off school to take care of his sick father, and he was married at 13. In 1887, he enrolled for a course at the University of Bombay, but did not stay there long before persuading his family to support him to go to England to become a barrister, so that he could return to India to gain a position like that of his father.

Gandhi enrolled for a law course at University College, London, and was an excellent student. He was all too aware of the clash of cultures between Eastern and Western values. One of his earliest difficulties resulted from being a vegetarian, but he was able to find a vegetarian restaurant in London. This is one of the first areas in which he was able to gain independence of thought, and this gave him confidence for ongoing struggles and conflicts.

Gandhi returned to India, shortly after the death of his mother, but found it almost impossible to get a job. At the time there were too many people seeking jobs in the legal profession in India and he was unable to take up a satisfactory post. He was therefore pleased to be offered a post working for a firm in Natal in South Africa.

However, South Africa was dominated by the apartheid mentality, with widespread segregation between the races. It was during this period that Gandhi became a radical activist for social reform, taking on the political mantel of his father. In 1894 he campaigned to prevent a Bill that set out to take away the vote from Indians in South Africa. The movement was unsuccessful but Gandhi had become a firm believer in radical politics to change society. He was now practising law in Durban and had formed the Natal Indian Congress, for which he was the secretary. Returning to India to bring his wife to South Africa he made some well-publicised speeches criticising the situation in South Africa. He returned to be faced by a hostile mob of white South Africans and narrowly escaped with his life. Gandhi was at the forefront of political activism against the hated apartheid regime, and was continually at loggerheads with the authorities.

Returning to India Gandhi became the focal point for Indian politics. During the First World War he had supported Britain, but increasingly he was to become alienated by heavy-handed British colonialism. This came to a head with the passing of laws in Britain which set out that those accused of 'sedition' could be imprisoned without trial. Gandhi organised non-violent protest against these laws – but they spilled over into violence.

By the early-1920s Gandhi had become a focus of protest against British colonialism. He became the central figure in the Indian National Congress, which led a boycott of British goods and services. The Congress movement organised massive civil disobedience of a non-violent kind with strikes, and non-cooperation with the authorities. However, Gandhi was worried that this would spill over into violence and eventually called off the protest. Gandhi was imprisoned for six years (although he only served the first two).

Increasingly, Gandhi was worried about the way in which India was splitting into a divided community based on Muslims and Hindus, and clashes between these communities were often hostile. Gandhi's way of dealing with these divisions was to look for a peaceful resolution, based on prayers for peace and spiritual fasting.

Gandhi organised a series of peaceful protests against the symbols of British colonialism. One of the most celebrated of these was the protest against the tax on salt. To combat this, Gandhi organised a mass march of people to the Arabian Sea where people made their own salt by evaporating seawater.

Gandhi was appointed to represent the Indian people in discussions about change which were held in London. These talks foundered and on his return to India he was imprisoned with a number of other Indian Congress leaders.

While in jail Gandhi and the others heard that a new constitution that was being planned for India, discriminated against the lowest caste members of society – the 'untouchables'. Gandhi organised a fast in protest against this and lost a lot of strength. It was feared that he would die, and his death would have ignited the powder keg against the colonialists. This led to a rapid rewriting of the constitution.

From the mid-1930s Gandhi resigned from the National Congress to concentrate on 'grassroots' development issues in India, based on developing thriving networks in rural areas of India. Gandhi's teaching was inspired by the ideal of *swaraj* (self-government), which for him meant not only getting rid of the burden of colonial rule, but also a process through which village people became self-reliant, and through which they would gain self-respect. He argued that it was ridiculous for Indians to import cotton cloth from abroad, when India produced vast quantities of raw cotton.

He therefore encouraged rural people to spin and weave themselves, arguing that 'Homespun' was the most valuable of all textiles. He centred his activities on the region of Sebagram.

After the Second World War India became independent, and was then split into India and Pakistan. There continued extensive enmity between Muslims and Hindus breaking out into bouts of terrible violence. Gandhi played a major role in reducing the tension between the two communities. However, the part he played in the peace process led to his tragic death at the hands of extremists. He was shot on his way to evening prayers on 30 January 1948.

Key works

The Collected Works of Mahatma Gandhi (1958)

Ethics and economics

Perhaps the most important lesson that Gandhi teaches other economists is never to divorce ethics from economics. In *Young India* (3 October 1921) Gandhi wrote '*I must confess that I do not draw a sharp or any distinction between economics and ethics*'.

In Hinduism the term *dharma* is used to mean moral law, which is the sacred duty of a society. Gandhi (1958) wrote that '*If dharma and economic interests cannot be reconciled either the conception of that dharma is false or the economic interest takes the form of unmitigated selfishness and does not aim at collective welfare*'.

For Gandhi, therefore, there was no point in economics if it was not based on *dharma*. If traditional economics therefore fails to take a Gandhian approach then it has no substance in the domain of moral values. He was determined to try and create a new kind of economics. At the same time, he wanted to create systems that worked in the real world, and were thus pragmatic. This requires us to reappraise our value systems.

Independence

Gandhi was opposed to the principle of dependency. In India this most obviously took the form of dependence of a colony to the coloniser. This had an impact on all aspects of life, so that production and consumption in Indian society was determined by relationships with Britain. Gandhi argued that individuals could free themselves from this dependency by building their strength from grassroots level upwards. Rather than industrialising through economies of scale, India could build up its own local industries using local resources. Independence could be achieved by refusing to buy foreign imports, by building up domestic industries, and by not getting trapped in an ideology of consumerism. The spinning wheel was the vehicle for meeting local needs, and boycotting foreign goods could reduce consumer dependency.

Gandhi set up the *Swadeshi* movement to encourage people to become more independent. *Swadeshi* means 'home-grown'. During the 1930s Gandhi's Indian National Congress encouraged people to wear only *khaddar* (cloth made by spinning wheels in the villages). Gandhi justified this approach both in terms of political independence and on moral grounds, arguing that we have a responsibility to our own local community.

Small-scale production

Gandhi was opposed to the widespread use of mechanisation because he saw machinery as rapidly taking the place of people in the production process. He argued that it is self-evident that machines create unemployment by taking away the work of people. Moreover, the development of machinery leads to a concentration of power in the hands of capitalists and in urban areas at the expense of rural ones.

Gandhi's solution to the problem of industrialisation was that of self-employment by the people. However, he was not totally opposed to machinery, and felt that machinery that could be used on a small scale in local communities could be helpful. For example, he was in favour of the Singer sewing machine which supported human efforts, and surgical instruments which help in medical treatment. He was also in favour of the use of machinery in the public utilities, provided the state acted as a guardian to make sure that they were used in a socially beneficial way.

Decentralisation

One of Gandhi's major concerns was with the decentralisation of production through a process of village industries. Within the local market he was in favour of free market prices because he saw too much evidence of price controls leading to inefficiencies. In *Harijan* (November 1947) he stated that '*There are enough cereals, pulses and oil-seeds in the villages of India. The artificial control of prices the growers do not understand. They therefore refuse willingly to part with their stock at a price much lower than they command in the open market . . . Controls give rise to fraud, suppression of truth, intensification of the black market and to artificial scarcity.*'

Self-respect

Gandhi identified 'self-respect' as an essential ingredient of well-being. This is a dimension that is frequently ignored in conventional economic indicators of growth and well-being. Providing bundles of goods and services is important to individuals but it cannot buy self-respect. Gandhi felt that many Indian villagers had lost self-respect because of dependence on foreign markets, and because of unsanitary living conditions, underemployment, poverty and hardship. Real growth for the community therefore involved creating model villages in which everyone would be able to gain self-respect.

Model villages as a basis for grassroots development

Gandhi believed in building the economy from the local level upwards. At a local level it is essential to build up social structures in which people are able to gain self-respect, in which they can live in harmony with their resources base, and in which they do not create problems which spill out into the larger ecosystem, wider economy and society. He described what a model village would look like in the following way: '*It will have cottages with sufficient light and ventilation, built of a material obtainable within a radius of five miles of it. The cottages will have courtyards enabling householders to plant vegetables for domestic use and to house their cattle. The village lanes and streets will be free of all avoidable dust. It will have wells according to its needs and accessible to all. It will have houses of worship for all, also a common meeting place, a village common for grazing its cattle, a cooperative dairy, primary and secondary schools in which industrial (i.e. vocational) education will be the central fact, and it will have Panhayats for settling disputes. It will produce its own grains, vegetables and fruit, and its own Khadi. This is roughly my idea of a model village . . .* (Harijan, 9 January 1937).

However, Gandhi realised that his notion of model villages based on decentralised planning would need to be developed locally. He could not impose a solution for development on others. As he states in his *Collected Works*: *'I cannot speak with either the definiteness or the confidence of a Stalin or a Hitler as I have no cut and dried programme which I can impose on the villagers.'*

Limitation of wants

For Gandhi one of the *'distinguishing features of modern civilisation is an indefinite multiplicity of wants.'*

One of Gandhi's best-known statements was that *'The world has enough for everybody's need, but not enough for everybody's greed.'*

Another of Gandhi's 'disciples', Mira Behn, highlights the way in which modern society has lost touch with Mother Earth, writing in 1949 that *'The tragedy today is that educated and moneyed classes are altogether out of touch with the vital fundamentals of existence – our Mother Earth, and the animal and vegetable population which she sustains. This world of Nature's planning is ruthlessly plundered, despoiled and disorganised by man whenever he gets the chance. By his science and machinery he may get huge returns for a time, but ultimately will come desolation. We have got to study Nature's balance, and develop our lives within her laws, if we are to survive as a physically healthy and morally decent species.'*

In an incisive analysis of Gandhi's views of consumption behaviour Ajit Dasgupta (1993) argues that Gandhi's contribution to welfare economics comes from stating *'that an individual's welfare is best achieved not, as economic theory suggests, by attempting to maximise the satisfaction of a multiplicity of desires subject only to the prevailing budget constraint but rather by reflecting on his desires and trying to choose between them.'* Dasgupta argues that desire, satisfaction, happiness and welfare are not the same thing because:

1. Not all kinds of happiness add to welfare, e.g. drugs.
2. Not all kinds of desire-satisfaction contribution to happiness – because it seems that the more people get the more they want, leading to a slavery to desire.

Gandhi (1958) used this critique to question the whole notion of Western 'culture': *'If you have one room you will desire to have two rooms, three rooms, the more the merrier. And similarly you will have to have as much furniture as you can put in your house, and so on endlessly. And the more you possess the better culture you represent or some such thing.'*

Gandhi was keenly aware of the relationship between the wants of those who lived at the core of industrial society, and those who live at the periphery, seeing that poverty was largely a product of affluence. In one newspaper article he highlighted this point by stating: *'We are sitting in this fine pandal under a blaze of electric lights, but we do not know we are burning these lights at the expense of the poor'* (*Harijan*, 11 May 1935).

Conclusion

The world of today is not a Gandhian world of localisation, limitation of wants, and sustainability. Rather we are faced by an increasingly globalised world in which the gap between rich and poor is growing ever wider and in which the notion of *dharma* has little influence on patterns of growth. Gandhi has many followers particularly among ecologists, but very little influence in mainstream economic thinking. However, it seems inevitable that economists of every persuasion will have to give more serious thought to ways of blending morality with economics, and to developing growth patterns for consumption that are more compatible with the carrying capacity of Mother Earth.

Further Reading

ANJARIA, J.J. (1941–42) The Gandhian approach to Indian economics. *Indian Journal of Economics* 22, 357–366.

DASGUPTA, A. (1993) *A history of Indian economic thought.* Routledge, ch. 9.

GANDHI, M.K. Writings in *Young India, Harijan, Navajiban.*

GANDHI, M. (1958) *The collected works of Mahatma Gandhi.* Government of India, Ministry of Information and Broadcasting, Publications Division.

GUHA, R. AND MARTINEZ-ALIER, J. (1997) *Varieties of environmentalism: essays north and south.* Earthscan, ch. 8.

GUPTA, K.M. AND BEHN, M. (1992) *Birth centenary volume.* Himalaya Seva Sangh.

KUMARAPPA, J.C. (1938) *Why the village movement,* 2nd edn. Rajahmundry, Hindusthan Publishing.

KUMARAPPA, J.C. (1948) *The economy of permanence,* 2nd edn. Wardha, All India Village Industries Association.

PRABHU, R.K. (1966) *Industrialise – and perish!* Najivan Press.

Irving Fisher

(1867–1947)

FROM THE LATE NINETEENTH CENTURY ONWARDS, THE STUDY OF ECONOMICS HAD started to make great strides forward in the United States drawing inspiration from parallel studies in Britain and Continental Europe. It was not long, therefore, before a number of new and exciting insights in economic thinking began to flow from the other side of the Atlantic.

Irving Fisher stands out as the most renowned American economist of the first half of the twentieth century. He used mathematical approaches to explore the relationship between economic variables, and his statistical and quantitative approaches pioneered the development of modern day econometrics (the measurement of economic phenomena). Fisher's approach showed the importance of painstaking gathering and interpretation of statistics and the development of mathematical models.

Fisher's major contributions to economics consisted of:

1. Developing quantitative approaches to empirical research – for example in the development of index numbers, and

2. Creating key theories involving the relationship between the quantity of money in the economy and prices, and developing an explanation of the relationship between capital and interest.

Fisher was to lay the foundations of modern day understanding of the part that money plays in the economy.

Methodology

FISHER SET OUT TO DEVELOP SCIENTIFIC APPROACHES TO ECONOMICS AND USED highly organised mathematical approaches in the study of economic variables. He sought to develop a science of economics comparable to the study of physics and mechanics.

Like Marshall, Fisher was an excellent teacher and he liked to use mathematics, and graphical approaches such as diagrams and charts, to set out his ideas in a clear way.

As a teacher he liked to produce simple and easy to understand textbooks for his students to follow, and during his life produced over 2,000 published books and papers. He came to economics as a well-trained mathematician. From the outset Fisher sought through his work to provide the 'unification of the theoretical-quantitative and the empirical-quantitative approach'. He therefore used statistics as a source of evidence to underpin his economic analysis and to support the theories that he developed. This approach is widely used today in a range of areas of economic research.

Critics of the use of mathematics in the economy point to the dangers of starting with a hypothesis and treating it as a rigorously verified proposition. However, in the right hands, and providing the user is aware of the limitations of the approach, mathematics can be an invaluable tool. Fisher used mathematics for illustrative purposes and as a source of evidence to draw out the implications of lines of inquiry.

Biography

FISHER WAS A BRILLIANT STUDENT WHO SHOWED PROMISE FROM AN EARLY AGE particularly in the field of mathematics. His father, a Congregational Minister, died of tuberculosis just before Fisher went on to university. His father's illness and later his own ill health led Fisher to be passionate about healthy eating and living. Fortunately, his father left him a legacy of $500 to continue with his studies, but he now became the principal breadwinner, and so he had to supplement his income by tutoring other students.

Fisher was fortunate enough to study at Yale where he showed excellence in mathematics and other subjects. In those days there was less specialism on a degree course so his university studies covered social science, science, philosophy and mathematics. He particularly enjoyed physics and mechanics and the study of these subjects helped him to develop an understanding of the structure and functioning of systems. He was taught by the influential sociologist William Graham Sumner, who encouraged him to focus for his doctorate on mathematical economics. Fisher is reported to have commented that he did not know that such a subject existed.

Fisher's interest in mechanics and systems was evident when he produced his thesis for his research which involved the construction of a machine equipped with pumps, wheels, levers and pipes to illustrate a general theory of equilibrium in the economy and the relationship between the various markets and components of the economy and how they were interdependent. The thesis published in 1891 was the first one in pure economics awarded by Yale. He received his award from the Faculty of Mathematics because economics was not recognised as a separate Faculty at the time. His thesis showed his debt to the French mathematical economist Léon Walras (1834–1910) who had used mathematical modelling to create a general equilibrium model of the economy.

Fisher stayed at Yale throughout his career. He started teaching mathematics – then began teaching modules in economics. As a young economist he was able to benefit from a year's travel tour giving lectures in Europe, a period in which he was able to meet and discuss new ideas with European scholars. In 1898, Fisher was 31 years old and he was appointed professor of political economy at Yale. However, he was unfortunate to catch tuberculosis at the same time and he was forced to recuperate in warmer climates. This personal tragedy strengthened his support for healthy living and he became a crusader for better diet and exercise for the rest of his life.

In addition, he passionately supported a number of other causes; he campaigned for the prohibition of alcohol in the USA, arguing that this would lead to improved productivity of labour, and for better public health and healthy living. He campaigned in favour of the League of Nations seeing this as a means of creating greater harmony in the world and he was also in favour of monetary reform.

As a statistician he was a leading expert on index numbers. He invented the visible card index file system from which he earned a fortune. However, he did not foresee the stock market crash of 15 October 1929 and he lost both his own and his wife's money.

Fisher appears in the history books of this period because two weeks before he made the famous observation: 'Stock prices have reached what looks like a permanently high plateau.'

As a result of this remark Fisher lost some of his credibility. What he was trying to say was that the American economy at the time was strong and that share prices represented a fair valuation of this strength. However, we know that share prices are determined by perceived values rather than real values, and so when the public lost confidence the whole house of cards collapsed.

Fisher continued to teach at Yale for the remainder of his life, and is still recognised as one of the key figures of American economics.

Key works

Purchasing Power of Money (1911)

Theory of Interest (1930)

Marginal utility theory

In his doctoral dissertation Fisher set out to measure the utility that individuals gained from consuming goods, and to create a model of general equilibrium in the economy showing how, for example, a shock to demand or supply in one of ten interrelated markets altered prices and quantities in all markets and changed the incomes and consumption bundles of the various consumers.

He set out to measure utility in the form of 'utils'. He saw utility as consisting of a consumer's estimation of the desiredness of a good rather than its usefulness. While this work is of little interest to the modern student in terms of its content, its approach in terms of seeking to find mathematical measurements and relationships, and in modelling economic relationships in the form of a working model is extremely interesting and laid the foundation for Fisher's ongoing work.

Capital and interest

The greatest economist, John Maynard Keynes, who was to develop his own theory of interest, referred to Fisher as '*the great-grandparent, who first influenced me strongly towards regarding money as a "real" factor in the determination of the interest rate.*'

In his *Theory of Interest* Fisher argued that the interest rate is determined by two factors: the '*impatience to spend income and opportunity to invest it*'.

Fisher showed that there is a difference between the 'nominal rate of interest' and the 'real rate of interest'. The nominal rate is the rate that a borrower has to pay (or what a lender receives) in money terms. However, the real rate involves taking consideration of price changes, that is, the level of inflation. If individuals did not take into account inflation they would find that the real value of the interest they received would be worth less than they anticipated. For example, if the nominal rate of interest is 10 per cent and inflation is running at 3 per cent then the real rate of interest will only be 7 per cent.

Fisher argued that the real rate of interest depends on:

1. Individuals' attitudes towards consuming good now or in the future. At times when people are more impatient they will need a greater inducement to save (i.e. they would need to be paid a higher rate of interest), than they would if they were more patient and prepared to postpone their consumption of goods.
2. The productivity of capital – that is, how much extra income could be created by putting off present consumption in order to invest for the future.

Using a mathematical approach Fisher showed how these two factors would determine the rate of interest.

Fisher also introduced the concept of 'rate of return over cost'. Keynes was later to develop this idea into his 'marginal efficiency of capital'. Fisher argued that rational investors will only be prepared to take up an investment opportunity if the rate of return over cost of the investment is greater than the interest rate.

The quantity theory of money

Pick up any standard text on economics and you are almost sure to find a section on the 'Fisher Equation' or the quantity theory of money.

The quantity theory of money is generally used today to show the relationship between the quantity of money available in an economy and the price level. The quantity theory is used to support the view that monetary inflation (rising prices) results from an increase in the money supply either resulting from governments printing more notes, or allowing the increase in credit opportunities in the economy.

The quantity theory that Fisher presented in his *Purchasing Power of Money* in 1911 is without doubt Fisher's key contribution to economics. In fact Fisher's equation was a development of earlier work by another American writer Simon Newcomb (1835–1909) who presented the idea in a simple form in his book *Principles of Political Economy*.

Fisher set out the quantity theory into the formula:

$$MV = PT$$

Money (notes, coins, and bank deposits) is used to buy goods. At any one moment there is a given stock of money. This stock of money can change hands more quickly or slowly depending on the velocity of circulation. This spending takes place on goods and services and the level of spending depends on average price levels (P), and the number of purchases (transactions T) that take place in a particular period.

The money stock in circulation times its velocity equals the price level times the volume of trade.

Fisher's studies included statistical estimates of the various terms of the formula – M, V, P and T which was typical of the econometric approach that he liked to use.

Fisher was able to show that changes in the supply of money in the economy would lead to changes in the price level assuming that V and T remain relatively fixed. He used statistical studies to back up this line of reasoning. As a mathematician and statistician he accepted that V can fluctuate over time, and that to draw a clear connection between M and P you have to assume that V and T remain constant.

Based on his research Fisher stated that changes in these other variables were 'indirect influences', while the terms of the equation set out the 'direct influences'. Fisher was able to assert therefore that in the long run changes in the money supply would produce similar changes in the price level. He also identified that this relationship would involve what he termed a 'transition period' while it worked through. Today we refer to this as a 'lagged effect'.

In the course of time the simple quantity theory and Fisher's theories of interest have been developed into more sophisticated forms but they provide an important basis for monetary economics, and our understanding of the importance of changes in the money supply in the economy.

Conclusion

Fisher is highly regarded in the development of economic thought because of the organised and detailed approach that he developed in the use of econometrics and mathematical modelling. The breakthroughs that he made in developing the quantity theory and theories of interest attest to the power of the approach that he used in providing new tools and analytical frameworks for the economist to apply. He was able to raise the status of economics in America and pave the way for a host of twentieth century American economists.

Further Reading

FISHER, I.N. (1911) *Purchasing power of money*. Macmillan.

FISHER, I.N. (1930) *Theory of interest*. Repr. (1977). Porcupine Press.

FISHER, I.N. (1956) *My father Irving Fisher*. Cornet Press.

GALBRAITH, J.K. (1987) *A history of economics*. Penguin, ch. 12.

SCHUMPETER, J. (1997) *Ten great economists*. Routledge.

SPIEGEL, H.W. (1971) *The growth of economic thought*. Prentice Hall, ch. 27.

TOBIN, J. (1987) *The New Palgrave: a dictionary of economics*. Vol. 2. (eds. Eatwell, J., Milgate, M. and Newman, P.). Macmillan Press.

John Maynard Keynes

(1883–1946)

KEYNES IS REGARDED BY A LARGE NUMBER OF ECONOMISTS AS HAVING MADE THE MOST important contribution to economics in the modern era. Prior to Keynes, orthodox economics was pretty much wrapped up in what was referred to as the neoclassical consensus. Keynes' work was to shatter the cosy security of traditional views. The neoclassical economists had painted a picture of a naturally ordered economic world which tended naturally towards full employment, and in which the market system led to a rational allocation of economic resources. Say's Law showed how the macro-economy cleared in the same way as did individual markets in the microeconomy.

However, Keynes was an economist who was used to dealing with the real world, having served on a number of influential committees in matters relating to money, finance, trade, and the organisation of the production and distribution of goods. He had a feel for the 'real economy' as well as the 'money economy' and his common sense and experience of the real world told him that the 1920s and 30s was a period in which the market was failing. As a witness to the widescale unemployment of the time he realised that it was a folly to stand back and wait for the market to clear.

Keynes appreciated that saving was not always a good thing in the macroeconomy. While saving is helpful in providing surplus funds for investment, if investors fail to take up these savings and re-spend them, then demand can fall in the economy causing a potentially devastating downward spiral in the economy. Keynes therefore introduced the concept of the 'paradox of thrift'. Thrift, while appearing to be a virtue and an engine to growth, can lead to a downturn in the economy. A number of writers including Schumpeter and Kalecki have drawn out the implication of Keynes' paradox of thrift to suggest that this could provide a strong case for a more even distribution of income in society.

Keynes suggested that the way out of a downturn in the economy is a countervailing injection in demand. In particular the government can play an important role in pumping demand back into the system by deficit financing – that is, spending more than it takes in revenue.

Perhaps the most significant contribution that Keynes made was in changing the dominant emphasis in economics from the study of the microeconomy to macroeconomics. Following Keynes, many of his contemporaries increasingly began to focus on issues such as unemployment, the role of the government in the economy, and later the causes, consequences and cures for inflation. Keynesian ideas were picked up by the Americans Hansen and Samuelson, who popularised his work, making it more accessible to the general reader and influencing politicians of the left and right on both sides of the Atlantic well into the 1970s.

Keynes was all too aware of the influence that the ideas of economists can have in the real world, famously stating that: *'The ideas of economists and political philosophers, both when they are right and when they are wrong, are more powerful than is commonly understood. Indeed the world is ruled by little else. Practical men, who believe themselves to be quite exempt from any intellectual influences, are usually the slaves of some defunct economist. Madmen in authority, who hear voices in the air, are distilling their frenzy from some academic scribbler of a few years back'* (Keynes 1936).

Methodology

ROBERT SKIDELSKY'S THREE-PART BIOGRAPHY OF KEYNES REVEALS HIM AS A THINKER who was committed to adversarial styles of engaging in discussion, which in many ways was a result of the teaching style that he was familiar with at Cambridge. From his student days Keynes was brought up to debate and discuss issues and defend a point of view against detailed criticism. Deirdre McCloskey (1996) describes Keynes' *General Theory* as *'a dialogic book arguing against this or that, especially the allegedly classical economists, rather than stating axioms and deriving theorems as though no opponent were in view'.*

Keynes was firmly of the opinion that the neoclassical economists could not see for looking, because they preferred to cling on to old theories which they deduced in a 'logical' way on the basis of flawed assumptions, rather than looking around them, at evidence such as the large numbers of factory closures, machines lying idle and men out of work. In the *General Theory* (1936) he likened neoclassical economists to Euclidean geometers in a non-Euclidean world: *'who, discovering that in experience straight lines apparently parallel often meet, rebuke the lines for not keeping straight – as the only remedy for the unfortunate collisions which are occurring. Yet in truth, there is no remedy except to throw over the axiom of parallels and to work out a non-Euclidean geometry. Something similar is today required in economics. We need to throw over . . . postulate(s) of the classical doctrine and to work out the behaviour of a system in which involuntary unemployment in the strict sense is possible.'*

Skidelsky also attests to Keynes' open-minded approach to thought. He cites the example of Keynes' reply on being accused of changing his mind. Keynes' retort was *'When I get new evidence I change my mind. What do you do?'*

Eric Roll (1973) sees the evolution of Keynes' ideas as *'a continuous process of renovation and reformulation of established doctrines and, in the end, of their transformation into something new.'* He argues that the main thrust of Keynes' work was on issues of practical policy, based on the practical work that Keynes was involved in – monetary reform, reparations payments, exchange rate reform, etc. In carrying out this work Keynes was able to test out the neoclassical theory of Marshall and Pigou that he had been schooled in against the light of his own experience. He was able to develop theories and ideas based on his own experience coupled with a process of reasoning and arguing out cases.

Keynes believed that the weakness of the neoclassical system was the way in which it was based on a number of special axioms that were required to demonstrate the self-correcting tendency of the free market system. Keynes believed that these axioms were untenable both in theory and more importantly in terms of real experience. He took a long time in preparing his ideas for publication, first subjecting them to an ongoing dialogue with fellow colleagues and students at Cambridge in order to identify and understand the full range of counter arguments that would be put up against his claims to knowledge.

In preparing the *General Theory* he sought to convey his message in everyday English rather than in the confusing symbols of pseudo-mathematics that had been popularised in the neoclassical tradition. He stated (1936): *'It is a great fault of symbolic pseudo-mathematical methods of formalising a system of economic analysis . . . that they expressly assume strict independence between the factors involved and lose all their cogency and authority if this hypothesis is disallowed, whereas, in ordinary discourse, where we are not blindly manipulating but know all the time what we are doing and what the words mean, we can keep "at the back of our heads" the necessary reserves and qualifications and the adjustments which we shall have to make later on, in a way in which we cannot keep complicated partial differentials "at the back" of several pages of algebra which assume that they all vanish. Too large a proportion of recent "mathematical" economics are mere concoctions, as imprecise as the initial assumptions they rest on, which allow the author to lose sight of the complexities and interdependencies of the real world in a maze of pretentious and unhelpful symbols.'*

Biography

KEYNES WAS THE SON OF THE WELL-KNOWN CAMBRIDGE LOGICIAN, AND MATHEMATICIAN John Neville Keynes. He studied at Eton where he proved to be a first-rate scholar, before going up to Cambridge, where he was taught by Alfred Marshall, and Arthur Pigou. During this period Marshall sent a note to the elder Keynes stating *'Your son is doing excellent work in Economics. I have told him that I should be greatly delighted if he should decide on the career of a professional economist.'* In his university exams he received good, but not outstanding marks. Initially he was more interested in maths than economics, and his first published work was on probability theory.

He then went on to take the civil service exams. However, again he did not receive the top marks in the economics section of the paper and later remarked that *'I evidently knew more about economics than my examiners.'* Keynes' connections with the civil service opened up a number of important doors for him, because he was an excellent administrator, and able to synthesise large quantities of detailed information into coherent reports. Working in an advisory capacity to governments and official bodies he had access to lots of detailed statistics, outlines, views and opinions of how the economy works as a living reality. As a result he was able to develop a good insight into real world relationships, rather than the theory-based approaches that were common among the neoclassical economists of his day. Initially he worked in the India Office for two years before returning to Cambridge to lecture in economics.

He then took up a number of key advisory positions which gave him access to the important data of his day, as well as placing him at the heart of all the key issues. In 1913 he worked on the Indian Currency Commission, focusing on monetary reform in India, providing him with a good grasp of monetary economics. This soon led to a position working for the Treasury where he showed a flair for current economic issues. In 1919 he worked as a Treasury representative at the peace conference in Versailles. He was not happy with the way that peace terms were negotiated at this conference, realising that by crippling Germany this would create a hotbed of dissent, which would lead to further antagonism. His work, *The Economic Consequences of the Peace* (1920) was critical of the scale of reparations and led to his resignation in 1919. This work was widely read and for the first time brought Keynes to the attention of the wider public.

At the same time he was offered the editorship of the *Economic Journal* and this provided Keynes with a vehicle for presenting a stream of ideas about economics.

Keynes' next major work, *A Tract on Monetary Reform*, written in 1923 against a background of the turbulence of the inter-war period, involved an attack on the Gold Standard which was regarded as a keystone of international economic relations. As ever, Keynes argued that the economic apparatus needed to be relevant to the situation of the day. He felt that the conditions that favoured the Gold Standard in the nineteenth century no longer existed. He was in favour of stable prices rather than a stable exchange rate, and felt that the Gold Standard (as a stable exchange rate) was a threat to price stability. The core of Keynes' argument was that rigid adherence to the Gold Standard would prevent countries from pursuing their own domestic policies. Inflation in the rest of the world would cause a country like the USA or Britain to gain gold which would have an inflationary effect within its own borders, and deflation would work in the opposite direction.

Shortly after the publication of this book, Winston Churchill announced that Britain would go back on the Gold Standard at the pre-war parity of $4.86 to the pound. As a result the pound was seriously overvalued, threatening the competitive position of British exporters, and confidence in the whole system when Britain was forced to back out. Keynes produced a pamphlet that was strongly critical of Churchill – *The Economic Consequences of Mr Churchill* (1925).

In his 1930 two-volume work, *A Treatise on Money*, Keynes started to develop an alternative approach to monetary economics to that presented by the traditional quantity theory. The seeming inability of monetary policy at the end of the 1920s to control price inflation had led Keynes to draw attention away from monetary factors. Instead he developed a theory in which income was seen as dependent on the behaviour of investment rather than on the stock of money. At the same time Keynes began to draw out an outline of international monetary institutions, such as the International Monetary Fund, to manage international money flows.

However, Keynes' major contribution to economics came with the publication of the *General Theory* in 1936. This is probably the most significant work in economics that has ever been written and has since led to the publication of thousands of books examining the importance of Keynes' ideas, and hundreds of thousands of papers and journal articles. Indeed, it can be argued that the multiplier effect of the injection in demand for articles about Keynes may on its own have staved off several recessions in economic activity. The *General Theory* was the product of Keynes' thinking over a number of years, and he received considerable support from colleagues at Cambridge in the development of his ideas. During the early 1930s a group of academics would meet regularly to discuss Keynes' lectures, first meeting in Richard Kahn's room and later in a larger room at Trinity College. Keynes' rarely attended these meetings of what was referred to as the 'Circus', but would receive reports on what was said at these meetings by Richard Kahn (who was instrumental in developing the multiplier effect). Keynes' *General Theory* was to have a ripple effect on its publication in changing people's thinking about the way in which the economy is organised. Initially, the impact was felt in Cambridge, before working outwards to the rest of the world. Keynesian ideas were taken on board and developed by the American economists Alvin Hansen, Paul Samuelson, James Tobin and John Kenneth Galbraith, who popularised Keynesian ideas and introduced them to a range of influential politicians.

Keynes' ideas were developed during a period of despair in which it seemed increasingly likely that people might turn to fascism or communism as radical alternatives to the capitalist system.

However, Keynes was concerned with saving capitalism rather than destroying it. For example, he was critical of communism stating that '*How can I adopt a creed, which, preferring the mud to the fish, exalts the boorish proletariat above the bourgeois and the intelligentsia who, with whatever faults, are the quality in life and surely carry the seeds of all human advancement?*' (1936).

As Keynes' thought conquered economic opinion, and as full employment became a goal of government policy, it seemed that a new Keynesian era had ushered in a period of prosperity. In the period following the Second World War recessions were short-lived and relatively harmless compared with the 1920s and 30s and much of the credit for this period of prosperity has been attributed to Keynes.

Keynes the man was far more than an economist. He had a broad range of interests that he developed throughout his life. During his student days at Cambridge he was influenced by the philosopher George Moore who believed in an 'ideal utilitarianism', which associated an individual's moral duty to perform an action with that action's capacity to produce the greatest possible good in the world. However, Moore didn't go so far as to define what he meant by 'good'. Moore also stated that each individual should be the judge of their own moral obligations. The implication was that as individuals we should be true to ourselves rather than conforming to society's conventions. This view was shared by a number of Keynes' close friends, a number of whom went on to make up what was known as the Bloomsbury set of artists and thinkers. Many of Keynes' friends and associates openly flouted conventional patterns of behaviour of the time (for example, in the development of relationships with partners of both sexes). Moore also emphasised the importance of 'the enjoyment of beautiful objects', and 'the pleasures of human intercourse'. Keynes went on to marry the distinguished Russian ballerina, Lydia Lopokova, who Schumpeter (1952) describes as proving '*a congenial companion and devoted helpmate – "in sickness and in health" – to the end.*'

Keynes played a significant part in giving Kings' College, Cambridge such an eminent status, and played an important role in managing the finances of the College.

Schumpeter (1952) explains that *'His extracurricular interests were many, and each of them he pursued with joyful alacrity . . . The Keynesian touch is that with him recreation was creative. For instance, he loved old books, niceties of bibliographic controversy, details of the characters, lives, and thoughts of men of the past. Many people share this taste which may have been fostered in him by the classical ingredients in his education. But whenever he indulged it, he took hold like the workman he was, and we owe to his hobby several not unimportant clarifications on points of literary history. He also was a lover and, up to a point, a good judge of pictures, to a modest extent also a collector. He thoroughly enjoyed a good play, and founded and generously financed the Cambridge Arts Theatre, which no one who went to it will forget. And, once upon a time, an acquaintance of his received the following note from him, evidently dashed off in high good humor: "Dear . . . if you wish to know what at this moment exclusively occupies my time, look at the enclosed." The enclosure consisted of a program or prospectus of the "Carmago Ballet".'*

Key works

General Theory of Employment, Interest and Money (1936)

General Theory

On New Year's Day, 1935, Keynes wrote to George Bernard Shaw: *'To understand my new state of mind, however, you have to know that I believe myself to be writing a book on economic theory which will largely revolutionise not I suppose at once but in the course of the next ten years the way the world thinks about economic problems.'*

The classical and neoclassical economists had primarily been concerned with the way in which markets operate (e.g. through supply and demand analysis), and with the distribution of income in society. For example, Keynes quoted Ricardo's famous statement to Malthus that political economy is concerned with an enquiry *'into the laws which determine the division of the produce of industry amongst the classes who concur in its formation.'* Keynes, in contrast, was more concerned with the macroeconomy and with the overall level of aggregates such as national income, employment and output.

Keynes' most significant contribution to economics was in showing that the ideas of classical economics were not relevant to the time or the society in which he was living. In the 1920s it was blatantly obvious that the economy was not clearing at anywhere near full employment. As a realist, Keynes believed that truth depended on a particular set of assumptions being true to the context to which they related. The notion of classical macroeconomic equilibrium at full employment was clearly irrelevant to Britain, America and many other countries at the time. In his *General Theory* (1936) he set out that *'The postulates of classical theory are applicable to a special case only and not to the general case, the situation which it assumes being a limiting point of the possible positions of equilibrium. Moreover, the characteristics of the special case assumed by the classical theory happen not to be those of the economic society in which we actually live, with the result that its teaching is misleading and disastrous if we attempt to apply it to the facts of experience.'*

Will Hutton (2001), in his assessment of Keynesian economics argues that the neoclassical economists' world was characterised by economic actors who are rational beings, able to treat decisions about the future as if they were being made in the present (with all the knowledge required to make these decisions being freely available) and that money does not complicate the process of exchange. Keynes (and Hutton) argue that these conditions don't exist – we don't have enough information to make rational decisions, we don't know what will happen in the future, and money distorts the real economy. As a result, the market is not likely to clear in a simple way to form an equilibrium position. Rather, economic actors have to cope with a confusing picture in which it is difficult to calculate what will happen in the market. Decisions about demand will be different from decisions about supply, and decisions about the future will be different from decisions about the present.

Keynes' *General Theory* set out that the chief problem of economics is not concerned with the establishment of prices in the market, or with questions of distribution of income, but with the determination of the level of output and employment. He identified the situation in which the market clears at full employment, as just one possibility among many.

The consumption function

Keynes developed the concept of the 'consumption function' to show that as income increases incrementally, then consumption falls as a proportion of this additional (marginal) income. In simple terms, as people become richer, they save more.

The demand for money

Keynes then argued that there was no guarantee that as savings increased that they would be taken up in extra investment. He outlined a number of precautionary reasons why people might hold on to their money:

1. To make transactions.
2. As a precaution against some unforeseen contingency.
3. To speculate. They might hold cash so that they can later benefit from changes in interest rates.

The transactions and precautionary motives for holding money are unstable, particularly when the economy is not at full employment, so that variations in national income will cause upward and downward movements in transactions.

The speculative demand for money would be highly volatile.

The liquidity trap

Keynes identified conditions in which the demand for money could be highly or totally elastic. Changes in the quantity of money would be absorbed completely in speculative balances. He referred to this as the 'liquidity trap'. In this situation increases in the supply of money would be absorbed totally for speculative purposes, and would have no effect on prices or income (thus putting paid to the notion of the *Quantity Theory of Money*).

Keynes identified this situation as arising when interest rates are so low, that yields on bonds, and shares will also be low. Investors will not see any point in buying shares or bonds, they will simply hold on to their money.

Given this interpretation, money plays a much less important role in the economy than had previously been suggested.

The relationship between saving and investment

Keynes agreed with the classical economists that savings and investment in the economy must be equal. However, he did not believe that this had to occur at the full employment point. When income is saved rather than spent, this can lead to a reduction in aggregate (total) demand in the economy, triggering off a reduction in output and incomes. This downward spiral continues until savings are reduced.

The economy moves towards equilibrium where intended saving and intended investment, and actual saving and actual investment are equal. This can be at any level of employment. Drawing on his own experience this concept of underemployment equilibrium was all too obvious in the 1920s and 30s.

In Keynes' analysis investment played a prominent part. The inducement to invest depended on the relationship between the anticipated rate of return on different amounts of investment (shown in the marginal efficiency of capital schedule) and the interest rate. Investors would make marginal increments in their investment up to the point at which the returns on investment (the marginal efficiency of capital) were equal to the cost (interest rate). He emphasised the role of expectations in determining the expected rate of return on investment, and placed a strong emphasis on the volatile nature of investment.

General unemployment

The neoclassical economists recognised a number of types of unemployment including seasonal unemployment (e.g. of workers in the tourist trade at off-season times), and frictional unemployment (as workers change jobs, in the normal course of events). However, the neoclassical economists didn't recognise general unemployment, which arises when aggregate demand in the economy is not sufficient to guarantee full employment. Keynes identified workers as being involuntary unemployed if they would like to work, but are not able to do so because of general demand deficiency.

The deflationary gap

Keynes showed that the level of output and employment of resources depends on the following:

1. Total demand for goods and services in the economy (aggregate demand), and
2. Total supply of goods and services in the economy (aggregate supply).

Keynesian economists have illustrated this relationship by means of aggregate demand and supply curves.

As with microeconomic supply curves, the aggregate supply curve will slope upwards from the bottom left as the economy increases its output, towards higher prices, but there will always be a limit to supply and this is at the point where factors of production are fully employed. At this point the supply curve will be vertical (given the current state of technical progress). The aggregate demand curve will slope downwards from the top left because, as prices fall, total demand for goods and services will tend to increase.

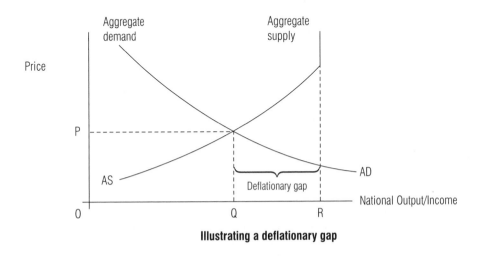

Illustrating a deflationary gap

The actual level of national income (Q) is where the aggregate supply and aggregate demand curves intersect. The difference between the equilibrium national income and the full employment position shows the extent to which it is possible to expand national income to minimise the employment of resources. This difference between national income and the full employment position is known as the deflationary gap (QR).

Manipulating aggregate demand

Keynes believed that aggregate demand might need to be manipulated in order to create desired levels of employment in the economy. To do this it would be necessary to adjust one or more of the components of aggregate demand. The components of aggregate demand are:

- *Consumption* itself. Keynes showed that consumption is largely a function of income.
- *Investment* in capital equipment. Private investment largely depends on the level of business confidence. When the economy is doing well business people are likely to invest. During a downturn, business people lose confidence in the economy and cut back on investment expenditures.
- *Net exports.* The relationship between exports and imports depends on the competitiveness of a country's foreign trade sector.

- *Net government spending*. The government's budget position depends on whether it spends more money than it takes in revenue, or not. Neoclassical economists believed in a balanced budget where government spending plans were balanced by taxation.

Having examined the components of aggregate demand Keynes believed that investment was the most volatile of these aggregates. He argued that during a downturn in the economy business people would become reluctant to invest. As a result savings would not be initially channelled into investment. This would lead to demand deficiency in the economy, causing supply to be reduced, and an ongoing downturn in economy activity until savings were once again in balance with investment at a lower level of national income.

Keynes' solution to the deflationary gap was to suggest government intervention in the economy. This could take a number of forms, for example:

- Increased government spending to stimulate demand.
- Reductions in taxes, to encourage consumers to spend more.

Keynes' solution to the deflationary gap was therefore the deficit budget.

He even suggested that a recession could be halted by burying money under the ground and allowing people to dig it up and spend it. Of course, he recognised that this was not a serious solution to unemployment, but made the point clear that the cause of a recession was demand deficiency.

Reflecting on the era in which Keynes was writing, Galbraith (1987) states that against a backcloth of the terrible privations and hardship that was the reality of the 1920s and 30s, *'There remained one – just one – course. That was government intervention to raise the level of investment spending – government borrowing and spending for public purposes. A deliberate deficit. This alone would break the underemployment equilibrium by, in effect, spending – wilfully spending – the unspent savings of the private sector. It was a powerful affirmation of the wisdom of what was already being done under the force of circumstance.'*

The multiplier effect

Keynes borrowed the idea of the multiplier effect from another Cambridge economist, Richard Kahn.

The multiplier effect shows how a small change in expenditure can lead to a much larger change in incomes and spending. The original change in demand is multiplied several times.

For example, if business people reduce investment by £1m and this leads eventually to an overall fall in spending of £3m, we can say that the multiplier is 3:

$$\text{Multiplier} = \frac{\text{Overall change in demand}}{\text{Original change in investment}} = \frac{£3m}{£1m} = 3$$

We can illustrate the multiplier effect in a city with a large university. When students arrive in October with plenty of spending money, the local economy begins to boom.

Shops, cafés, bookshops take on more part-time and full-time staff, who receive wages for their work. These wages are then spent in the town or city and the multiplier effect continues. The original increase in spending by students is multiplied around the local economy. However, in the summer holidays, the reverse happens as students leave town and lots of jobs disappear, leading to a localised recession.

The same principle for the multiplier can be extended to the national and international economies.

The accelerator effect

The accelerator effect is another way of showing how changes in demand in the economy can lead to a dynamic downward or upward effect. The accelerator principle shows that where there is a small change in the production of consumer goods (following a change in demand for them) there is likely to be a much larger change in investment in capital goods required to make the consumer goods. For example, a book publisher is engaged in printing economics books and has 100 standard machines in operation. As the lifespan of each machine is 20 years, five machines are typically replaced each year. If during one year, demand for economics books rises by 20 per cent (and the firm is already working at full capacity), the firm will now need 120 machines in operation and so will have to buy 20 new machines as well as replace the five which are worn out. A 20 per cent rise in demand for books has caused an increase in the number of machines required from five to 25, a 400 per cent increase in demand for capital goods. If the short-term peak demand of 120 machines is not maintained, over-capacity will soon develop and then the accelerator works in reverse. As a result of over-capacity a decline in demand for consumer goods will result in a sharper decline for capital goods.

Conclusion

Keynes' ideas transformed economics, and continue to raise the status of economists. Today, for example, it is widely accepted that economists can play a prominent and useful advisory role in helping governments to form economic policy. In the immediate post-war period governments of all political persuasions gave a prominent place to the creation of full employment in the economy. The means that governments typically employed to secure full employment were government demand management policies.

Up until the end of the 1970s governments were only too pleased to use deficit financing, because it increased the part that they could play in managing the life of their nations. However, by the 1970s it had become apparent that there were serious problems associated with deficit financing, and it seems likely that Keynes would have been one of the first to point out these flaws. Keynes believed that economic policy should be relevant to the circumstances that prevailed in the real world. It is likely that he would have been highly critical of government expenditures on projects that yielded low rates of return as was the case with a large number of schemes supported by governments in the 1960s and 1970s.

Government deficit budgets helped to worsen the cost-push inflation that was a feature of the 1970s, and it was obvious that deficit financing was not the way forward any longer. The quantity theory of money came back into fashion and the monetarism of Milton Friedman and others. The emphasis in economics in Britain, and the United

States in particular switched from managing demand in the economy to seeking to find ways of making supply more efficient. In a new era of neoliberal resurgence Keynesian techniques appeared to become less relevant.

A number of criticisms have been levelled at Keynesian ideas. One that is put forward by hardened neoclassical economists is that Keynes' ideas did not provide a General Theory at all – it is the neoclassical theory that provides the General Theory. These economists argued that the unemployment of the 1920s and 30s was simply caused by inflexibility within the economic system, such as rigidities which prevented prices from moving in a downward direction, caused, for example, by the strength of trade unions. These economists are the ones that today demand flexibility throughout the economy, for example flexibility in the labour market including the removal of minimum wage and maximum hours legislation.

A second source of criticism is put forward by monetarists such as Friedman who argue that Keynesian demand management has a lagged effect. If the government increases spending in a recession, it will take time for this extra spending to impact on the economy. By then, the correct policy might be to be seeking to reduce expenditure.

A third source of criticism relates to the inflationary impact of deficit budgets that was discussed earlier.

However, there continues to be strong support for Keynes among those who, like Keynes, were opposed to convention and the conventional wisdom. Will Hutton (2001) sees Keynesianism as a challenge to the entire intellectual tradition that sees 'the state' as being limited; and the liberty of the individual as paramount. Hutton sees the significance of Keynes as lying in the notion that *'the common interest cannot be guaranteed by the felicitous interaction of private interests, but must rather be asserted in the collectivity of individuals in the form of the State.'* In this Keynes was opposed, and continues to be opposed, to traditional Anglo-Saxon values of the individual and the market place. Supporters of Keynes argue that as a defender of capitalism he did more for the working people of this country than Bakunin, Luxembourg, Marx and Engels ever did.

 Further Reading

BACKHOUSE, R.E. (2002) *The Penguin history of economics*. Penguin, ch. 13.

BREIT, W. AND RANSOM, R. (1982) *The academic scribblers*. The Dryden Press, ch. 7.

BUTLER, E. (1985) *Milton Friedman: a guide to his economic thought*. Gower.

DAVIDSON, P. (1994) *Post Keynesian macroeconomic theory*. Edward Elgar.

GALBRAITH, J.K. (1987) *A history of economics*, Penguin, ch. 17.

HUTTON, W. (2001) *The revolution that never was: an assessment of Keynesian economics*. Vintage.

KEYNES, J.M. (1920) *The economic consequences of the peace.* Macmillan and Co Ltd.

KEYNES, J.M. (1923) *A tract on monetary reform.* Macmillan and Co Ltd.

KEYNES, J.M. (1925) *The economic consequences of Mr Churchill.* Hogarth Press.

KEYNES, J.M. (1930) *A treatise on money. Macmillan.*

KEYNES, J.M. (1936) *The general theory of employment, interest and money.* Macmillan and Co Ltd.

LEIJONHUFVUD, A. (1979) *On Keynesian economics and the economics of Keynes.* Oxford University Press.

MCCLOSKEY, D. (2000) Keynes was a sophist, and a good thing, too. Eastern Economic Journal, 1996, in *How to be human, though an economist.* University of Michigan Press.

ROLL, E. (1973) *A history of economic thought,* 4th edn. Faber and Faber.

SCHUMPETER, J.A. (1952) *Ten great economists: from Marx to Keynes.* George Allen and Unwin.

SPIEGEL, H.W. (1971) *The growth of economic thought.* Prentice Hall, ch. 26.

Friedrich Hayek

(1899–1992)

THE TWENTIETH CENTURY WAS ESSENTIALLY THE CENTURY OF THREE GREAT ECONOMISTS – John Maynard Keynes, Friedrich Hayek and Milton Friedman. It was also a period that provided a watershed between nineteenth-century liberalism, and the growing influence of state socialism. As the century wore on it seemed to many that the role of the state in running the economy would become increasingly important. However, by the end of the century, this trend had been reversed – in great measure as the result of the influence of liberal economists like Hayek and Friedman whose ideas influenced key world leaders, most notably Margaret Thatcher and Ronald Reagan from the late 1970s.

In Britain the influence of Hayek on the Thatcher era is illustrated by a well-known story that at a key Conservative Party meeting in the late 1970s, one of Thatcher's colleagues had prepared a paper arguing that the middle way was the pragmatic path for the Conservative party to take. Before he had finished introducing his paper, the new Party Leader (Margaret Thatcher) reached into her briefcase and took out Friedrich von Hayek's book, *The Constitution of Liberty*. Interrupting the speaker, she held the book up for all to see. 'This', she said sternly, 'is what we believe', and banged Hayek down on the table.

Hayek is today regarded to be the most prominent member of the Austrian school of economics which has been highly influential in shaping neoliberal economic thinking in recent years. His support for freedom and democracy was shaped by his own experiences of the totalitarianism of Nazi Germany. He was determined that societies would not slip back down the slippery path to a state dominated society and his life and work was committed to democratic ideals, freedom and economic liberty.

Hayek was a great believer in gaining experience from the lessons of the past. In his most widely known political work (1944) he wrote that *'although history never quite repeats itself, and just because no development is inevitable, we can in a measure learn from the past to avoid a repetition of the same process.'* In particular, he was concerned that society did not repeat the mistakes of the period of National Socialism in Germany when the Nazis had created a totalitarian society. He was a great believer in individual freedom drawing inspiration from John Stuart Mill's ideas about individual liberty. He stressed the importance of economic freedom.

It is interesting to note that Hayek's ideas only began to be influential towards the end of his life. Like Keynes he realised that it takes a long time for the ideas of economists to be widely accepted. In his inaugural lecture at the London School of Economics, on 'The Trend of Economic Thinking' (1933) he stated that *'the views at present held by the public can clearly be traced to the economists of a generation or so ago. So that the fact is, not that the teaching of the economist has no influence at all; on the contrary, it may be very powerful. But it takes a long time to make its influence felt.'*

Methodology

HAYEK BELIEVED IN INTELLECTUAL CURIOSITY. INDIVIDUALS SHOULD BE OPEN TO NEW ideas rather than simply seeking evidence that support their preconceived ideas. He was strongly influence by the ideas of the philosopher Karl Popper. Popper's approach was based on the idea of falsification. Instead of seeking evidence that backs up and provides supporting evidence for our ideas – we should instead seek to find evidence that contradicts our ideas. It is more fruitful to find cases which contradict our ideas than simply to keep on building up more evidence that seems to prove our argument. Hayek argued that propositions of ethics, politics and economics could be tested in the same way as those in the sciences using a spirit of enquiry and an openness to falsification.

In an essay on 'Being an Economist' (1933) Hayek wrote that *'nearly all of us come to the study of economics with very strong views on subjects which we do not understand. And even if we make a show of being detached and ready to learn, I am afraid it is almost always with a mental reservation, with an inward determination to prove that our instincts were right and that nothing we learn can change our basic convictions.'* Hayek was strongly opposed to this approach, seeing the study of economics as an opportunity to reappraise our own thinking in order to know more rather than building on our prejudices. He felt that too many of the economists of his generation were more concerned in producing popular ideas which added to their own esteem rather than facing harsh realities. In particular, he felt that the post-war Keynesian orthodoxy, however well intentioned, led down the path to socialism, and gave too much power to the state. He felt that the lessons of history had not been learnt.

Hayek felt strongly that knowledge is limited and tenuous. In an article on methodological approaches ('Two Types of Mind', 1991), he argued that he himself was a 'puzzler' or 'muddler' rather than a 'master' of his subject.

Hayek believed in the use of natural science methods in economics, which he characterised as 'scientism'. His ideas clashed with those of Keynes because he believed in allowing the natural forces of the market to determine social relations in the economy rather than allowing human intervention in the economy through the government. He defined theoretical economics (1991) as aiming *'at explaining those uniformities in the economic activities of society which are not the result of deliberate design but the produce of the interplay of the separate decisions of individuals and groups, thereby excluding from it all non-market phenomena'* as opposed to Keynes who called for purposeful action by means of public policies.

Hayek's entire approach to economics emphasises the limited nature of knowledge. For example, information about supply and demand is dispersed among many consumers and producers. Only the market is capable of communicating all of this information to individuals operating within the market. The market will therefore beat the state every time in providing the information required to make rational economic decisions.

FRIEDRICH HAYEK WAS BORN IN 1899 AND WAS PART OF A FAMILY OF INTELLECTUALS in Vienna, Austria. He studied at the University of Vienna where he received doctorates in 1921 and 1923. At the time, the University of Vienna was one of the leading centres for the study of economics in the world, and the Austrian school of economists was very influential. Although he was enrolled at the university to study law his prime areas of interest were economics and psychology. Hayek's interest in economics stemmed from his desire to improve the conditions of people in society, at a time when poverty was obvious in parts of Vienna.

At the time, socialism seemed to provide the way forward for dealing with inequality and social problems and was supported by a number of European intellectuals. In 1922, however, the influential Austrian academic and writer Ludwig von Mises produced his famous book which in English bears the title 'Socialism'. Later, Hayek (1944) was to say that '*To none of us young men who read the book when it appeared, the world was ever the same again.*'

Mises' book was an attack on central planning, arguing that only the existence of a market makes it possible to establish values for items that go into production. Mises argued that socialism cannot achieve an efficient utilisation of resources.

Hayek was strongly influenced by the persuasiveness of Mises' argument and with a number of other prominent Austrian intellectuals began to meet together to discuss ideas at Mises' Privatseminar (a seminar which was held every other Friday at the University of Vienna) and also periodically invited prominent intellectuals from the UK, America and elsewhere. Hayek acknowledged his debt to von Mises when he wrote (1991) that '*There is no single man to whom I owe more intellectually.*'

Mises' position, however, was considered extreme; for example, he saw no role for government at all. This extremism meant that over time Mises' influence became detached from the mainstream of economic thought.

Hayek's intellectual curiosity and intelligence impressed von Mises and on graduating Hayek was asked to work under Mises in a government office examining the nature of business cycles combining theoretical and empirical approaches. In 1927 Hayek became the Director of the Institute for Business Cycle Research.

Hayek helped to develop understanding of the nature and causes of business cycles and his first book, *Monetary Theory and the Trade Cycle* (1929) analysed the effects of credit expansion on the capital structure of the economy. This study showed how expansion in the money supply could lead to an artificial boom in the economy that could not be sustained.

Because of the influence of Austrian explanations of the trade cycle Hayek was invited to give a series of lectures at the London School of Economics, and in 1930–31 he became Professor of Economic Science and Statistics at the LSE. In 1935, he published one of his key works, *Prices and Production*, that was to be cited in his award of the Nobel Prize for Economics in 1974. In this work Hayek presented his trademark view that *'The price system will fulfil its . . . function only if competition prevails, that is, if the individual producer has to adapt himself to price changes and cannot control them.'*

Hayek's ideas were frequently in contradiction with those of the leading British economist John Maynard Keynes, but the two always got on well on a personal level. During the bombing of London during the Second World War Keynes arranged for Hayek to be safely housed in one of the Cambridge colleges.

Hayek's work was based on non-government interference in the economy, while Keynes saw government intervention as the route to make the capitalist system survive and flourish. Hayek never set out a full-scale attack on Keynes' *General Theory of Employment*, although his work is clearly at odds with the Keynesian thesis.

In the 1950s Hayek and a number of other Austrian economists were invited to teach in America and Hayek joined a number of other influential economists including Milton Friedman at the University of Chicago. Increasingly Hayek's interest moved from economics to politics and psychology. However, following his award of the Nobel Prize in 1974 there was a widespread revival of interest in his ideas – to the extent that Hayekian influence was to become the dominant economic and political influence in the UK, the United States and elsewhere from the late 1970s onwards.

Key works

Monetary Theory and the Trade Cycle (1929)

Prices and Production (1935)

The Road to Serfdom (1944)

Key Ideas

Theory of the trade cycle

The trade cycle is made up of a series of booms and recessions which characterise patterns of economic growth and slowdown over a period of time. In the period following the First World War economists were seeking for an explanation for this phenomenon, particularly in the light of the Great Depression of the 1920s.

The Mises–Hayek theory of the trade cycle explained the 'cluster of errors' that characterises the business cycle. This Austrian version of the trade cycle based on empirical research and theory shows how fluctuations in macroeconomy activity can come about which lead to an ongoing cycle.

Credit expansion, made possible by the artificial lowering of interest rates, misleads business people who are led to engage in ventures that would not otherwise have appeared profitable. The false signal generated by credit expansion leads to mal-coordination of the production and consumption plans of economic actors. This mal-coordination first manifests itself in a 'boom', and then, later in the 'bust' as the time pattern of production adjusts to the real pattern of savings and consumption in the economy.

The road to serfdom

Hayek's *The Road to Serfdom* was surely one of the most important texts produced in the twentieth century because of its influence on the policies of Margaret Thatcher and Ronald Reagan which in turn led to the revival of classical liberal thinking in the West and in many other parts of the world. The overall effect was to roll back the socialist influence which had been steadily growing during the twentieth century and continued until 1979 when Thatcher was elected in the UK. The problems of socialism that Hayek had observed in Nazi Germany and that he saw beginning to re-emerge in Europe led him to write *The Road to Serfdom*.

Hayek's road which led to serfdom was that of socialism – and his book was addressed 'To the Socialists of all parties' by which he meant that unwittingly politicians from a range of parties had adopted state controls which were leading to a reduction of the role of the free market in running the economy. The first chapter of *The Road to Serfdom* was titled 'The Abandoned Road' – by which Hayek referred to the abandonment of the free market principles of the nineteenth century.

Hayek was particularly worried that the road to socialism inevitably moved society towards totalitarianism and away from democracy stating that *'Few are ready to recognise that the rise of Fascism and Nazism was not a reaction against the socialist trends of the preceding period, but a necessary outcome of those tendencies'* (Hayek 1944).

Hayek stated that *The Road to Serfdom* was essentially a political document, seeking to prevent countries from repeating the mistakes of history and taking the world back towards totalitarianism. It was not surprising that Margaret Thatcher was attracted to these ideas which echoed her own dislike of socialism.

Hayek (1944) argued that it was not evil people that were dragging society down the road to serfdom but misguided ones: *'Is there a greater tragedy imaginable than that in our endeavour consciously to shape our future in accordance with high ideals, we should in fact unwittingly produce the very opposite of what we have been striving for?'*

Liberalism

Hayek (1944) associated liberalism with progress stating that *'During the whole of this modern period of European history the general direction of social development was one of freeing the individual from the ties which had bound him to the customary or prescribed ways in the pursuit of his ordinary activities. The realisation that the unhampered efforts of individuals were capable of producing a complex order of economic activities could come only after this development had made some progress. The subsequent elaboration of a consistent argument in favour of economic freedom was the outcome of a free growth of economic activity which had been the undersigned and unforeseen by-product of political freedom.*

Perhaps the most significant result of the increase in individual liberty in Western Europe was the marvellous growth of science that followed. Previously the few attempts made towards a more extended industrial use of mechanised inventions, some extraordinarily advanced, were promptly suppressed and the desire for knowledge stifled, so long as the beliefs of the great majority were binding for all. That the inventive faculty of man had been no less in earlier periods is shown by the development in some industries which, like mining or watch-making, were not subject to restrictive controls.

Only since industrial freedom opened the path to the free use of new knowledge, only since everything could be tried – if somebody could be found to back it as his own risk – has science made the great strides which in the last hundred and fifty years have changed the face of the world.

Wherever the barriers to the free exercise of human enterprise were removed men soon became able to satisfy ever-widening ranges of desires. And, while the rising standard soon led to the discovery of dark spots in society, which men soon became no longer willing to tolerate, there was probably no class that did not benefit substantially from the general advance.'

However, Hayek also argued that society should not stick rigidly to rough rules of thumb such as *laissez-faire*, that is, leaving everything to the market (here Hayek moved away from von Mises). Hayek believed that government could play a role in making the market better, for example, by removing monopoly powers and other restrictions to trade.

Hayek believed that the problem for liberalism was that it had been too successful in that it had led people's expectations to rise – everyone wanted more of the good things of life – and they wanted them quicker – failing to realise that the mechanism that was delivering growth was freedom in the economic and political sphere.

He stated (1944) that *'Liberalism came to be regarded as a "negative" creed because it could offer to particular individuals little more than a share in the common progress – a progress which came to be taken more and more for granted and was no longer recognised as the result of the policy of freedom. It might even be said that the very success of liberalism became the cause of its decline. Because of the success already achieved man became increasingly aware of and unwilling to tolerate the evils still with him which now appeared both unbearable and unnecessary.'*

The failures of socialism

Hayek (1944) argued that socialism offers false promises to individual members of society and that it takes away individual freedom: *'To ally these suspicions socials began increasingly to make use of the promise of a "new freedom". The coming of socialism was to be the leap from the realm of necessity to the realm of freedom. It was to bring "economic freedom", without which the political freedom already gained was not worth having ... To the great apostles of political freedom the word had meant freedom from coercion, freedom from the arbitrary power of other men. The new freedom promised however, was to be freedom from necessity, release from the compulsion of the circumstances which inevitably limit the range of choice of all of us, although for some very much more than for others.'*

Marx had promised *'From each according to his ability to each according to his need'*, but of course, provided that everyone subjugated their individual will to the collective will of the state. At the start of his chapter 'The Inevitability of Planning' – Hayek cites Mussolini who stated that *'We were the first to assert that the more complicated the forms of civilisation, the more restricted the freedom of the individual must become'*.

The Road to Serfdom forces supporters of socialism to confront an additional problem, over and beyond technical economic ones. If socialism requires the replacement of the market with a central plan, then, Hayek pointed out, an institution must be created that would be responsible for creating this plan. Hayek called this institution the 'Central Planning Bureau'.

To put the plan into practice and to manage the flow of resources, the Bureau would have to exercise broad discretionary power in economic affairs. Yet the Central Planning Bureau in a socialist society would have no market prices to act as guides. It would have no way of knowing how to efficiently allocate resources. The absence of a pricing system, Hayek argued, would be the key weakness in socialism. He also stated that it is likely that those who would rise to the top in a socialist system would be those with a comparative advantage in exercising discretionary power and who were willing to make unpleasant decisions. It was inevitable that these people would abuse the system to achieve their own ends.

Events seem to have provided evidence to support Hayek's assertion as witnessed by tyrannical rule and misapplication of resources by tyrants such as Stalin, Mao, Hitler, Pol Pot, and Caecescu.

The efficient use of information in the free market

Hayek argued that the use of information in society is one of the tremendous advantages of a free market over a planned economy in that the voluntary cooperation of individuals utilises far more information and knowledge than any single individual possesses or than the government can possess. Individuals adjust their activities on the basis of how others' actions affect their own situations; and the interactions and voluntary cooperation among individuals give rise to better and wiser social institutions than the state can create. Human society is thus too complex for state planners. To understand and find the best solutions to social questions, the government would have to know what all the separate people know, and that is beyond the reach of any one person or any one authority.

Monetary instability

The focus on both Mises' and Hayek's approaches was on the non-neutrality of money. The way money is injected into the economic system tends to affect the structure of relative prices and, by affecting relative prices, tends to influence the allocation of resources along alternative product uses.

Conclusion

Between 1945 and 1979 it seemed as if thinkers like Hayek had lost the debate against those in favour of state intervention in the economy – most prominently John Maynard Keynes. Keynes argued that the state had an important role to play in preventing economies from economic crises which caused widespread unemployment. Keynes argued that at times when there was a shortfall of demand in the economy, the state should step in to increase its own spending and to encourage citizens to spend more money to create a demand for goods and, hence, more jobs.

However, Keynes' policies, although they were initially successful, lost momentum during the 1970s and 80s as they increasingly led to inflation resulting from inefficient state expenditure, coupled with rising levels of unemployment as world economic growth slowed down.

Hayek's ideas were able to regain widescale credibility in the 1990s in the wake of the election of free marketers in the USA and the UK and the collapse of Eastern European economies hampered by the shackles of inefficient state planning. Today, in large parts of the world the liberal economic ideas of Hayek are in the ascendancy, although Hayek would have been critical of high levels of continued state control – he might feel that we are still on that road to serfdom. From the 1980s onwards Hayek's ideas were much talked about and he should be seen as one of the major influences in the revival of free market/neoliberal economics.

 Further Reading

BACKHOUSE, R.E. (2002) *The Penguin history of economics.* Penguin, ch. 10.

HAYEK, F.A. (1929) *Monetary theory and the trade cycle.* Jonathan Cape.

HAYEK, F.A. (1933) The trend of economic thinking. Inaugural lecture at the London School of Economics, 1 March.

HAYEK, F.A. (1935) *Prices and production.* Routledge.

HAYEK, F.A. (1941) *The pure theory of capital.* Chicago University Press.

HAYEK, F.A. (1944) *The road to serfdom.* Chicago University Press.

HAYEK, F.A. (1991) *The trend of economic thinking: the collected works of F.A. Hayek,* Edited by W.W. Bartley III and S. Kresge, Vol. III. Routledge.

SPIEGEL, H.W. (1971) *The growth of economic thought.* Prentice Hall, ch. 23.

Joan Robinson

(1903–1983)

J OAN ROBINSON WAS AN EXCEPTIONAL ECONOMIST, WITH A REMARKABLE GIFT OF pulling together the threads of a range of different perspectives on economics. She gained prominence in 1933 when she developed a theory of competitive markets lying between the extremes of perfect competition and monopoly. As Galbraith (1987) states, she did not stop there but for the next fifty years went on to pursue a dazzling range and variety of enquiry into economic issues. As a member of the Cambridge school of economics she was strongly influenced by Keynesian thinking, but she was equally versed in the neoclassical economics of Marshall, as well as researching Marx's economics to identify those elements that were appropriate to her own period. Robinson identified a lot that was helpful in Marxist economics but argued that modern day Marxists did not help the Marxist cause because they insisted on hanging on to too much of Marxist ideology that had been clearly discredited. She identified a post-Keynesian agenda which took into account the problems of inequality in society, growth models for developing societies, and the importance of the environment. She placed a strong emphasis on the importance of time in economics, and the need for economists to take a more dynamic approach based on change over time. Robinson was highly critical of the ultra-theoretical approach of classical economics particularly in relation to competitive models and laws relating to international trade. By examining the real world she was able to develop models of competition and trade that were far more representative of how things happen.

Methodology

J OAN ROBINSON SET OUT TO POSE QUESTIONS AND SEEK WAYS OF FINDING ANSWERS to those questions. Her early work involved asking questions about how firms competed with each other in the market place. However, in the wake of the Keynesian revolution she realised that there were more important questions to investigate and turned her attention to issues involving the macroeconomy, particularly in relation to growth over time. The questions she posed were related to issues that were relevant to the real world. She believed in simplification as a tool of analysis, but this simplification needed to be of relationships that were relevant to the real world. She was highly critical of economists who developed theories in 'empty boxes' – her boxes were full of real facts. In the conclusion to her book, *Economic Heresies* (1971) she stated: '*It is easy enough to make models on stated assumptions. The difficulty is to find the assumptions that are relevant to reality. The art is to set up a scheme that simplifies the problem so as to make it manageable without eliminating the essential characteristics of the actual situation on which it is intended to throw light.*'

She was particularly frustrated by neoclassical models based on abstraction. For example, she criticised conventional trade theory because '*The argument is usually conducted in terms of static comparisons of equilibrium positions of a model which has the following characteristics. There are two countries which represent the whole trading world. Each country is in a stationary equilibrium with given "resources" fully employed. There is perfect mobility of labour between occupations within each country and no mobility between countries. The value of imports is equal to the value of exports.*

These characteristics of the model exclude discussion of any question which is interesting in reality' ('The Need for a Reconsideration of the Theory of International Trade', 1973a).

In the textbook that she co-authored with John Eatwell, another Cambridge economist, in 1973, she outlined an appropriate method to be employed by economists in the use of a modelling approach providing that realistic assumptions are made: '*The doctrines, interpretations, and theories that make up the tradition of economic teaching are developed and expounded by a method of analysis peculiar to the subject. The method is to select from the flux of history (including the present as history) entities such as commodities, prices, monetary units, cultivable land, productive equipment, employers, workers, and owners of wealth, specify the economic environment in which they are to interact, and set them up in a model in which their interactions are worked out by a kind of quasi-mathematical logic.*

A model represents an hypothesis about reality. In the natural sciences, hypotheses can be tested by evidence drawn from experience. But an hypothesis about society cannot be tested, in the manner of the well-developed sciences, by controlled experiments in a laboratory, or by exact observation of unchanging regularities in nature. Economics has to rely on the experiments thrown up by events, and these experiments are not controlled; too many things are happening at once. If the predictions of a model turn out to be more or less correct, it may be by accident. The reasoning that led to the prediction is not necessarily vindicated by the result. If the predictions turn out to be wrong, it is hard to know in what respect the model was at fault, or concrete analysis based on it erroneous. The relations between a model and the reality it hopes to reflect are never clear-cut and are always subject to a variety of interpretations.'

Robinson and Eatwell (1973) argued that models are essential simplifications because '*a map at the scale of 1:1 is of no use to the traveller.*' They stated that '*The art of setting up models is to cut out all complications inessential to the point at issues, without eliminating the features necessary for safe guidance.*'

Robinson and Eatwell (1973) insisted that models need to be based on social reality: '*The most essential element to include in any piece of analysis is an indication of the nature of the social system to which it is applied. Economic relationships are relationships between people.*'

Another important aspect of Joan Robinson's methodology was that she sought out information from a range of sources and perspectives and gave credit to her sources of inspiration. She made friends with a number of interesting economists from across the globe who shared similar interests to her, including the Polish economist Michael Kalecki and the American J.K. Galbraith who both spent time at Cambridge during the 1930s. She was always concerned to pick out the good bits of analysis that could be found among the detritus of discarded ideas. At the same time she was particularly attached to critical thinking and stated that '*The purpose of studying economics is not to acquire a set of ready-made answers to economic questions, but to learn how to avoid being deceived by economists.*'

Robinson was wary of the claim that economics is a science, and stressed the normative nature of economics particularly in relation to policy making. In an essay on Marx, Marshall and Keynes (1960) she stated that: '*Economic doctrines always come to us as propaganda. This is bound up with the very nature of the subject and to pretend that it is not so in the name of "pure science" is a very unscientific refusal to accept the facts.*

The element of propaganda is inherent in the subject because it is concerned with policy. It would be of no interest if it were not. If you want a subject that is worth pursuing for its intrinsic appeal without any view to consequences you would not be attending a lecture on economics. You would be, say, doing pure mathematics or studying the behaviour of birds.'

Robinson clearly understood that her own view of economics was coloured by her own biography, and her concern with issues such as greater equality and the elimination of poverty.

Biography

JOAN ROBINSON WAS BORN JOAN VIOLET MAURICE. SHE WAS BROUGHT UP IN A FAMILY of five children, four of whom were girls. Both her mother and father came from distinguished families, and there was a strong element of social conscience in the biographies of her forbears, for example, her grandmother (on her mother's side) had founded the Alexandra Hospital for Children with Hip Disease in London. The family had strong connections with Cambridge University.

Her father, Major General Sir Frederick Maurice came to national prominence when he accused Lloyd George's government of deceiving Parliament about the true strength of the British army on the Western front at the start of the First World War. The army was not prepared to meet the German onslaught and was driven back almost to the Channel ports. Maurice set out these details in a letter to *The Times*. The letter effectively ended Maurice's military career. However, he was aware of this likelihood and was able to pass on to his children the value that being true to one's conscience is more important than material success.

At school Robinson was a hard working and extremely able student. During her time at St Paul's School in London she carried out voluntary work in a settlement house for poor people, and this social concern went on to inform her thinking and actions throughout her life. In 1921 she won a scholarship to Girton College Cambridge, where she read economics from 1922 to 1925. She was there when Alfred Marshall died in 1924.

Robinson studied at Cambridge at a time when it was patently obvious that traditional neoclassical economic ideas were not providing the solutions to the problems of unemployment. However, she was fortunate to be there at the time when Keynes' and his circle of friends were developing a new challenge to the classical orthodoxy.

She stated that: *'I was a student at a time when vulgar economics was in a particularly vulgar state. There was Great Britain with never less than a million workers unemployed, and there was I with my supervisor teaching me that it is logically impossible to have unemployment because of Say's Law.*

Now comes Keynes and proves that Say's Law is nonsense (so did Marx, of course, but my supervisor never drew my attention to Marx's views on the subject). Moreover (and that is where I am a left-wing Keynesian instead of the other kind), I see at a glance that Keynes is showing that unemployment is going to be a very tough nut to crack, because it is not just an accident – it has a function. In short, Keynes put into my head the very idea of the reserve army of labour that my supervisor had been so careful to keep out of it' (Robinson 1973a).

On graduating from Cambridge Robinson began to tutor a number of students, and from this began to develop the teaching skills which were to make her such an effective communicator with others. She had the knack of presenting complex ideas in an easy to understand fashion.

At Cambridge she met the economist Austin Robinson, who was a young lecturer at the University, and the two left for India where Austin had secured the post of tutor to the Maharajah of Gwailor. It was during this period that Robinson gained *'her first glimpse of the economically under-developed world'*. This helped to further the normative streak that underpinned all of her work in seeking to secure better conditions for poorer members of any society.

Robinson was convinced that there should be a much greater level of equality in society. She sought to identify ways in which economics could contribute to a society based on full employment, where growth in living standards was the norm, and in which the motivation for social improvement was based on ethical humanitarian principles rather than self-interest. She identified inequality in the distribution of income as one of the key flaws of capitalist society.

However, Robinson was at odds with socialist dogma. She sought to create a synthesis between Marshallian neoclassical economics, new Keynesian demand management approaches, and Marxist ideas about the long-term progress and development of society.

The Robinsons returned from India in 1929 and set up once again at Cambridge. Joan Robinson set to work rewriting the theory of the firm, identifying imperfect competition as a key intermediate state between monopoly and perfect competition. This was groundbreaking work which immediately gave her international status. However, she did not rest on her laurels. At the time the new Keynesian revolution was just breaking, and Robinson realised the significance of Keynes' ideas and the importance of developing a much better understanding of the macroeconomy. Robinson appreciated that

Keynes had provided a clear and effective criticism of classical orthodoxy in relation to short-term equilibrium.

In 1931 Robinson and a small number of other economists at Cambridge were invited to join a group which came to be given the name 'the Circus'. The group was set up on the suggestion of the young economist Pierro Sraffa and included Joan and Austin Robinson, as well as others such as Richard Kahn who was to go on to develop the idea of the multiplier effect. The group originally met at Kahn's rooms at Kings' College, but later became a wider seminar group meeting at Trinity College. The focus for the discussions tended to concentrate on working out in more detail some of Keynes' ideas that were outlined in his lectures. Keynes rarely attended the seminars but after the meetings *Kahn would report orally to Keynes the subject matter and lines of argument* (1973a).

In 1937, Joan Robinson published a very well-received book *Introduction to the Theory of Employment* in which she built on Keynesian ideas, and discussed some principal concerns of her own, such as the impact of 'beggar my neighbour' policies whereby trade restrictions imposed by one country lead to 'tit for tat' retaliation so that everyone loses out.

During the 1940s Robinson became particularly interested in Marxist economics. Although she was highly critical of many ideas in Marx, particularly the labour theory of value, she was attracted to the historical approach to development and Marx's ideas about the accumulation of capital over time which she saw as providing a useful growth theory about the development of capitalist society.

Marx showed how societies were rarely in equilibrium, and that tensions developed within an existing system requiring change. Robinson appreciated the emphasis on time and change. This influenced Robinson to develop theories based on the examination of history and disequilibrium rather than the classical emphasis on equilibrium states.

Marx's ideas also appealed to Robinson's dislike of the excesses and injustices of the capitalist system.

A key influence on Robinson was the Polish economist Michael Kalecki who Robinson persuaded to visit Cambridge in the mid-1930s. Kalecki had been wrestling with similar problems to Keynes, and was keenly interested in the work of Keynes and his colleagues. Kalecki developed a model of the failure of the economy to achieve equilibrium at full employment that was similar to that formulated by Keynes. Kalecki's theory was based on the Marxist division of society between employers and capitalists. Kalecki argued that national income was shared between capitalists and workers. As a general rule workers spend all of their income. In contrast, capitalists can spend their income (profits) or save it. It was thus the action of capitalists which triggered off the trade cycle and which determined the aggregate level of expenditure in the economy. Kalecki also integrated macroeconomic demand theory with the theory of the firm, arguing that the greater the level of monopoly power, the more potential employees had to squeeze the share of national income accruing to labour. Robinson was a keen admirer of Kalecki's work and the two enjoyed disagreeing with each other on a range of theoretical issues. Robinson (1973a) acknowledged her debt to Kalecki when she wrote: *'I learned far more, over thirty-five years, from the arguments with Kalecki that I had lost than from those that I won.'*

Robinson's work on Marxian economics led her to take an increasing interest in socialist economies in the post-war period. In 1952 she visited the Soviet Union and made six visits to China, a country for which she had a great deal of affection. It must be remembered that it was unusual for Western academics to have access to the Eastern bloc in any great measure during this period. In China, she visited cooperatives and communes as well as factories and universities, and was able to develop a working knowledge of how Chinese communism worked in practice. She was able to write a series of articles for the *Monthly Review*, a magazine that presented political and economic views principally from a Marxist perspective. During the 1960s she produced a variety of papers examining aspects of the economies of China, Cuba and other state socialist economies. Many liberal economists therefore perceived her work as being coloured by a red or at least bright pink tinge.

Robinson's enthusiasm about some of the benefits of socialism earned her criticism from a variety of sources at a time when there was considerable tension between East and West. Robinson was highly critical of the weapons race and of American military power. She argued that in a world of inequality and widespread poverty, there was no justification in building economic growth around military expenditure. During the 1960s her ideas were enthusiastically welcomed by those opposed to the war in Vietnam. However, while Robinson was interested in the ideas of Marx, she was above all a Keynesian socialist.

One of Robinson's major contributions was in presenting Keynes' ideas in a way that was intelligible to the lay reader. She was an excellent communicator and produced a number of papers explaining Keynesian and post-Keynesian ideas in an interesting way.

From the 1950s she was involved in an ongoing 'debate' with American economists based at Harvard and MIT in Cambridge, USA. A number of Cambridge USA economists had done some excellent work on developing Keynes' ideas, usually by building mathematical modelling techniques. These economists included Paul Samuelson and Robert Solow who had developed a theory of growth. Robinson termed these economists 'bastard Keynesians'. She felt that these economists had too readily sought to blend Keynesian ideas back into a neoclassical consensus, based on the notion of equilibrium, economic growth, and the distribution of income in line with neoclassical assumptions. In contrast, Robinson sought to develop a more critical post-Keynesian agenda which questioned existing patterns of developing capitalist society and posed challenges to the existing distribution of incomes, the exploitation of the environment, and so on.

From the 1960s onwards she was attracted to the ideas of the American economist J.K. Galbraith whose work was highly critical of consumerism and the role of large companies in the USA. Galbraith's book, *The Affluent Society*, identified the ills of American society in which private affluence is matched by 'public squalor', and the neglect of 'collective goods' which could benefit all members of society and particularly the poor. Galbraith set out that the level of poverty in the USA was 'a disgrace'. He was highly critical of the way in which companies in the USA set out to create needs among consumers rather than in giving priority to meeting the needs of consumers. In his book *The New Industrial State*, he showed how effective businesses and other organisations are in organising the production of consumer goods, but once again was critical of the failure to meet the needs of all members of society. Galbraith and Robinson thus both shared a post-Keynesian agenda which posed serious ethical questions about the nature and purpose of economic activity. Galbraith (1987) wrote about Robinson that her work set out *'to comfort the afflicted and afflict the comfortable'*. The same could equally be said of Galbraith.

Above all Robinson was concerned with economic issues that were relevant to the real world and to helping to meet the needs of ordinary people. During her lifetime the nature of economics was transformed, from an over-emphasis on theory to much more real concerns. Robinson was pleased with this change and in her *Notes on the Theory of Economic Development* (1955) stated: *'I began by saying that the students of to-day are to be pitied because economic theory is growing faster than it is possible to learn it, but at least they have the consolation that nowadays it is concerned with interesting subjects.'*

Key works

The Economics of Imperfect Competition (1933)

The Long Period Theory of Employment (1936)

Essays on the Theory of Employment (1937)

Collected Economic Papers (1951, 1960, 1965, 1973, 1980)

Economic Heresies: Some Old-fashioned Questions in Economic Theory (1971)

After Keynes (1973)

An Introduction to Modern Economics, with John Eatwell (1973)

What Are the Questions? And Other Essays (1980)

Imperfect competition

In her famous 1933 book, *The Economics of Imperfect Competition*, Robinson introduced the idea of imperfect competition at the same time as E.H. Chamberlin produced similar ideas in the USA. Robinson was not happy with the classical economists' emphasis on perfect competition which was a theoretical state in which markets were divided into lots of small companies producing identical products, in which firms could not set prices in the market but had to take a price from the market, and in which consumers had perfect knowledge of prices being charged by all the firms in the market. The perfect market supported the free market economy in that it led to an efficient use of resources.

At Cambridge, Robinson was a friend of a young Italian economist, Pierro Sraffa, who in 1933 published a paper, *The Theory of Monopolistic Competition*, arguing that the analysis of firms should be in terms of monopoly rather than competition – because decreasing costs of production were widespread. As a result the threat to firms being able to sell more products did not come from cost constraints, but from demand constraints as markets fail to absorb all of the product of individual firms.

Robinson could see that this idealised state was unreal and so developed a more sophisticated theory of the market based on an array of intermediate possibilities between perfect competition and monopoly – imperfect competition. Robinson argued that competition is never perfect and so firms are faced with a downward sloping demand curve. If they want to sell larger quantities they have to do so at lower prices. Sellers usually have a significant power to control price, perhaps by advertising in order to build brand loyalty.

Robinson's notion of imperfect competition provided a radical critique to existing classical analysis which was based on the assumption that firms produce up to the point at which the marginal cost of producing an additional unit of a product is equal to price so that resources are used in an efficient way. However, Robinson observed that during the slump (when she was researching) firms were not producing at full capacity, and that they were producing at output levels at which their marginal costs of production were actually falling. In the real world of the 1920s and 30s most firms were producing at outputs below their capacity, with falling marginal costs, and simply adding a margin for profits over and above their average production costs.

The theory of imperfect competition provided a radical critique to a wide range of assumptions on which classical models of the economy were based, for example the notion that wages are equal to the marginal product of labour. Drawing on empirical evidence Robinson (1973b) was able to assert '*In general in modern industry, it seems that the wage bill is about half of the value added. In the typical case, then, the value of marginal product of labour is twice the wage.*'

Robinson went on to show that an important intermediate case between that of monopoly and perfect competition is that of oligopoly where there are only a small number of competitors in the same industry.

Robinson and Eatwell (1973) described how oligopoly comes about in the following way: '*Since profits feed growth, and growth feeds profits, the output of successful firms expands faster than the total output of industry, and they eat up or knock out unsuccessful competitors. Heavy investments can be undertaken only by strong firms, commanding large sums of finance, and covering many ventures so that the failure of one or two would not be fatal.*

Nowadays, in many markets, there are only two or three such firms in operation – an oligopoly – and these firms are not interested in cutting prices in such a way as to destroy each other's gross profits. Moreover, a barrage of advertisement, exclusive deals with retailers, and so forth, make it extremely hard for an outsider to break into their preserves.'

Chamberlin and Robinson examined imperfect competition from different perspectives. Chamberlin saw imperfect competition as providing many benefits to the consumer in the form of varied products and opportunity for wider choice. In contrast, Robinson pointed out the wastes of imperfect competition and the way in which it restricted welfare. She was in favour of government intervention to make markets work better.

Providing support for Keynesian theory

Robinson was a keen supporter of the central Keynesian idea that the market economy on its own would not necessarily create a full employment equilibrium. Her earlier work on imperfect competition had led her to a frustration with classical economics, and its inability to explain real events and relationships. She referred to this as a crisis in economic theory. For example, she refers to an occasion when Hayek was explaining the classical system at Cambridge – 'he covered a blackboard with triangles' and in her view followed the existing orthodoxy by suggesting that the slump was caused by consumption. Robinson (1971) explains what happened next:

'R.F. Kahn, who was at that time involved in explaining that the multiplier guaranteed that saving equals investment, asked in a puzzled tone, "Is it your view that if I went out tomorrow and bought a new overcoat, that would increase unemployment?" "Yes", said Hayek "But" pointing to his triangles on the board "it would take a very long mathematical argument to explain why".

This pitiful state of confusion was the first crisis of economic theory.'

Robinson believed that Keynesian ideas prevailed over the previous orthodoxy of classical economics. She argued that the 25 years following the Second World War provided a vindication of Keynes' rejection of classical ideas.

She stated that: *'Keynes was arguing against the dominant orthodoxy, which held that government expenditure could not increase employment. He had to prove, first of all, that it could. He had to show that an increase in investment will increase consumption – that more wages will be spent on more beer and boots whether the investment is useful or not. He had to show that the secondary increase in real income is quite independent of the object of the primary outlay. Pay men to dig holes in the ground and fill them up again if you cannot do anything else.'* ('The Second Crisis of Economic Theory', 1973a).

Robinson (1973a) believes that Keynes' ideas proved to be accurate and that in the post-war period *'there certainly was a great increase in economic wealth in 25 years without a slump. This was especially true in the countries which were initially not allowed to dissipate their resources on arms and could put all their investment into productive forms . . . Capitalism with near-full employment was an impressive spectacle.'*

Moving forward from Marx, Marshall and Keynes

Robinson was in a particularly privileged position in that she had been exposed at first hand to the teaching and ideas of Marshall and Keynes while at Cambridge. In addition, she was an avid reader of Marx. She lived through a period in which Keynesian ideas became the orthodox means of controlling the economy and in which the Eastern bloc and China engaged heavily in state socialism. She travelled widely, and was always interested in listening to the views of others. As a result she was able to develop extensive critiques of Marx, Marshall and Keynes – and to identify new questions that needed to be asked to move economics forward.

She saw Marx, Marshall and Keynes as providing three views of capitalism. She saw Marx as a representation of revolutionary socialism, Marshall a complacent defence of capitalism and Keynes the disillusioned defence of capitalism.

She argued that *'Each point of view bears the stamp of the period when it was conceived. Marx formed his ideas in the grim poverty of the forties. Marshall saw capitalism blossoming in peace and prosperity in the sixties. Keynes had to find an explanation for the morbid conditions of "poverty in the midst of plenty" in the period between the wars. But each has significance for other times, for in so far as each theory is valid it throws light upon essential characteristics of the capitalist system which have always been present in it and still have to be reckoned with.'* ('Marx, Marshall and Keynes', 1960).

Robinson criticised the Marxists of her day for hanging on religiously to a pure Marxist ideology when it was apparently obvious that some of Marx's economic ideas such as the labour theory of value, were clearly flawed. She felt that they would be better employed concentrating on those bits of Marxist theory that were clearly relevant, such as Marx's notion of the expansion of capitalist society over time based on the accumulation of capital. Marx suggested that eventually this could lead to a crisis of capitalism based on the inability of capitalists to sustain sufficient demand for the products of the capitalist system. Robinson felt that Marx's theory of growth and capital accumulation was worth taking seriously (see the notes below on capital accumulation).

Robinson criticised Marshallian economics, because of its assumption that in general it was based on the belief that full employment and growth was the natural state of affairs. Robinson (1960) would have liked to see more discussion of macroeconomic questions. Marshallian economics *'concentrates attention on the details of relative prices, the fortunes of individual firms and supply and demand of particular commodities, while leaving the main outline into which those details fit extremely hazy.'* Marshall identified the engine for growth in the economy as being the energy of entrepreneurs which governs capital accumulation. However, for Marshall events like slumps were regarded as the exception to the rule of macroeconomic equilibrium – *'a slump occurs when confidence fails – investment declines, unemployment reduces the demand for consumer goods and so multiplies itself* (Robinson 1960).

Robinson criticised Keynesian economics for stopping with short-term equilibrium positions in developed economies. She would have liked the Keynesians to go on to examine long-term growth, and capital accumulation. She also felt that Keynesian theory could only really be applied to developed economies in which there was already productive capacity in existence. In her view Keynesian ideas failed to provide answers to the problems of a country *'which suffers from a lack of productive capacity or on the kind of unemployment that arises from having too little capital to be able to offer work to all available labour . . . Where lack of productive capacity is the problem, merely generating demand only leads to inflation, and expenditure for its own sake – building pyramids instead of railway – is clearly not what the situation demands'* (Robinson 1960).

Robinson realised that the way forward was not to set yourself up as a Marxist, Marshallian, or Keynesian economist but to draw on what was most helpful from all of these perspectives.

Robinson therefore saw that the most important questions that economists needed to answer were those about long-term growth. In the event, governments increasingly relied on stop-go economic policies – pumping expenditure into the economy to avoid unemployment, and cutting back when inflation set in, leading to a period of slow growth and instability.

Developing a post-Keynesian theory of distribution

Robinson was highly critical of 'Keynesian' economics in its failure to tackle the issue of poverty in society. She wrote (1973b) that '*Capitalism with near-full employment was an impressive spectacle. But a growth in wealth is not the same thing as reducing poverty. A universal paean was raised in praise of growth. Growth was going to solve all problems. No need to bother about poverty. Growth will lift up the bottom and poverty will disappear without any need to pay attention to.*' Robinson was thus concerned to identify ways of dealing with poverty in society, particularly in relation to long-term growth models. In her view (1973b), when Keynesian ideas became the conventional wisdom, there was '*just one simple omission; when Keynes became orthodox they forgot to change the question and discuss what employment should be for.*'

One of the key influences on Robinson's thinking was the Polish economist Michael Kalecki, who visited Cambridge in 1936 and shared his ideas with members of the Cambridge School. Kalecki was working on his book, *The General Theory of Employment*, that was heavily influenced by Keynesian ideas.

Kalecki had a different interpretation to Keynes as to how an increase in investment brings about an increase in saving. Keynes felt that increases in investment would work through the system according to how much individuals would want to save.

Kalecki's alternative explanation was that an increase in investment brings about increased saving because it increases profits relative to wages.

Kalecki set out a balance sheet of Gross National Product on the basis that GNP is divided between workers and capitalists, in the form of wages and salaries to workers, and gross profits to capitalists. Assuming that workers spend what they earn, then gross profit will be equal to gross investment and capitalists' consumption.

Gross National Product (income perspective)	Gross National Product (expenditure perspective)
Gross profits	Gross investment Capitalists' consumption
Wages and salaries	Workers' consumption

Kalecki then set out to answer the question of whether profits determine capitalists' investment and consumption, or whether capitalists' investment and consumption determine profits.

The answer that Kalecki gave was that capitalists might decide to consume and invest more in a given period than in the previous one, but they cannot decide to earn more. His view was therefore that investment and consumption decisions determine profits.

Kalecki summed up this view by stating that '*The workers spend what they get and the capitalist get what they spend*' (Robinson, 1966).

Although Robinson recognised that it was not quite that simple in a modern industrial economy in which real wages are rising, the basic principle holds that workers receive their wages individually and this feeds into consumption, while the capitalists receive what they spend as a class.

In any case, the economic model as it stood, whether under a neoclassical or Keynesian model for the economy, did very little to deal with the problem of poverty.

Robinson felt that poverty in the midst of plenty was as much a problem in a full employed economy as it was during the slump.

Capital accumulation

Robinson believed that Keynes should have moved on from explaining how full employment can be achieved in the short period in capitalist societies to long-term explanations of a growing economy with full employment. To this end she carried out her own investigations into conditions favouring economic growth in the long term, which she published in her paper, 'Notes on the Theory of Economic Development' (1955). In this paper she noted that Keynes had turned classical ideas of saving and investment on their head. The classical economists believed that saving was required to create investment, thus providing a justification for capitalism, and income from property *'the rentier had the right to be rewarded for the noble self-sacrifice of not consuming all his wealth.'* So Keynes' argument that saving is a cause of unemployment was deeply shocking to the existing order. According to Keynes the development of wealth *'depends not upon prudence but upon energy'* (Robinson, 1960).

Robinson (1960) criticised Keynesian theory for not looking at the impact of adding to the stock of capital over time – *'Keynes said very little about the long term'*. Robinson could see that in line with Marx's ideas about capital accumulation – that there was a real danger that this might slow down, and that demand in the economy might not be sufficient to keep encouraging growth in the economy, leading to a potential crisis.

She pointed to the difficulties of maintaining long-term full employment equilibrium in the following way:

'A statement of the conditions for steady progress suggests that there is no necessary and inevitable collapse of capitalism in prospect. At the same time, it shows how hard it is for the conditions for stability to be satisfied and how many weak points there are in the mechanism that keeps the system running.

Let me repeat the conditions required:

1. *The balance of forces between workers and employers must be such as to keep real wages rising with output per head. This is essential. It is also desirable, though less important, that prices should be stable; that is to say, that the rise of real wages comes about by a rise of money wages step by step with productivity.*

2. *Technical progress must be neutral, so that the shares of wages and of profit remain constant.*

3. *Accumulation must be sufficient to keep the stock of capital expanding as fast as output per man rises. The animal sprits of the entrepreneurs must never flag, so that the system is kept continually at stretch, and technical progress must be sufficient to enable it to be so.*

4. *Thriftiness must be maintained so that saving bears a constant proportion to income.*

5. *The monetary system must operate in such a way as to permit investment to proceed at the required rate.*

6. *Limitation of natural resources must be overcome by technical progress which makes it possible to substitute capital for those resources which are growing scarce'* (Robinson 1960).

The key point that Robinson stresses about long-term capital accumulation is that while in the short period during a slump thriftiness is a problem in that it makes the problem worse – in the long term saving by capitalists is essential to growth. In the long period high levels of savings that are then turned into investment lead to growth in the economy – leading to rising real wages for employees.

The time factor

One of Robinson's most important contributions to economics was in the emphasis that she gave to time. In particular she stressed the fact that we cannot predict the future. Traditionally, economic theory had worked on the assumption that it was possible to treat the past, present and future as if they were predictable events. Robinson (1973a) states that this is nonsense: *'Once we admit that an economy exists in time, that history goes one way, from the irrevocable past into the unknown future, the conception of equilibrium based on the mechanical analogy of a pendulum swinging to and fro in space become untenable. The whole of traditional economics needs to be thought out afresh.'*

Taking this view of time means that economic forecasting and assumptions about the future become unpredictable. Economists therefore need to be wary of making assumptions about the predictability of the micro- or macroeconomy whatever their perspective is. This applies equally to Keynesian economists (many of whom have fallen into the old trap) as it does to classical economists.

Robinson also stressed the importance of taking time into consideration when examining diagrams, such as demand and supply diagrams. Using this approach she encouraged students to think of these diagrams as three-dimensional maps. In one axis we can represent price and on the other quantity, but we must not forget time.

In the text she produced with John Eatwell (1973) she set this out in the following way: *'The diagram then represents a slice of time "today" with the past behind it. We are comparing possible positions, not representing changes. It is impossible to move from one point to another by changing past history. Any movement must be in the dimension of future time.'*

Socialism in developing economies

Joan Robinson saw socialism as a valid alternative pathway to economic growth in society that could be far more effective in tackling inequality in distribution than capitalism. In her text *An Introduction to Modern Economics* (with John Eatwell, 1973) she set out a chapter on socialist states showing how they are organised to deal with a range of economic problems.

Robinson championed the advantages of state socialism particularly in terms of providing an alternative model for long-term capital accumulation and economic growth which could achieve better results if the planners' actions were brought in line with consumer requirements.

She showed how socialist plans could be designed to ensure adequate training and development of beneficial sectors of the economy. She showed that trade cycles would not exist in socialist economies, and that a dynamic local economy could be developed around well-organised plans. She showed how only limited inflation would be likely to occur in a socialist economy in which prices would be fixed centrally.

However, she was well aware of the failings of over-regimented socialism. She was critical of Soviet repression in Poland and Czechoslovakia, and was opposed to centralised dogma. She saw lack of political freedom as a major weakness of these systems.

In a paper on 'Socialist Affluence' (1973a) she set out the weakness of the Soviet system by taking the example of Czechoslovakia: 'The economic system developed for the purpose of rapid accumulation was imitated from the Soviet Union and contained features which were not at all appropriate to the requirements of a small country highly dependent upon international trade. Moreover the Soviet system imposed not only necessary but also unnecessary hardships upon the consumer, for instance, the elimination of individual tradesmen, such as cobblers. The planners were taught to think that only investment goods were "serious" and neglect of consumer interests became a virtue in itself.

The dogma that, under socialism, the share of investment devoted to Department I which was identified with heavy industry, must exceed the share of Department II, meant a continuous effort to accelerate accumulation. The dogma was disputed, for instance in Poland in 1956, but policy in Czechoslovakia continued to be dominated by it. When the rate of growth slackened and actually came to a halt, the authorities could think of no remedy except more investment.'

Here, Robinson was criticising the sort of tunnel vision that was eventually to lead to the collapse of communism in the late 1970s.

Pollution

Another of Robinson's major concerns was with the environment, and she saw environmental damage as one of the most obvious manifestations of the capitalist economists' obsession with material growth. She wrote that: 'Pollution and the irreparable loss of resources, both for production and pleasure, provide the most obvious and notorious objection to the doctrine that the free play of market forces in a regime of laissez-faire leads to beneficial result for society as a whole. Some economists try to recapture lost ground by advocating that a price be put upon the damage that pollution does, and industry be obliged to pay it. This would mean that firms who found it sufficiently profitable to poison us could buy the right to do so' (Robinson and Eatwell, 1973).

Like many environmental economists of today she identified the obsession with 'growth' as one of the root causes of environmental degradation. 'The whole argument is obfuscated by the conception of "growth". In recent years, it has been fashionable to measure the success of a national economy by its rate of growth of GNP. GNP is a statistical measure of the sales value of goods and services at the prices ruling at some base date. The index, in the nature of the case, cannot take account of any values not expressed in money. It is necessarily an imperfect measure of what used to be called the "moral and material progress of the nation". It is, at best, a measure of the growth of economic power in the world market. The British have given themselves an inferiority complex because their rate of "growth" has been relatively slow in the postwar era. Now the cry is raised *that growth causes destruction and ought to be stopped. A better argument for the anti-pollutionists would be that, if the true costs of production were included in the calculation of GNP, growth might very well be negative, so that it is really they who are in favour of positive growth'* (Robinson and Eatwell 1973).

However, Robinson felt that common sense could prevail, if the debate about the environment was presented in terms of the needs of our children, and their children. She set out that: *'Proposals for policy necessarily run into conflicts of interest and incompatibility of judgements. Every participant in the debate has his own prejudices. But there is one prejudice which is fairly widespread, that is, in favour of bringing up healthy children. The best hope for the anti-pollutionists is to enlist this sentiment on their side of the case'* (Robinson and Eatwell 1973).

Conclusion

There is a strong case for arguing that Joan Robinson was one of the most important economists of all time. The sheer range of her ideas coupled with her ability to synthesise viewpoints from a range of perspectives while still being aware of essential differences sets her above others who wrap themselves up in the more confined spaces of a particular view of the world. Robinson was keen to learn from others and to champion 'worthy causes'.

CICARELLI, J. AND CICARELLI, J. (2000) *Joan Robinson: a bibliographical biography*. Greenwood Press.

FEIWEL, G.G. (ed.) (1989) *Joan Robinson and modern economic theory*. New York University Press.

GALBRAITH, J.K. (1987) *A history of economics, the past and the present*. Penguin, ch. 14.

HARCOURT, G.C. (1991) Joan Robinson (1903–1983), in P. Aresti (ed.), *A biographical dictionary of dissenting economists*. Elgar.

KEYNES, J.M. (1936) *The general theory of employment, interest and money*. Macmillan and Co.

RIMA, I.H. (ed.) (1991) *The Joan Robinson legacy*. M.E. Sharpe.

ROBINSON, J. (1955) *Notes on the theory of economic development*. Annals de la Faculté de Droit de Liège.

ROBINSON, J. (1960) *Collected economic papers*, Vol. II. Basil Blackwell.

ROBINSON, J. (1966) *Kalecki and Keynes – in problems of economic dynamics and planning*. Oxford.

ROBINSON, J. (1971) *Economic heresies, some old-fashioned questions in economic theory*. Macmillan.

ROBINSON, J. (1973a) *Collected economic papers*, Vol. IV. Basil Blackwell.

ROBINSON, J. (ed.) (1973b) *After Keynes*. Basil Blackwell.

ROBINSON, J. (1980) *What are the questions? And other essays*. M. E. Sharpe.

ROBINSON, J. (2002) The economics of imperfect competition. *Robinson's collected works*. Palgrave.

ROBINSON, J. (2002) The long period theory of employment. *Robinson's collected works*. Palgrave.

ROBINSON, J. (2002) Essays on the theory of employment. *Robinson's collected works*. Palgrave.

ROBINSON, J. AND EATWELL, J. (1973) *An introduction to modern economics*. McGraw-Hill.

SPIEGEL, H.W. (1971) *The growth of economic thought*. Prentice Hall, ch. 25.

Paul A. Samuelson
(1915–)

S AMUELSON IS THE MASTER CRAFTSMAN OF MODERN ECONOMIC TECHNIQUES AND theories who was able to pick up the baton passed on by Keynes. He is an avid reader and researcher into a range of different issues involving economic theory enabling him to develop an all-round understanding of economic relationships. His work has covered a dazzling array of topic areas based on his interests at the time. In an autobiographical note (1992), he wrote that: ' *"What are you working on now?" This is a question I have been asked all my life. And never in my life have I known how to answer it. At any one time I have several balls in the air. And always there is an inventory of questions just below the threshold of my explicit attention. Some of these slumber in that limbo for two decades. There is no hurry; they will keep. Some morning (or at night in a dream) the evolving wheel of chance will turn their number up.*'

Samuelson regards economics to be a science of the bourgeoisie, arguing that it is less effective at providing policies and solutions in non-capitalist societies. He himself came from a middle-class family background to parents who had prospered in American society. He developed an interest in economics from an early age and by the age of 22 had written his *Foundations of Economic Analysis*, which was full of insight. Samuelson quickly mastered the economic theory that was around in his younger days and then set out to build new ideas and theories at a faster rate than any of his contemporaries.

Keynes had moved the emphasis in economics to macroeconomics. Samuelson was then able to develop this new body of theory and to popularise the subject both through his astonishingly popular textbook, which over the years has sold millions of copies throughout the world, and through the news columns which he regularly turned out, including regular articles for *Newsweek* magazine and the *New York Times*. It was Samuelson who first brought Keynesian ideas to the general attention of the American public. His textbook *Economics* provided a synthesis of the best of neoclassical and Keynesian ideas, discarding a lot of irrelevant clutter. As a writer, Samuelson had a clear sense of audience, being able to tailor his newspaper articles to a wider audience than for his specialist technical articles. Samuelson was the first American to win the Nobel Prize for Economics. The Swedish Royal Academy in its award citation, said, '*Professor Samuelson's extensive production, covering nearly all areas of economic theory, is characterised by an outstanding ability to derive important new theorems and to find new applications for existing ones. By his contributions, Samuelson has done more than any other contemporary economist to raise the level of scientific analysis in economic theory.*'

Sir Eric Roll places Samuelson in a historical light as the principal founder and codifier of 'New Economics'. He is particularly adept at outlining macroeconomic relationships. He defines macroeconomics as *'the study of the aggregate performance of the whole GNP and of the general price level'* (Samuelson 1948).

Samuelson's key strength lay in his ability to use mathematics to outline sets of economic relationships. He was able to draw on existing pieces of economic theory and to draw out inferences from these theories using the tools of mathematical analysis. Much of Samuelson's work has been of a theoretical rather than an empirical nature.

IN OUTLINING HIS METHODOLOGY, SAMUELSON MAKES IT CLEAR THAT IT IS NOT something that he spends a great deal of time in thinking about. He paraphrases George Bernard Shaw in stating that *'Those who can, do science; those who can't prattle about its methodology'* (Samuelson 1992).

Samuelson's natural enthusiasm for economic issues and problems has meant that he has always found lots of interesting problems to investigate using a range of tools and techniques. In an autobiographical note (1992) he stated that *'I have been blessed with an abundance of interesting problems to puzzle out. Many artists and writers run into long fallow periods when new creative ideas just will not come. Luckily, that has not been my experience . . . One tackles the most important unsolved problem at hand. Then the next one.'*

While Samuelson spends a lot of time in developing theories, he emphasises that his *'first and last allegiance is to the facts'*. Samuelson places himself firmly in the camp of induction in carrying out his economics, and is highly critical of modern-day Ricardians *'who believed that by thinking in one's study one could arrive at the basic immutable laws of political economy'* (1992).

Samuelson is sceptical of the ability of economists to outline objective truths stating that *'Precision in deterministic facts or in their probability laws can at best be only partial and approximate. Which of the objective facts out there are worthy of study and description or explanation depends admittedly on subjective properties of the scientists.'* He argues that what is seen as important depends on the predisposition of the researcher and that ways of seeing help to impose themselves on or to distort the data. However, in spite of these reservations, Samuelson is still of the view that when examining the rise and fall of new systems of ideas *'what ultimately shapes the verdicts of the scientist juries is an empirical reality out there.'*

Samuelson is strongly associated with mathematical economics. For example, he used mathematics, and mathematical representations to draw out a dynamic model of the link between the multiplier and accelerator effects, and illustrated Keynes' short-term economic equilibrium by drawing the Keynesian Cross showing the relationship between national income and national expenditure.

However, Samuelson's emphasis on mathematical techniques has been strongly criticised by a number of influential economists who argue that a mathematical modelling approach can abstract from reality. For example, John Blatt (1983) is particularly critical of what he sees as the 'Samuelson approach'. Blatt argues that in pure mathematics it is appropriate to work from a set of 'axioms' (that is, initial assumptions which are accepted without further question) these axioms being generally accepted among mathematicians. These axioms or 'rules of the game' must be substantially the same for all investigators. He states that Samuelson's work, in particular *Foundations of Economic Analysis* (1947), created a set of axioms which lie at the heart of modern economics. This book and a number of other works provided the accepted conventional truth for pure mathematical economics. Blatt (1983) states *'Paul Samuelson . . . has postulated an economic universe, and the entire mathematical economics profession has swallowed his universe whole and is dancing in accordance with the rules he has laid down for that universe.'* The rules set out by Samuelson became the *'fully objective standard of professional judgment of competence in pure economic theory.'*

The main criticism that Blatt levels at the Samuelson approach is that the mathematical modelling used is at one remove from reality, and the tendency has been to move away from reality in the direction of mathematical abstraction. Blatt is not opposed to the use of mathematics in economics (he is a mathematician) but he believes that mathematics should be used to explore reality rather than abstractions.

Although Samuelson is a firm believer that a scientific approach needs to be applied in economics, he recognises that this is underwritten by the ethical stance and beliefs of the researcher, as can be seen from his statement that: *'Although positivistic analysis of what the actual world is like commands and constrains my every move as an economist, there is never far from my consciousness a concern for the ethics of the outcome. Mine is a simple ideology that favours the underdog and (other things equal) abhors inequality'* (Samuelson 1992).

Biography

PAUL SAMUELSON WAS BORN IN 1915 IN GARY, INDIANA – A TOWN THAT BENEFITED from its geographical location 'where coal meets ore at the tip of Lake Michigan'. His father was a pharmacist with his own chemist store, and his mother came from a relatively wealthy family (her grandfather had emigrated to America from Poland at the time of the Gold Rush). The family practised the Jewish religion, and Samuelson remarks that economics has a particularly affinity for Jewish people because of its entrepreneurial associations, and also because Jews at times feel marginalised in society, enabling them to develop critical perceptions and enabling them to move thinking forward.

The Samuelson family moved to Chicago in 1923, and as a result Paul was to go on to study at the University of Chicago, one of the spiritual homes of twentieth-century free market economics. It did not take Samuelson long to develop a thirst for economic understanding. It was a subject in which he excelled.

Samuelson (1992) informs us in outlining his life philosophy that 'Many economists . . . became economists, they tell us, to do good for the world. I became an economist quite by chance, primarily because the analysis was so interesting and easy – indeed so easy that at first I thought that there must be more to it than I was recognising, else why were my older classmates making such heavy weather over supply and demand? (How could an increased demand for wool help but lower the price of pork and beef?)'

Samuelson (1992) wrote that 'I was born an economist on January 2, 1932, which means that chronologically I was about sixteen and a half years of age.' It was on this date that he attended his first class at the University of Chicago, to hear the lecturer discuss the ideas of Robert Malthus. He found the discourse interesting and easy to follow. Samuelson was to find his economics studies full of interesting issues. He says that he took to economics in the way that his daughter responded to ice cream the first time it was put on her tongue – 'she went wild'.

Samuelson believes that he came to economics at the right time, because in the early 1930s it was obvious that new ideas were needed to deal with the key issues of the time and the conventional wisdom was not half way adequate. As he recalls (1992), 'Yes, 1932 was a great time to be born an economist. The sleeping beauty of political economy was waiting for the enlivening kiss of new methods, new paradigms, new hired hands, and new problems. Science is a parasite; the greater the patient population the better the advance in physiology and pathology; and out of pathology arises therapy. The year 1932 was the trough of the great depression, and from its rotten soil was belatedly begot the new subject that today we call macroeconomics.'

In an essay on Isaac Newton, Keynes had written that Newton's genius lay in being able to focus on scientific problems for long periods of time until he was able to work out the solution to them. Samuelson had a similar ability with economic problem solving. He was able to focus on an issue that was puzzling scholars and then draw out new and coherent ways of tackling these puzzles.

Writing about his postgraduate days Samuelson (1992) recalled that: 'In those days thinking about economics filled my every hour'. He married Mary Crawford a fellow graduate student in economics and with her wrote his doctoral dissertation 'Foundations of Economic Analysis'. He talks of developing some of the theorems for this work 'while sitting in the front seat of a car being driven westward at 70 miles an hour by my wife'.

Samuelson was taught by a number of famous and interesting lecturers including Frank Knight and Aaron Director (Milton Friedman's brother-in-law). He shared classes with Friedman and George Stigler (another Nobel laureate).

In 1935 Samuelson won a fellowship, awarded to the eight most promising graduates, to carry out postgraduate study providing they moved on to another university. The award would pay for all of their study. Samuelson chose to go on to Harvard. He freely admits that he chose Harvard because of its reputation as an 'Ivy League' college. He was fortunate to have some excellent teachers including Alvin Hansen, Joseph Schumpeter and Wassily Leontief and fellow students included John Kenneth Galbraith and James Tobin.

Working in such exalted company certainly motivated Samuelson and in no time he had a string of publications to his name in both micro- and macroeconomics.

He was particularly fortunate to work alongside Alvin Hansen who had done as much as anyone to build on the foundations of Keynesian thinking. Hansen was a good communicator and was able to make Keynes' ideas more understandable to a wider audience. In 1939 Samuelson produced a paper that was well received, on the dynamic relationship between the multiplier and the accelerator effects. He was offered a teaching post at Harvard in 1940, but felt that his talents were not being fully used. Some commentators, including Samuelson, argue that there was a clear element of anti-Semitism in the University at the time, while others point to some personal disagreements between Samuelson and senior colleagues. In any case he was offered a professorship at the nearby MIT (the other half of the American Cambridge).

At MIT Samuelson proved to be an excellent teacher and the content of what he taught is clearly set out in his book *Economics* (1948) that was published after the war and continues to sell millions of copies. This was a follow up to his earlier *Foundations of Economic Analysis* (1947) which used a mathematical approach to formalising economic theory.

The book followed the Keynesian line that unemployment could be cured by a combination of government spending and tax reductions, and that inflation could be cured by reducing government spending and raising taxes.

'Samuelson' became the standard economics text across the world, and many influential figures learned their economics from this book. John F. Kennedy used Samuelson as an economic adviser, as did Presidents Johnson and Carter. The Kennedy era was the highpoint of US Keynesianism in which deficit government spending and tax cuts were used to create employment. In 1961 he was the author of the 'Samuelson Report on the State of the American Economy to President-Elect Kennedy'. Samuelson served on a number of government committees particularly in relation to economic development and employment.

While Friedman, and the Chicago school advocated the free market, Samuelson championed Keynesian demand management and government intervention in the marketplace. However, he has always resisted heavy-handed government. He puts down his distrust of too much government to the McCarthy era in America and the witch hunt of 'communists', at a time in which Samuelson was put on the blacklist.

Samuelson sees society as being made up of a community of interdependent people and is highly critical of the atomistic nature of individualism. In an essay on 'Modern Economic Realities and Individualism' (1999) he wrote *'Just as there is a sociology of family life and of politics, there is a sociology of individualistic competition. It is not a rich one. Ask not your neighbour's name; enquire only for his numerical schedules of supply and demand. Under perfect competition, no buyer need face a seller . . . Carry the notion of the individual to its limit and you get a monstrosity, just as you do if you carry the notion of a group to its limit. Yet get not Nietzsche's superman, nor even Mill's imperfect-perfect Victorian entitled to his own mistakes. You get Wolf-Boy.'*

Samuelson's work essentially provides a synthesis between Keynesian and market economics. He bestowed particularly harsh criticism of President Nixon's Republican economic agenda writing at one stage (1975) in the downturn in the world economy *'If you turn this recession upside down you will read clearly on its bottom, "Made in Washington".'*

From the late 1950s onwards Samuelson increasingly saw inflation as being the major problem facing the US economy. In 1958 he wrote '*The history of the Twentieth Century – America's Century! – has been pretty much a history of rising prices . . . Inflation is itself a problem.*'

In 1991 MIT established in his honour the Paul A. Samuelson Professorship in Economics.

Today, Samuelson's book continues to be a best seller, although its style and accessible approach has also been used by a number of other (usually American) writers, so that it has to vie with other competitors to make the essential reading list of university courses.

Key works

Foundations of Economic Analysis (1947)

Economics, an Introductory Analysis (First of many editions, 1948)

Deriving testable conclusions

In his *Foundations* Samuelson borrowed ideas from mathematics and science to examine an approach to producing 'operationally meaningful theorems' in economics – in other words 'hypotheses about empirical data which could conceivably be refuted, if only under ideal conditions'.

Stable equilibrium

As a basis for Samuelson's mathematical approach he claimed that a key to tackling problems were the twin concepts of equilibrium and stability.

Here Samuelson based his thinking on two assumptions.

1. That equilibrium is based on the maximisation of a particular state. So for example, equilibrium will exist in the market when (a) for example, the firm is maximising its profit, and (b) when the consumer is maximising utility.
2. The system is stable, if it is disturbed then it will return to the equilibrium position.

Samuelson believed that these assumptions provided the basis for deriving lots of meaningful theorems which would help economists to tackle economic problems related to the consumer, the firm, the economy, etc.

The Keynesian Cross

Samuelson presented Keynes' ideas of aggregate demand management in the form of the Keynesian Cross. Samuelson regarded this cross to be as significant as the Marshallian Cross because it provided a rationale for post-war fiscal policy.

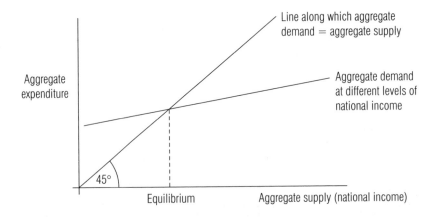

The Keynesian Cross

The Keynesian Cross, which tutors usually refer to as the 45 degree diagram, has on the vertical axis expenditures in euros for consumption and investment goods. The horizontal axis shows the euro value of national income or product. At any point on the 45 degree line, national expenditure will be equal to national income/product. In other words at any point on this line aggregate demand will equal aggregate supply.

The problem is that the equilibrium level where demand equals supply in the economy at a moment in time may be less than that required to create full employment. In Keynesian terms a deflationary gap exists in this situation.

Samuelson showed that the government can close this gap by increasing its own expenditure. The government doesn't have to increase its expenditure by the full amount that demand is short of the full employment supply level. This is because of the multiplier effect.

For example, if the full employment supply level is at €100,000, and the current equilibrium level of supply in the economy is €90,000 then €10,000 of extra spending is required. The government only needs to spend a proportion of this €10,000 because of the multiplier effect.

The multiplier effect was developed by a colleague of Keynes, Richard Kahn (1905–89). Kahn showed that increases in government expenditure (and other fresh injections of demand into the economy) are multiplied out in a mathematical way. New workers are taken on for public works projects who then re-spend their money. This increased level of consumption is received as incomes, perhaps by shop workers who then re-spend their money back into the economy.

It is also possible to have a situation when aggregate demand is in equilibrium with aggregate supply at a point to the right of the full employment point. In this situation an inflationary gap occurs, requiring government to reduce spending in the economy, by lowering its own expenditure and raising taxes.

Trade off between unemployment and inflation

In 1958 A.W. Phillips showed a negative relationship between inflation and the unemployment rate in the UK – low unemployment was associated with high inflation and vice versa. Richard Lipsey followed this up by claiming that the shape of the 'Phillips curve' was based on the fact that if the demand for labour exceed supply then the price would rise (pushing up inflation).

Samuelson and Robert Solow followed up this work by uncovering a similar relationship in the USA, and argued that the Phillips curve could underpin thinking about government policy. When unemployment is rising then the government could pump more demand into the economy, when it is falling the government could take deflationary measures.

The 'grand neoclassical synthesis'

By the early 1960s Samuelson had been swayed by Alvin Hansen, and the English economist John Hicks to believe that an equilibrium model of the economy could be set out combining Keynesian ideas with those of neoclassical economics. Samuelson was particularly interested in the mathematical notion of equilibrium. Later versions of his *Economics* set out to show how a perfectly competitive market place which maximised returns to buyers and sellers could be combined with an efficient macroeconomic equilibrium. Samuelson referred to this as the *'grand neoclassical synthesis'*. With this change in emphasis the door was once again open for returning to free market models of the economy. In the 1970s inflation increasingly became the major concern for economic policy-makers, which led to criticisms of Keynesian budget deficits. The emphasis switched back to a neoliberal version of the economy in which the money supply and interest rates were seen as the route to creating equilibrium in the economy. In simple terms Samuelson's synthesis is based on the belief that nations today can successfully control either depression or inflation by fiscal or monetary policy.

The role of government in the economy and public goods

Samuelson believes that the government has a key role to play in securing economic stability in the economy and equity. He believes that the free market is unlikely to automatically achieve these ends. The market is good at allocating goods and making things run smoothly but it doesn't have a conception of fairness. He refers to *'rationing by the purse'*. The evils of the market need to be weighed up against its benefits in pragmatic terms, and then modifications need to be made to make it work better.

Samuelson provided a rationale for government intervention in some cases, namely:

- Paternalistic policies voted upon by the electorate which felt that the market solution was not optimal.
- Redistribution of income.

- Regulation of industries which exhibit increasing returns.
- A myriad externality situations where public and private interests diverge.

In his own view there are all sorts of situations where government can intervene in a useful way, ranging from health and welfare, education and training, to urban renewal projects. He does not see government involvement in these areas as interference – it is simply getting involved to correct weaknesses in the market system.

Samuelson drew a distinction between private consumption goods and public consumption goods. Private goods are ones which when purchased means there are less available for everybody else, like buying a ticket to a concert, or purchasing goods in shop.

Public goods are ones which when they are provided are provided for everybody, nobody is excluded. *'Each individual's consumption of such a good leads to no subtraction from any other individual's consumption of that good'* (Samuelson 1948).

Frequently quoted examples include the services of a lighthouse, or the existence of a healthy non-polluted environment. If one individual benefits from a public good that does not limit the enjoyment of another person. A 'pure' public good is the ideal state of public good provision.

Samuelson argued that the amount of public goods supplied tends to be less than the amount that is socially desirable. Because everyone benefits, nobody has an incentive to pay. In a similar way, a problem of externalities or public 'bads' like pollution is that the actions of individuals cause harm for others.

The existence of public goods and negative externalities is said to provide a good case for government intervention. The government should play a part in providing public goods when the market does not provide enough of them, and in taxing or penalising the production of public 'bads'.

Samuelson showed that even in theory it is highly problematic for government to be able to provide combinations of public and private goods in order to maximise welfare, even with the existence of a computer that is able to calculate the true preferences of all consumers.

Dynamic adjustments in the market

Samuelson shows that markets are subject to dynamic forces which are not always easy to predict. In a static model the market or the economy adjusts back to an equilibrium state. In reality the situation is likely to be far more dynamic. For example, in his famous work on the relationship between the accelerator (which shows the impact of changes in consumption on investment in the economy), and the multiplier effect, he showed through mathematical reasoning that with different values for the marginal propensity to consume in the economy (the percentage of additional income that a consumer receives that they go on to spend) there could be all sorts of different impacts resulting from the reaction of income to changes in investment. In some situations there might be a downturn in the economy, while in others there could be rapidly accelerating growth. It is therefore necessary to have a clear understanding and knowledge of such factors as savings ratios, and business optimism at any one time and in a specific economy.

Inflationary pressures

From the 1950s onwards Samuelson was all too aware that inflation was becoming the major problem affecting the economy. In his report to Kennedy in 1961 he set out that *'A careful survey of the behaviour of prices and costs shows that our recent stability in the wholesale price index has come in a period of admittedly high unemployment and slackness in our economy. For this reason it is premature to believe that the restoration of high employment will no longer involve problems concerning the stability of prices.'*

Samuelson warned that as unemployment fell, prices would be likely to rise. He talked about a new kind of inflation – which he referred to as 'cost-push'. Cost-push inflation is *'a force that operates year in and year out, whenever we are at high employment, to push up prices. It's a price creep, not a price gallop but the bad thing about it is that, instead of setting in only after you have reached overfull employment, the suspicion is dawning that it may be a problem that plagues us even when we haven't arrived at a satisfactory level of employment.'*

Samuelson argued that the emphasis should be maintained on achieving full employment but that new ways of improving efficiency should be created through the supply side of the economy, particularly through efficient markets.

A 'humane economy'

Samuelson argues in favour of a 'humane economy', recognising that this will lead to a trade off against economic efficiency. He is thus neither for the free market or for state control but for a well-reasoned mixture (a Third Way) that will achieve greater social welfare than the free market. At the same time, however, he wants to see a synthesis in which decision-making processes are based on a well-thought out economic rationale.

Samuelson is critical of controlled socialist societies because he believes that they *'are rarely efficient and virtually never freely democratic'*. He argues that often the best examples of free markets are totalitarian states where the government is able to enforce the rules of the market on society – for example, Taiwan and Singapore.

What Samuelson (1992) says he would like to see is a humane economy *'that is at the same time efficient and respecting of personal (if not business) freedoms'*. He goes on to say: *'Much of producing and consuming decisions involve use of the market mechanism. But the worst inequality of condition that result from reliance on market forces – even in the presence of equality of ex ante opportunity – can be mitigated by the transfer powers of the democratic state. Does the enhancement of equity by the welfare state take no toll in terms of efficiency? Yes, there will be some trade-off of enhanced total output against enhanced equality, some trade-off between security and progress. I call the resultant optimising compromise economics with a heart, and it is my dream to keep it also economics with a head.'*

Revealed preference and indexes of welfare

One of Samuelson's earliest contributions in economics was that of the notion of 'revealed preference'. He argued that it was fruitless developing theories of consumer demand that were not based on empirical evidence. The revealed preference of a consumer is simply the choice that they reveal through their actions. Previously demand theory had been based on the notion of utility that a consumer derives from a purchasing activity – but utility is a difficult concept because consumers all have different motives.

Samuelson uses the same sort of logic to question the exactness of a range of indexes that are used in economics to measure economic welfare, for example, indexes of prices and national income. Samuelson argues that the effects of changes in these indexes on welfare can't be exactly measured even in theory, because there will always be some bias which will make even the most ideal index number subject to some ambiguity.

Conclusion

Samuelson had a tremendous impact on twentieth-century economics, not least because his book was so widely read. He was also influential in introducing a Keynesian agenda to President Kennedy and the Democratic Party in the USA. Samuelson's economics is very much that of the mixed market, and he has sought to identify appropriate areas for government intervention, including the role of macro-economic stabilisation in relation to unemployment and inflation. Samuelson's mathematical work created a framework for economic analysis based on a set of key axioms. In addition he provided a view of how economists could develop a more dynamic perspective of adjustments to equilibrium.

 Further Reading

BACKHOUSE, R.E. (2002) *The Penguin history of economics.* Penguin.

BLATT, J. (1983) How economists misuse mathematics, in A. Eichner (ed.), *Why economics is not yet a science.* Macmillan.

BRETT, W. AND RANSOM R. (1982) *The academic scribblers.* The Dryden Press.

CANTERBERY, E.R. (2001) *A brief history of economics, artful approaches to the dismal science.* World Scientific, ch. 11.

SAMUELSON, P.A. (1939) Interactions between the multiplier analysis and the principle of acceleration. *Review of Economic Statistics,* May, 75–78.

SAMUELSON, P.A. (1947) *Foundations of economic analysis.* Harvard University Press.

SAMUELSON, P.A. (1948) *Economics, an introductory analysis,* 1st edn. Mcgraw-Hill.

SAMUELSON, P.A. (1969–1980) *Nobel Lectures, Economic Sciences.*

SAMUELSON, P.A. (1992) My life philosophy; policy credos and working days, in M. Szenzberg (ed.), *Eminent economists, their life philosophies.* Cambridge University Press.

SAMUELSON, P.A. (1999) Modern economic realities and realism, in J.E. Stiglitz (ed.), *The collected scientific papers of P.A. Samuelson.* MIT Press.

SILK, L. (1974) *The economists.* Basic Books.

SPIEGEL, H.W. (1971) *The growth of economic thought.* Prentice Hall, ch. 27.

Robert M. Solow
(1924–)

ONE OF THE KEY PROBLEMS FACING ECONOMISTS IS THAT OF EXPLAINING HOW economies grow over time. This is of central importance because in a world of finite resources and growing population it is essential for economies to grow in a sustainable way in order to meet the needs of the people of the world. While Keynesian and neoclassical economic models provided an explanation of short-term equilibrium positions for the macroeconomy, there was still a lot of work to be done in the 1950s on identifying growth models over time. Robert Solow's major contribution to economics was in outlining a clearer picture of the growth process than had previously been available.

A number of economists have sought to shed light on the process of growth. Adam Smith identified a modernisation process of economic growth based on increasingly sophisticated economic relations leading to capitalism. Marx had identified social and economic growth as involving a series of revolutions with capitalism being just one stage on the road to advanced communism. W.W. Rostow in his book *The Stages of Economic Growth* (1960), which he presented on the title page as 'A non-Communist Manifesto', as a critique of Marx's view of the development of society over time, outlined a number of stages that societies go through in the process of 'growth'. Rostow identified these stages as:

- The traditional society
- The preconditions for take off
- The take off
- The drive to maturity, and
- The age of high-mass consumption.

Rostow argued that as societies became more advanced more funds could be channelled into investment in new technologies, which would enable them to take off into a sustained period of growth. He looked for historical examples of societies experiencing take-off, for example Britain during the Industrial Revolution, and so on. One of the problems of his work, however, is that it was based largely on an inductive approach and broad generalisation from carefully selected data, rather than detailed empirical research.

The Harrod–Domar model of growth based on work carried out by Sir Roy Harrod and Esvey Domar at the start of the 1940s set out to identify the conditions required for an economy to grow at a steady state. Working separately Harrod and Domar identified basically the same theoretical model of growth based on the capital–output ratio (the number of units of capital to produce a unit of output) and the Keynesian saving–investment equality, and an assumption about the propensity to save. In the Harrod–Domar model the number of workers per machine in any industry is assumed to remain constant. Harrod and Domar showed that an economy would be capable of steady growth at a constant rate if the fraction of income saved (national saving rate) was equal to the product of the capital–output ratio and the rate of growth of the effective labour force. Only in this situation could the economy keep its stock of plant and equipment balanced with its supply of labour so that steady growth could occur. Harrod and Domar showed that the conditions required to create steady growth would be exceptional rather than the normal run of things.

In this model investment not only acts as a component of demand (as stated in the Keynesian model) but additionally (something Keynes neglected) it is an important component of supply. Therefore investment needs to grow at a sufficient rate to generate enough income (given the existing multiplier) to buy enough goods (given the marginal propensity to consume) to justify the existing level of equipment and plant. Given this model it appears that capitalism is basically unstable because it is necessary that increases in total demand must be matched by industrial capacity to supply the required level (of growing) demand.

Given the Harrod–Domar model the economy is more likely than not to be lurching from upturn to downturn – an increase in investment (and thus in aggregate demand) increases profit margins and prices, leading to a reduction in consumption. In contrast, a fall in investment (and thus in aggregate demand) reduces prices relative to wages leading to a rise in consumption.

In 1956 Robert Solow was able to rewrite growth theory in an article entitled, 'A Contribution to the Theory of Economic Growth' which was to provide the substance for a number of books that Solow was later to write on this subject. The Solow version of growth was more reassuring because it showed that capitalist growth patterns were not nearly as unpredictable as Harrod and Domar had indicated.

In particular, Solow was able to identify the role of technology in the growth process, and to create a theoretical framework which better enables economists to discuss and identify the range of factors involved in economic growth both through empirical and theoretical analysis. Solow provided the backbone for what is referred to as a neoclassical growth theory which seeks to explain the contribution of various inputs to the overall growth of output in the economy. Moreover, Solow's explanation of growth showed how the path of economic growth is a relatively stable one, rather than the unstable one envisaged by the Harrod–Domar model.

Methodology

SOLOW IS IN FAVOUR OF ECONOMISTS DEVELOPING A GOOD TECHNICAL COMPETENCE IN areas in which they specialise rather than claiming to be able to develop general theories covering a range of issues. He suggests that the dilemma facing economists is *'Whether to have more and more to say about less and less, or . . . less and less to say about more and more.'* Solow prefers the first course of technical specialism as evidenced by his own focus on growth theory, and issues related to labour markets. Solow is opposed to economics trying to build a 'Theory of Everything', largely because the social institutions around which the economy is structured are continually evolving over time. As a result *'economics must pay close attention to local institutions, because they matter for behaviour'*. The implication is that we can't use a 'one size fits all' type of analysis across economies and across time, we need to be much more aware of institutions on the ground in specific contexts. He goes on to state that *'It is sometimes said that economics done in my preferred piecemeal way results in just a whole bunch of little models, connected to each other only tenuously at best. I can live with that. It is much better than insisting on a single unified model that is wrong about nearly every particular thing'* (Solow in Szenzberg 1992).

His work combines theoretical reasoning, for example in building a model of economic growth, that could then be worked out in more detail by mathematical techniques, coupled with empirical evidence, particularly in relation to factors leading to the growth of the US economy.

In addition, like Adam Smith he is a keen believer in 'common sense'. He is aware that in creating economic models we frequently simplify from the reality of the real world. He states that *'every piece of empirical economics rests on a substructure of background assumptions that are probably not quite true'*. He recognises, for example, in attributing growth to particular influences that small errors in assumptions made about relationships can become magnified in further mathematical calculations so that they only provide rough and ready measures. He likes to quote the warning issued by a leading student of basketball statistics that *'No amount of (apparent) statistical evidence will make a statement invulnerable to common sense.'*

Solow believes in using every bit of evidence that is available to us if it helps us to develop useful insights. He prefers fresh insight to methodological purity arguing that *'we have to piece together what we can from casual observation, questionnaires, folk beliefs, historical narrative, and anything that comes to hand'* (Solow in Szenzberg 1992).

Biography

SOLOW'S BIOGRAPHICAL NOTES TO HIS NOBEL PRIZE ACCEPTANCE SPEECH SHOW THAT she did not come from a privileged educational background. He was born in Brooklyn, the eldest of three children. His grandparents were immigrants to the United States. However, he was more fortunate than his parents and grandparents in being able to go to university and won a scholarship to Harvard in 1940.

His generation were still very much aware of the hardship of the depression years in America and the wider world. At Harvard he began to develop an interest in economics and sociology (having been taught by the eminent American sociologist Talcott Parsons).

However, with America's entry into the Second World War, Solow realised that there were more pressing concerns than academic study and so he joined the US army serving in North Africa, Sicily and Italy during the war years. He sees this period as having been a positive learning experience, stating that *'I think that those three years as a soldier formed my character. I found myself part of a tight-knit group, doing a hard job with skill and mutual loyalty, led by one of the most remarkable men I have ever known, who never wavered from the path of humour and decency'* (Solow 1987). This experience prepared him for teamwork situations, which in later years he was able to again experience, first when working in a team of Economic Advisers to the US government, and later in the collegiate atmosphere of the economics department of the renowned MIT in Cambridge, Massachusetts.

Returning to Harvard, Solow picked up his studies in economics, and was greatly influenced by the teaching of Wassily Leontief, another famous Nobel Laureate, who was an excellent communicator of economic theory. Leontief carried out a lot of influential work examining inputs and outputs of major industries in the United States from 1919–39 showing the interconnected nature of industries, and drawing up mathematical models to show how these relationships worked. During his student days, Solow took a keen interest in statistics, and in order to follow this further spent a year at Columbia University, which had a number of specialist teachers in this field.

Solow was then hired by the Economics Department of MIT to teach courses in statistics and economics. However, being allocated an office immediately next to that of Paul Samuelson who was always pleased to share his ideas, Solow began to concentrate more and more on macroeconomic theory.

In the 1950s Solow focused his attention on economic growth models, and was interested in the Harrod–Domar interpretation that a steady state of growth could only be achieved when the saving rate equalled the product of the capital–output ratio and the rate of growth of the effective labour force. Solow could see that if the Harrod–Domar model was correct then it would be extremely unlikely for the economy to advance at a steady rate because of the different facts/influences affecting the various parts of the model. Solow (1987) identified these influences in the following way: *'the saving rate was a fact about preferences; the growth rate of labour supply was a demographic-sociological fact; the capital-output ratio was a technological fact.'*

Key works

'A Contribution to the Theory of Economic Growth' (1956)

Growth Theory and Exposition (1970)

Neoclassical growth theory

Most economists would agree that Solow's major contribution to economics was in setting out neoclassical growth theory, giving a key place to technology in growth.

In this model changes in output can be set out in functional notation as:

$$Y = Af(L,K)$$

where L denotes variations in labour inputs; K denotes variations in capital inputs, and A denotes technological progress.

Solow was critical of the Harrod–Domar model for its failure to take account of technological progress. Solow showed that capital and labour inputs are infinitely substitutable one for the other in production (Harrod and Domar had assumed that production required fixed ratios of the inputs to production). He also felt that because Harrod and Domar had written in a period in which the ideas of economists were shaped by the harsh reality of the depression of the 1930s, they were too influenced by the apparent instability of the capitalist system that was a feature of that period. Another criticism he had (1987) of the Harrod–Domar model was that it suggested that *'If the condition for steady growth in a labour-surplus economy is that the saving rate equal the product of the growth rate of employment and a technologically determined capital-output ratio, then a recipe for doubling the rate of growth was simply to double the saving rate, perhaps through the public budget.'* However, Solow was aware that an increase in saving could also reduce demand in the economy thus having a negative effect on growth.

Solow's (1970) view is that *'Growth theory was invented to provide a systematic way to talk about and to compare equilibrium paths for the economy'*.

In recent years empirical studies in developed countries indicate that technological progress (often referred to as productivity growth) is the most significant contributor to growth, requiring a further examination of the factors leading to technological change.

More recently economists have sought to address the question of identifying components of technological progress. One of the key findings of this research has been that investment in training and education – that is, enabling the labour force to make better use of capital equipment – is an important contributory factor in technological progress.

Edward Denison played a major role in the process of 'growth accounting' seeking ways of refining Solow's technological component of growth into constituent parts. Using empirical evidence Denison showed that for the period 1929–82 in the USA, one quarter of economic growth could be attributed to increased labour input of constant educational level and 16 per cent to increased educational qualifications of the average worker. The growth of 'capital' accounted for 12 per cent, and 11 per cent to improved allocation of resources (principally switching of resources from low productivity agriculture to higher productivity industry). Eleven per cent of growth could be accounted for by economies of scale, and 34 per cent due to the 'growth of knowledge' – that is, technological progress in a narrow sense.

Neoclassical growth theory makes the assumption that countries which are less developed will be able to catch up with countries already experiencing faster rates of growth as a result of technological progress – a process known as convergence. However, empirical evidence indicates that this catching up (convergence) is not taking place. One of the explanations of this lack of convergence is that there is not sufficient investment in human capital (in education and training) in countries that are less developed.

Phillips curve

Working with Paul Samuelson, Solow applied the Phillips curve trade off between unemployment and inflation to the US economy for the 1950s and 60s. At the time it appeared that this was a stable relationship, although from the 1970s onwards this broke down and led to Friedman's expectations augmented Phillips curve.

Wage inequality

In the dispute as to whether growing wage inequality (in the United States) since the 1970s stems from the growth of technology, or from the growth of international trade, Solow argues that more evidence tends to point the finger at technology. He argues that advances in technology have increased the demand for highly skilled and educated workers, while the demand for poorly educated workers with few skills has declined. Solow sees the question of wage inequality as being a major social and economic issue because wages are the principal component of income for most households, and low income and the social evil of poverty go hand in hand.

He is not in favour of explanations which suggest that wages for unskilled workers have fallen largely as a result of competition from workers in low-wage economies. He holds this view because (1) wage inequality began to grow before low-wage economies started to industrialise, and (2) the USA does not import heavily, and goods from the low-wage economies only make up a small percentage of total US imports.

Solow cites evidence showing that low-wage men have been hit hardest by growing inequalities and traces this back to the 1940s, although differences become most marked in the 1970s. Since 1989 the trend to growing inequality has continued both for men and women.

Welfare reform

Solow is critical of notions in America and Europe that it is a simple process to transfer people from welfare programmes to work, by reducing welfare benefits and expecting people to become more reliant. Solow argues that at a microeconomic level this will simply reduce wages for the lowest paid in the economy as competition for jobs increases. Solow likens it to a process of musical chairs in which those that fail to sit on a chair when the music stops lose their job, as more job seekers come onto the market. Forcing the poor into work isn't necessarily helpful because for a number of people (e.g. those who look after young children) the costs of working are often high. Ultimately it is the poor who pay for a workfare scheme rather than the taxpayer. At a macro-level too depressing wages can lead to a fall in demand in the economy, which has a negative effect on economic growth.

Solow is not opposed to the idea of welfare to work if the idea is thought through carefully. However, he says that it would be a costly initiative if done properly because it would involve creating more jobs (through the public sector and through subsidy of the private sector) to take up the increased supply of labour. He is also in favour of schemes that combine work with welfare, enabling poorer people to work part of the time and receive welfare part of the time, in line with their needs and requirements. In this way they would be able to maintain their dignity as well as a steady income. He argues that it is too simplistic to argue that work is better than welfare.

Conclusion

An understanding of factors contributing to economic growth is one of the most important parts of economics. Solow's major contribution to this field was that of identifying the important part that technology plays in growth. Subsequent writers have been able to build on this idea by further seeking to break down technological progress into sub-elements, in order to better identify ways of analysing contributions that can be made to growth by activities such as education, training, use of resources, economies of scale, etc. Solow is clear that we must avoid trying to rely too heavily on mathematical techniques and statistics to set out hard and fast relationships; rather we need to look at the weight of evidence and use our common sense judgement to identify appropriate pathways to growth. In recent years we have become far more critical of the 'growth' process. This criticism comes from two main sources. The first of these is an ecological and environmental critique of growth that questions the validity of measuring growth in terms of 'goods' and the use of measures like GDP that fail to take account of environmental capital. The second critique is of capitalist growth patterns that benefit the core of the capitalist world at the expense of the periphery and the rich within a nation at the expense of the poor. There is a vast literature relating to 'dependency theory' – the notion that the poor world has become dependent on the rich world for its own development – and the real path to growth is to break away from dependency, by the rejection of neoliberal models of economics including neoclassical growth theory.

 **Further Reading**

CANTERBERY, E. (2001) *A brief history of economics*. World Scientific, ch. 13.

CYPHER, J.M. AND DIETZ, J.L. (1997) *The process of economic development*. Routledge, ch. 4.

DOMAR, E.D. (1940) Capital expansion, rate of growth and employment, *Econometrica*, April.

HARROD, R. (1939) An essay in dynamic theory. *Economic Journal*, March.

ROLL, E. (1983) *A history of economic thought*. Faber & Faber, 3rd edn, ch. 12.

ROSTOW, W.W. (1960) *The stages of economic growth*.

SOLOW, R. (1956) A contribution to the theory of economic growth. *Quarterly Journal of Economics*, February.

SOLOW, R. (1970) *Growth theory: an exposition*. Oxford University Press.

SOLOW, R. (1987) Nobel Prize acceptance speech in Mahler, K. (ed.), *Nobel Lectures*. Economic Sciences.

SOLOW, R. (1998) Guess who pays for workfare? *The New York Review*, XLV (17).

SZENZBERG, M. (1992) *Eminent economists, their life philosophies, Robert Solow*. Cambridge University Press.

John von Neumann
(1903–1957)

GAME THEORY PROVIDES AN ALTERNATIVE EXPLANATION OF HOW MICROECONOMIC decisions made by lots of individual economic actors create equilibrium market conditions. Adam Smith showed how the marketplace in which individuals pursue their own self-interest can lead to the best possible outcomes for all. The game theorists, John von Neumann and John Nash provided a mathematical explanation of how equilibrium situations can arise in 'game' situations in which all of the players are happy with their game strategy, thus providing an alternative approach to equilibrium in situations involving self-interest. Von Neumann and Nash both believed that they had developed theories that were 'better' than those provided by the neoclassical economists.

John von Neumann was the eccentric mathematical genius who developed 'game theory' and sought to apply it to a range of applied fields including economics. The term 'strategy' may be a better description of what von Neumann referred to as games. The scientist Jacob Bronowski (1979) recalls travelling in a taxi with von Neumann during the Second World War, and being given the following explanation: *'I naturally said to him, since I am an enthusiastic chess player, "You mean, the theory of games like chess." "No, no," he said "Chess is not a game. Chess is a well-defined form of computation. You may not be able to work out the answers, but in theory there must be a solution, a right procedure in any position. Now real games," he said, "are not like that at all. Real life is not like that. Real life consists of bluffing, of little tactics of deception, of asking yourself what is the other man going to think I mean to do. And that is what games are about in my theory".'*

Von Neumann played a significant role in the mathematisation of economics, which continued to gain impetus from the 1970s onwards. His *The Theory of Games and Economic Behaviour* (1994) written with Oskar Morgenstern, established an alternative approach to mathematical modelling to the neoclassical economists' mathematical attempts to establish a General Equilibrium Theory. Von Neumann and other subsequent writers on game theory including John Nash (1928–) have given mathematics a far more prominent place in economics syllabuses particularly in microeconomics where game theory applications are used in describing market situations, models of international trade, and have a wide application in industrial economics.

Some people find game theory to be a fascinating subject for study, and believe that it has wide application to a range of situations in life with particular relevance to economics. For example, Kreps (1990) stated that *'nowadays one cannot find a field of economics (or of disciplines related to economics, such as finance, accounting, marketing, political science) in which understanding the concept of a Nash equilibrium is not nearly essential to the consumption of the recent literature . . . the basic notions of non-cooperative game theory have become a staple in the diet of students of economics.'* In contrast, other people find it trivial because it strips down human action to simple assumptions about the choices that players make, and ignores a range of contextual factors, and institutional relationships that are of importance in any social situation. Others like Rizvi (1994) argue that *'contemporary applications of game theory serve only as very particular examples and do not have the force of a general approach to economic problems'.*

VON NEUMANN'S WORK INVOLVED APPLYING MATHEMATICAL APPROACHES TO GAME situations, that is, ones in which players are engaged in processes of devising strategies. Essentially, he used a deductive approach, involving computing the various possibilities in a given game situation. Most of the game situations that von Neumann and Morgenstern outlined were based on deducing outcomes based on limiting sets of assumptions, related to situations which approximate to games (including economic ones) in the real world.

VON NEUMANN CAME TO ECONOMICS FROM MATHEMATICS. HE DEVELOPED GAME theory as a mathematical concept and quickly realised that it can be applied to a range of real life situations – for example, his advice was sought by the American President Eisenhower in identifying mathematical (game theory) strategies on how to respond to the nuclear threat from the Soviet Union. Fortunately, von Neumann's ideas were not taken up for he advocated getting in a nuclear strike first rather than waiting to see how the situation developed.

Von Neumann was born in Hungary, and was one of a number of intellectual émigrés from that country to the United States in the inter-war period. By the time he arrived in the USA in 1931, he had already published a number of important short articles.

In 1928, at the age of 25 he had produced a brilliant article on 'game theory'. Mathematicians have always been interested in modelling and calculating probabilities related to games of chance such as throws of the dice, and the likely outcome of the spin of a roulette wheel.

However, as we have already seen von Neumann was principally interested in games of strategy in which the chosen actions of players depend on their perception of what other players will do. In such a game of strategy, a player would be unwise to devise their own strategy without consideration of what the other players will be doing. Von Neumann's work was thus concerned with working out mathematically the implications of operating in different ways in the theory of games.

János von Neumann was born in Budapest. It was not until he moved to America that he was to change his name to John or 'Johnny'. He was born into a wealthy Jewish family, his father being a banker. He was brought up in a large extended family in an apartment in Budapest. He was brought up in a Hungary in which anti-Semitism was commonplace, but the family were not overly religious, and for most of his adult years von Neumann held agnostic beliefs. From childhood János was endowed with a photographic memory, and the family took delight in showing off the ability of their son to recite pages of the telephone book to their guests. The family had an extensive library and von Neumann was encouraged to read widely and to learn and recite much of what he had learnt. At school his academic talent was quickly spotted and he was encouraged to follow a special mathematics programme.

It is possible that von Neumann would have continued to live and work in Europe, if he had not been living in a period of increasing nationalism and anti-Semitism in central Europe. In 1919 the Communists took over in Hungary, and the political and economic climate became unfavourable to wealthy established families. In the early 1920s politics in Hungary took on an anti-Semitic turn, when the nationalists seized power and during a period that was referred to as the 'white terror', 'traitors' were sought out including Jews who were seen as playing a significant part in the Communist uprising.

John von Neumann was part of an exodus of about 100,000 people who fled from Hungary. Many of the intellectuals eventually ended up in the United States. Before migrating to America, von Neumann studied science at the University of Berlin and the Swiss Federal Institute of Technology in Zurich, before completing a PhD in mathematics from the University of Budapest. He then took up teaching posts at the University of Berlin and Hamburg, before being offered a permanent teaching post at Princeton in the United States. However, he was to do little teaching. Most of his academic life was spent on research and theoretical speculation. John von Neumann was an excellent problem solver with a lightning quick brain, and he was employed as a consultant and advisor by a number of 'think tanks' in the United States, particularly working in the field of national strategy including the RAND Corporation. Von Neumann was widely regarded as a mathematical genius so that he was frequently called on to help in the solving of complex mathematical problems.

Accounts of the life of von Neumann tend to focus on his eccentricity and quirks of his personality. For example, Paul Strathern's *Dr Strangelove's Game, A Brief History of Economic Genius* (2001) which starts and finishes with an examination of the life of von Neumann, paints a picture of von Neumann as '*a mysterious figure with a Hungarian accent, his crippled body confined to a wheelchair, (who) would be whisked by limousine from his bed at Walter Reed Hospital in Washington to the White House*' to provide advice to the President about nuclear strategy during the Cold War with the Eastern bloc. Strathern also recounts the way in which von Neumann applied game theory in his tempestuous relations with two wives, writing to his second wife '*I hope you have forgiven my modest venture in double-crossing.*'

William Poundstone's biography of von Neumann, *Prisoner's Dilemma* (1993), paints the picture of von Neumann as an individual with powerful intellect, but with a limited ability when it comes to personal relations (what is referred to today as having low 'emotional intelligence'). Herman Goldstine in his book *The Computer from Pascal to von Neumann* (1972), recounts *'As far as I could tell, von Neumann was able on once reading a book or article to quote it back verbatim; moreover he could do it years later without hesitation. He could also translate it at no diminution in speed from its original language into English. On one occasion I tested his ability by asking him to tell me how the* Tale of Two Cities *started. Whereupon, without any pause, he immediately began to recite the first chapter and continued until asked to stop after about ten or fifteen minutes.'*

In 1939 von Neumann was approached by another Austro-Hungarian, Oskar Morgenstern to work collaboratively on a book about game theory and its application to economics. Morgenstern had studied economics, but had a low opinion of the existing output of the subject. He felt that game theory would provide an important way of transforming the mathematical usefulness of the subject. Morgenstern was another eccentric character, but the two rubbed along well together.

They believed that economists needed to go back to step one in developing a science of economics based on game theory. In their introduction to the book (1944), they stated *'We hope to establish satisfactorily . . . that the typical problems of economic behaviour become strictly identical with the mathematical notions of suitable games of strategy.'*

While it took some time for other economists to develop more than a passing interest in the Theory of Games, this approach has had much more prominence in economic study today and added an important impetus to the mathematisation of the subject. Game theory application can be seen as another attempt by the economics profession to try and create a scientific basis to the study of economics, particularly with a growing loss of confidence in neoclassical General Equilibrium Theory.

Work on game theory was given further momentum by the ideas of John Nash, who developed the concept of the Nash equilibrium. A Nash equilibrium is a choice of strategy whereby no individual player can gain by playing differently, assuming that their opponents keep to their prescribed strategies. As a young man, Nash presented his new ideas to von Neumann, who was dismissive of Nash's new insights, failing to listen fully to Nash's arguments and stating that what Nash had to say was 'obvious'.

This stung Nash into refining his ideas, and going on to win the Nobel Prize for Economics in 1994 for 'pioneering analysis of equilibria in the theory of noncooperative games.' Nash was, like von Neumann, flawed when it came to 'emotional intelligence' and ability to interact with others. E. Ray Canterbery (2001) describes him as having one consistency; *'he was "compulsively rational," the adjective contradicting the noun. He turned life's decisions – whether to say "hello," where to bank, what job to accept, who to marry – into mathematical rules divorced from emotion, convention, or tradition.'* Although a mathematical genius, Nash suffered from episodes of paranoid schizophrenia and for three decades from the age of 30 suffered from hallucinations, delusions, and confusion. He eventually recovered from this severe period of mental disturbance and in the 1990s was able to continue with some of his mathematical work.

It is interesting to note that the principal work of game theorists was carried out by individuals who, while they were brilliant at theorising and making calculations, had little of the human and social skills of empathy and the ability to build close relationships with others, bringing us back to Oscar Wilde's criticism that *'An economist is someone that knows the price of everything but the value of nothing.'*

Key works

The Theory of Games and Economic Behaviour (with O. Morgenstern, 1944)

Games

In developing an understanding of game theory it is helpful to first develop an understanding of the terminology used.

A *game* can be defined as a situation in which the intelligent decisions of players are interdependent.

Each *player* (decision maker) will try to maximise their individual *payoff* (return).

For example, in a market in which a small number of producers are competing, the payoff might be the profit they receive.

In order to succeed in the game each player must choose a strategy. The *strategy* is the plan for the game providing details of how the player will act in different situations. The strategy chosen by different players will depend on the strategies that are chosen by the other players.

The economist is interested in equilibrium situations in the game. *Equilibrium* exists when each player chooses the best possible strategy given the strategies that are chosen by other players. This situation is described as the *Nash equilibrium*. At this point no player will want to change their strategy, since they have already based their strategy on what the other players will do.

Another important distinction in game theory is made between games in which participants can make binding agreements among themselves – referred to as *cooperative games*, and ones in which they can't make binding agreements – *non-cooperative games*.

Zero-sum games

One of von Neumann's major contributions to game theory was in the explanation of what are described as zero-sum games. These are situations in which the total payoff or winnings from a game are fixed in advance. A popular example is the game of poker where players put money in a central pot, and winnings are taken from this pot. One person's win from the pot is another person's loss. Clearly, this sort of theory can be applied to competitive markets and other economic situations in which one player's strategy can help them to benefit at the expense of rivals.

There is a range of situations from everyday life that are zero sum. For example, where two neighbours sell a field to a builder for a given sum of money, then this determines the size of the pot. The two neighbours then must bargain for their share of this finite pot. The neighbours will seek to employ the strategy that enables them to take most from the pot. If one player's strategy enables them to earn an extra £1,000, the resulting effect will be that their neighbour loses £1,000.

The players prefer some of the possible outcomes of the game to others and their strategy in the game will involve seeking to secure a preferred outcome.

The term 'zero-sum society' is used to describe the way in which one person's gain in a modern society is equal to someone else's loss.

Utility

Von Neumann applied the concept of *utility* that was widely known in economics to preferences expressed on a numerical scale. It is helpful in a game situation to think of utility as the 'points' that a player tries to win. In games in which money is the reward, then money won will represent utility, utility will be gained from 'winning'.

A simple numerical example of a zero-sum game would be one in which the winner receives +1 point, and the loser –1. If there is a winner and a loser, the sum of the utilities will be zero. In game theory a two person zero-sum game is described as 'total war' because there can only be one winner and one loser.

Minimax

In a situation in which the outcomes for one player depend on the actions of others, what is the rational action of an individual player? Von Neumann's solution rested on the concept of the *minimax*, taken from the Latin *minimum maximorum*, the smallest among the largest, and *maximin* from *maximum minimorum*, the largest among the smallest.

We can illustrate von Neumann's arguments by means of a table. The figures in the table show payoffs, that is, gains to A relative to B. Both players seek to employ the best competitive strategy.

The table assumes that player A has three strategies available: I, II and III. The payoff from choosing each of the strategies is shown in the horizontal rows. The results from B's choice of strategies I, II and III are shown in the vertical rows.

Strategies of Player A	Strategies of Player B		
	I	II	III
I	12	24	6
II	14	20	16
III	10	4	12

The initial reaction from looking at the table is to suggest that Player A should choose strategy I – because this would give a payoff of 24 (the largest shown in the table if

Player B chose strategy II). However, in a competitive situation if Player A chose strategy I, then player B is likely to choose strategy III, which would only give A a payoff of 6 (the second to lowest payoff shown).

Studying the possible outcomes of the game in more detail suggests that in fact Player A should choose strategy II because with this strategy the payoffs will be relatively high (14, 20 or 16) whatever strategy B plays. If A plays strategy II and B chooses their best response I, then A will receive a payoff of 14, which is the largest of the smallest payoffs (maximin) resulting from the three strategies they could play (the other Mins would be 6 for strategy I and 4 for strategy III.

The rational strategy for B to play is strategy I, because this will prevent B from losing more than 14 to A. This is referred to as the minimax from B's point of view. It is the smallest of the largest amounts that B could lose to A.

The entry 14 is termed the 'saddle point' – because it is both the 'maximin' (for player A) and the 'minimax' (for player B). The saddle point represents the outcome of a game in which both players are working to competitive strategies.

Von Neumann applied the concept of the saddle point to zero-sum, two person games, introducing an element of chance into the games. Players would play these games on the basis of working out the probabilities of what their rivals were doing. The results of the games would tend to the saddle point, with minimax and maximin coinciding.

Von Neumann and Morgenstern applied a utility index to their theory of games, setting out a preference scale for given strategies to which they were able to attach numerical values.

Through the minimax theorem von Neumann showed the importance of acting in a rational way. Two players whose interests are completely opposed can settle on a rational course of action knowing that the other will do the same. This mutually desirable equilibrium is enforced by the self-interest and mistrust of the players.

Dominance

The term 'dominant strategy' is used to describe a strategy which produces at least as high a payoff as any other strategy in response to any strategy played by the other player. Von Neumann and Morgenstern (1944) explained dominance in the following terms: *'when there exists a group of participants each one of whom prefers his individual situation in x to that in y, and who are convinced that they are able as a group – i.e. as an alliance – to enforce their preferences, one outcome which can be called x will dominate over another outcome, y.'*

Nash equilibrium

The work of John Nash is particularly important because it provided an explanation or justification of how situations in which individuals are seeking their own personal self-interest (as set out by Adam Smith) can lead to a market equilibrium in a situation in which each player believes that they are implementing their 'best' strategy.

Nash concentrated on 'non-cooperative games' where coalitions between players are forbidden. He was primarily concerned with non zero-sum games and those involving three or more players.

He was able to take von Neumann's game theory further by showing that an equilibrium situation develops in non zero-sum games. Interestingly he also showed that in games where individuals' interests are not completely opposed it is more difficult to arrive at a rational solution, and the solutions arrived at may be less satisfying to the players of the game.

Applying game theory

Applications have been sought for game theory in a wide range of business and economic situations particularly in relation to competition between firms, and in a range of trading situations. The attraction of game theory is that it provides mathematical solutions enabling organisations (and economists) to calculate a range of possible outcomes to strategies in order to identify maximin and minimax positions. However, game theory approaches may be seriously flawed in relation to the real world – for example, von Neumann's suggestion that America should drop the bomb first.

Conclusion

Game theory provides an appealing approach particularly to microeconomic situations and ones where game players are competing against each other by formulating rival strategies. However, while it provides a broadly tenable approach to theoretical situations in which individuals are seeking to outdo one another, it is difficult to apply it to the real world unless we assume that rationality involves being completely selfish and self-interested. In searching for real life applications of game theory in economics we are led back to a question asked by Kreps (1990): *'To what question is "Nash equilibrium" the answer?'*

Another major weakness of game theory is that it assumes that people behave in a rational way. However, the reality is that many people do not behave in a rational way. A key problem, therefore, is that if a player assumes that other players are operating in a rational way (and they are not) then all of the calculations that they make about other players' actions will be unfounded.

Game theory only seems to apply to the real world when its own rigorous requirements are met. The problem with reality is that it tends not to apply the required assumptions of game theory.

It is helpful to economists to understand some of the simple mathematical theorems set out by von Neumann and Nash; however, it is important to recognise that they will only provide a highly limited understanding of real economic relations.

 Further Reading

BRONOWSKI, J. (1979) *The origins of knowledge and imagination.* Mcgraw Hill.

CANTERBERY, E.R. (2001) *A brief history of economics, artful approaches to the dismal science.* World Scientific.

GOLDSTINE, H.H. (1972) *The computer from Pascal to von Neumann*. Princeton University Press.

KREPS, J. (1990) *Game theory and economic modelling*. Oxford University Press.

NASH, J.F. JR (1959) Equilibrium points in n-person games. *Proceedings of the National Academy of Sciences of the United States*, vol. 46.

NASH, J.F. JR (1951) Non-cooperative games. *Annals of Mathematics*, 54.

POUNDSTONE, W. (1993) *Prisoner's dilemma: John von Neumann*. Penguin.

RIZVI, S. (1994) *Game theory to the rescue? Contributions to political economy*. Academic Press.

SPIEGEL, H.W. (1971) *The growth of economic thought*. Prentice Hall, ch. 28.

STRATHERN, P. (2001) *Dr Strangelove's game: a brief history of economic genius*. Hamish Hamilton.

VON NEUMANN, J. AND O. MORGENSTERN (1944) *The theory of games and economic behaviour*. Princeton University Press.

Milton Friedman

(1912–)

MILTON FRIEDMAN HAS BEEN ONE OF THE MOST INFLUENTIAL ECONOMISTS OF RECENT times. Not only is he an academic but he is also a writer who is able to put over his ideas to a mass audience. Friedman has used the mass media as a medium of communication by writing for popular magazines and journals and by regularly appearing on television to put over his ideas in an interesting and informed way.

Friedman is particularly associated with the Chicago school of thinking associated with the University of Chicago. His influential contributions have been in providing strong and coherent arguments for free enterprise economies, rolling back the influence of the state, and in providing a new version of the quantity theory of money, which has involved reworking Irving Fisher's ideas to show that increases in the money supply should be steady and controlled, and that broad fluctuations in the money supply will have disturbing impacts on economic activity. In the 1980s and 90s the terms 'Friedmanite economics' or 'monetarism' entered the popular vocabulary and were loosely associated with the notions that there is a danger of too much state interference in the economy and that too large increases in the supply of money could lead to inflationary pressures.

As a champion of the competitive free market economy Friedman's ideas have been widely adopted by those seeking to roll back the Keynesian post-war conventional wisdom, and they particularly influenced key world leaders such as Margaret Thatcher and Ronald Reagan. Friedman sees the free market as a necessary condition for the development of a modern democratic society. In his influential text *Capitalism and Freedom*, first published in 1962, Friedman set out that *'Viewed as a means to the end of political freedom, economic arrangements are important because of their effect on the concentration or dispersion of power. The kind of economic organisation that provides economic freedom directly, namely competitive capitalism, also promotes political freedom because it separates economic power from political power and in this way enables the one to offset the other.*

Historical evidence speaks with a single voice on the relation between political freedom and a free market. I know of no example in time or place of a society that has been marked by a large measure of political freedom, and that has not also used something comparable to a free market to organise the bulk of economic activity.'

In his preface to a more recent edition of *Capitalism and Freedom* (1982), Hayek notes that when his book was first published it was not widely noticed. However, he shows that his follow up book *Free to Choose* (1980), which was the subject of a popular television series, was reviewed in all of the relevant journals and magazines – indicating the change in popular opinion towards the competitive free market.

Methodology

FRIEDMAN SEES ECONOMICS AS PROVIDING AN ESSENTIAL TOOL KIT FOR INVESTIGATING and finding out relevant knowledge enabling us to make more informed policy decisions. He places great emphasis on the importance of using an appropriate methodology. His chosen methodology is that of 'positive economics'. A distinction between 'positive' and 'normative' economics was first developed by John Neville Keynes, the father of the celebrated English economist. J.N. Keynes (1891) made a distinction between *'a positive science . . . a body of systematised knowledge concerning what is; and a normative science . . . a body of systemised knowledge discussing criteria of what ought to be.'*

Friedman believes in the importance of distinguishing between the knowledge of 'what is' from judgements of 'what ought to be'.

Friedman (1953) stated in his book on this subject 'The methodology of positive economics' that normative policy conclusions must rest on predictions derived from positive economics about the consequences of alternative policies.

The development of positive economics therefore lies at the heart of economics. If we develop a better understanding of 'what is' then we are in a better position to have an informed discussion and to make rational decisions about 'what ought to be'. For example, if we have a better understanding of the relationship between increases in the money supply and price rises (through a study of 'positive economics'), we are then in a better position to make judgements about whether and in what circumstances the money supply ought to be allowed to increase and by how much ('normative economics').

Friedman sees economics as providing a tool kit that can be used in most circum-stances; for example, in setting out the legitimate role of the state, in deter-mining education and health policies etc. He stresses the importance of studying empirical evidence in order to better understand 'what is'. Armed with this empirical evidence it is easier to work out the implications of various alternative policies. As a methodological approach Friedman stresses the importance of formulating hypotheses as statements that can be tested in order to resolve disagreements over policy issues.

Much of Friedman's work has involved gathering detailed evidence in order to test hypotheses. For example, in the area of Friedman's New Quantity Theory of Money, Friedman collected a vast array of evidence to support his ideas.

Biography

I T IS POSSIBLE TO ARGUE THAT FRIEDMAN'S FAMILY BACKGROUND AND UPBRINGING could have led him towards either being a passionate advocate of competitive free markets or a critical opponent. He was not born to a privileged family, and as a result had to forge his own future in a highly competitive American society. His parents were in no position to bestow material wealth on the young Milton, but they were able through their example to establish the values of hard work, enterprise and a passion for knowledge. In a note on liberalism in *Capitalism and Freedom* (1962), Friedman wrote that *'The heart of the liberal philosophy is a belief in the dignity of the individual, in his freedom to make the most of his capacities and opportunities according to his own lights, subject only to the proviso that he does not interfere with the freedom of other individuals to do the same.'*

Milton Friedman was born in Brooklyn in 1912, the son of poor Jewish immigrants who had come to America from Ruthenia which at the time was part of the Austro-Hungarian Empire. His father dealt in wholesale dry goods, and his mother worked as a seamstress in a New York sweatshop under harsh working conditions. When the family moved the short distance across the Hudson River to Rahway, New Jersey, Friedman's mother ran a retail dry-goods store while his father commuted to his wholesale business in New York. When Milton was 15, his father died, leaving very little money for the family to live off. He was fortunate to receive a partial scholarship to attend Rutgers University and he was able to supplement this by working as a waiter in a local restaurant as well as doing some administrative work in a department store.

During his time at Rutgers he was influenced by Arthur F. Burns, who stressed the importance of gathering empirical evidence. He graduated in mathematics and economics and his tutors persuaded him to carry out further study in economics at the University of Chicago, which at the time was the home of many of America's best economists. His teachers at Chicago provided him with the seeds of approaches and ideas that influenced his thinking throughout his life. Frank Knight and Henry Simons were critical of the role of the state and were in favour of economic liberalism (Knight had a pessimistic view of the human race, arguing that the dominant trait was that of greed rather than altruism), Jacob Viner's classes developed a fascination in Friedman for economic theory; from Arthur Burns the young Friedman was to develop an appreciation of objective approaches to research and enquiry methods, and other teachers encouraged Friedman's interest in mathematics and statistics.

In his first year at Chicago, Friedman met Rose Director whose brother was already an influential economist. Rose Director was a first-class economist with good analytical skills. She was to become Friedman's wife and over the years they have collaborated on a range of books and research projects, so that it is almost impossible to distinguish between the work of the two Friedmans.

Financial circumstances made it impossible for Friedman to complete his course at Chicago, but he was able to take up a scholarship at the University of Columbia (tempted by the offer of $1,500 a year). At Columbia he was fortunate enough to work with Wesley Mitchell who influenced Friedman still further in the importance of using an empirical approach in economics.

Through Mitchell, Friedman built a close association with the National Bureau of Economic Research which further helped to underpin his emphasis on developing and using factual information. In 1937 Friedman took up a research project with the National Bureau of Economic Research investigating the professional structures of lawyers, doctors, accountants and others. This research formed the basis of Friedman's PhD thesis.

One of the major findings of his PhD (entitled 'Income from Independent Professional Practice') was that restrictions on the entry into professions such as medicine led to the numbers of doctors and others rising less quickly than the increase in the population. The effect was to drive up the costs of medicine to the consumer. Friedman contended that the medical profession collaborated in this restriction in supply in order to push up the incomes and hence 'profits' of medical professionals. This was a politically sensitive finding – and as a result Friedman was not allowed to have his thesis published until he had added some other 'reasons' why medical practitioners might earn 'economic rent'.

In 1939–40 Friedman was offered a post at the University of Wisconsin. However, there was a lot of in-fighting at the University, and when Friedman was offered a long-term contract there was some opposition from 'Conservatives', a number of whom suggested that having more than one Jew on the Faculty was too many. As a result Friedman decided not to stay.

Leonard Silk (1976) argues that these events helped to develop a wariness in Friedman of institutions: *'His wariness of institutions, even liberal and intellectual institutions, deepened. He decided that there was more freedom and security for Jews or other minority group members in the marketplace than in "institutions" – whether they were liberal or conservative, academic or political.'*

In the early 1940s Friedman began to take an interest in the role of money in the economy, and its relationship with inflation. It was from this study that Friedman was eventually to develop his new versions of the quantity theory of money.

In 1948 Friedman took up a post at the University of Chicago and from this base he was to produce most of his celebrated early work.

It was at this time that Friedman began to develop work that supported the competitive market economy. In his *Roofs or Ceilings? The Current Housing Problem* (written with George Stigler in 1946) Friedman argued that the free market would provide the best solution to housing shortages following the Second World War stating that:

'1. *In a free market, there is always some housing immediately available for rent – at all rent levels.*

2. *The bidding up of rents forces some people to economise on space. Until there is sufficient new construction, this doubling up is the only Solution.*

3. *The high rents act as a strong stimulus to new construction.*

4. *No complex, expensive, and expansive machinery is necessary. The rationing is conducted quietly and impersonally through the price system.'*

This early study of the role of the free market in housing is representative of his ongoing empirical work in a wide raft of policy-related issues, based on Friedman's view of the importance of 'positive economics' in providing evidence for policy making.

Working for the National Bureau of Economic Research involved Friedman working closely with Wesley Mitchell on Mitchell's prime area of concern, the Business Cycle. However, it became clear that the topic was too big for an individual to research all areas of it – so the work was portioned out among leading economists. Friedman was given the task of examining American monetary history. Friedman set out with Anna Schwartz to produce *A Monetary History of the United States 1867–1960*, which was eventually published in 1963. It was this work that was to provide the empirical and intellectual basis for the doctrine known as 'monetarism'. It was this work in particular that was to build Friedman's reputation as a leading economist whose research provided the evidence to support neoliberal political and economic decisions from the late 1970s onwards. It provided the basis for Friedman's assertion that *'inflation is always and everywhere a monetary phenomenon'* and the importance of providing a stable monetary framework for economic decision-making.

Friedman's book, appearing in the 1960s at a time in which governments had allowed the money supply to increase, provided a persuasive argument for a more controlled monetary expansion. Faced with the problem of inflation in the early 1970s governments and economists were increasingly influenced by Friedman's ideas with regards to monetary policy, and from the late 1970s we saw a neoliberal revival involving the rolling back of government influence.

In 1976 Milton Friedman received the Nobel Prize for economics, and from the 1970s onwards his work and that of Hayek have been particularly influential in shaping neoliberal economic thinking, as well as the politics of the market economy.

Friedman's work has not been restricted to academic books and journals. He is a great believer in popularising the subject. The book *Free to Choose* that was co-written with Rose Friedman in 1980 sold 400,000 copies in its first year, and was based on a popular television series under the same name. Over the years Friedman has written regular columns for leading newspapers and has constantly sought to present his ideas in a practical and easy to understand manner. With an amusing and informed manner of delivery Friedman was made for the mass media presentation of ideas that is so important in persuading a broad mass of people to support ideas in the modern age.

In the mid-1970s Friedman was heavily criticised by left wingers when he visited Chile and produced a paper giving his views on the high levels of inflation in the country. His paper was adopted by the Pinochet government and he was subsequently blamed for the shock treatment that the Chilean economy was subjected to by government policies to reduce inflation. This led to an orchestrated set of demonstrations at Friedman's public appearances including the award ceremony in Stockholm when he accepted the Nobel Prize. However, in the course of events Friedman felt justified in his prescription because unemployment and inflation both went on to fall substantially in Chile. He went on to argue that the recovery of the Chilean economy was one of the major turnarounds of the twentieth century.

Key works

Capitalism and Freedom (1962)

A Monetary History of the United States (with Anna Schwartz, 1963)

Free to Choose (with Rose Friedman, 1980)

Economic freedom

Friedman's core belief is in economic freedom. In *Capitalism and Freedom* (1962) he set out that *'As liberals, we take freedom of the individual, or perhaps the family, as our ultimate goal in judging social arrangements. Freedom as a value in this sense has to do with the interrelations among people.'*

Like Adam Smith, Friedman supported voluntary co-operation of individuals – the technique of the market place, as the best way of co-ordinating the economic activities of millions.

This technique of co-ordination is the best and only way of securing economic freedom. He states (1962) that *'The possibility of co-ordination through voluntary co-operation rests on the elementary – yet frequently denied – proposition that both parties to an economic transaction benefit from it, provided the transaction is bi-laterally voluntary and informed.*

Exchange can therefore bring about co-ordination without coercion. A working model of a society organised through voluntary exchange is a free private enterprise exchange economy – what we have been calling competitive capitalism.'

The role of the state

Friedman notes that in the 1920s and 30s intellectuals in Europe and America were increasingly in favour of expanding the role of the state. They argued that with the development of democratic societies, government could be used as an agent to make a better society. As the century moved on more and more people became convinced that economic tools such as Keynesian policies could be used to make the capitalist system work better through the benevolence of government.

However, by the 1960s Friedman was to reject this notion, and he argued the importance of weighing up the evidence for and against an increased role for the state. In his conclusion to *Capitalism and Freedom* (1962) he argued that *'We now have several decades of experience with governmental intervention. It is no longer necessary to compare the market as it actually operates and government intervention as it ideally might operate. We can compare the actual with the actual.'* He argued that if this comparison is made it is clear that government intervention has not had the desired result. While Marx and Engels had written in the Communist manifesto that *'The proletarians have nothing to lose but their chains. They have a world to win.'* The reality was that workers in Russia had far less freedom than in any Western state. At the same time a whole host of government measures in Western countries had failed – for example, regulation of the railways to protect consumers had led to increasing monopoly powers for existing railway companies; monetary reforms had led to inflation; support for farmers had led to the waste and embezzlement of funds; housing programmes had led to deteriorations in housing; social security programmes had led to rising numbers living off social security, and so on.

However, Friedman (1962) did see government as playing a useful role in society. He states that *'The existence of a free market does not of course eliminate the need for government. On the contrary, government is essential both as a forum for determining the "rules of the game" and as an umpire to interpret and enforce the rules decided on. What the market does is to reduce greatly the range of issues that must be decided through political means, and thereby to minimise the extent to which government need participate directly in the game.'*

The role of money in the economy

Perhaps the most fundamental contribution Friedman has made to economics has been in his study (with Anne Schwartz, 1963) of the importance of the role of money in the economy.

Friedman and Schwartz's detailed study of the relationship between money and prices during the Great Depression provided evidence that the Federal Reserve System in the USA helped to increase monetary instability. Their view was that the US Federal Reserve failed to provide adequate liquidity when the demand for money increased in the USA as a result of banking crises which led to a lack of confidence. The Federal Reserve had the power to increase liquidity but they failed to do so.

In *Capitalism and Freedom* (1962), Friedman stated that: *'I am myself persuaded, on the basis of extensive study of the historical evidence, that the difference in economic stability revealed by the crude comparison is in fact attributable to the difference in monetary institutions. This evidence persuades me that at least a third of the price rise during and just after World War I is attributable to the establishment of the Federal Reserve System and would not have occurred if the earlier banking system had been retained; that the severity of each of the major contractions – 1920–21, 1929–33, and 1937–38 – is directly attributable to acts of commission and omission by the Reserve authorities and would not have occurred under earlier monetary and banking arrangements. There might well have been recessions on these or other occasions, but it is highly unlikely that any would have developed into a major contraction.'*

The new quantity theory of money

The quantity theory of money as set out by Irving Fisher has already been examined. This seemed to have been discredited by a new Keynesian orthodoxy. Keynes argued that increases in the supply of money would be likely to be offset by demand – that people would hold onto new money that had been created, rather than using it to bid up prices. The conventional Keynesian wisdom suggested that increases in the money supply during a recession would have a positive effect in encouraging greater output and employment.

However, Friedman noted that 'easy money' policies had an inflationary impact, pushing up prices.

Friedman showed that the quantity theory of money could be looked at in a new way. He stated that the quantity theory is not essentially a theory of output, or prices, instead it is essentially a theory of the demand for money.

Using empirical evidence Friedman showed that the demand for money is in fact highly stable so that increases in the money supply are likely to lead to changes in prices.

In Friedman's analysis money is treated as another type of 'capital' asset that individuals hold within their overall portfolio of such assets, for example, goods, shares, and other investments.

An individual holds cash, not because this provides them with an income in the strict sense, but in a broad sense it does provide an income or return because money benefits the individual because it is instantly available, it can be converted into other assets, and it can be used for unforeseen expenditure.

Money, thus, is a capital asset providing a string of future services. The demand for money, therefore, is fairly stable in order to be used to fulfil these functions. Determinants of the demand for money would include the total wealth of individuals, their anticipation of future price rises, the yield on alternative capital assets and so on. Most of these remain fairly constant.

With this new theory of the importance of money, Friedman was able to show that the quantity of money has a direct influence on the economy.

The permanent income hypothesis

Another related idea of Friedman, based on extensive research into spending, was his 'permanent income' hypothesis of the consumption function. The consumption function shows the proportion of income that is consumed. As people become richer they typically spend a smaller proportion of their income.

Friedman modified traditional views of the consumption function by showing that consumption is related to their income over a period of time rather than at a moment in time. Even though we may receive our income at given intervals, for example at the end of each month, we tend to think of it as a smooth and regular flow over a period of time. Our expenditure pattern is also determined by our expected future income – with people expecting their incomes to rise over time. Spending is thus based on longer-term expectations about incomes smoothed over a period of time.

This finding added further weight to Friedman's view of the stable demand for money. He showed that the demand for money, like all forms of consumption, is based upon calculations of permanent income rather than actual income at a moment in time.

Monetarism

From studying the demand for money, Friedman turned next to an analysis of appropriate policies for dealing with the supply of money. His study of the Great Depression showed that a contraction in the money supply by the central authorities lay at the heart of the crash.

Friedman believed strongly that short-term measures to alter the supply of money in the economy have a destabilising effect. A major reason for this is a lagged effect of changes in the money supply. If the central bank increases the money supply during a depression this will take time to have an effect on economic activity and prices. By the time the policy had an impact, it might be inappropriate (perhaps a contraction in the money supply would be required). Friedman is thus strongly opposed to short-term tinkering with the money supply. He is also highly critical of central banking authorities' inability to define and measure the supply of money.

Rather than the central authorities changing the money supply in a discretionary way, Friedman believes that it is more sensible to create a monetary rule – expanding the money supply at a stable rate, regardless of the circumstances of the moment.

Friedman's version of monetarism is thus based on two central principles:

1. The change in the money supply is the only key influence on the overall level of spending and economic activity, and
2. In order for the central bank to create a climate that creates prosperity and stable prices, then it needs to increase the money supply in a stable and well-publicised manner at a rate related to the real rate of growth of the economy.

In a section in his early book *Capitalism and Freedom* (1962) on the control of money Friedman set out his view that *'In the present state of our knowledge, it seems to me desirable to state the rule in terms of the behaviour of the stock of money. My choice at the moment would be a legislated rule instructing the monetary authorities to achieve a specified rate of growth in the stock of money. For this purpose, I would define the stock of money as including currency outside commercial banks plus all deposits of commercial banks. I would specify that the Reserve System should see to it that the total stock of money so defined rises month by month, and indeed, so far as possible, day by day, at an annual rate of X per cent, where X is some number between 3 and 5. The precise definition of money adopted, or the precise rate of growth chosen, makes far less difference than the definite choice of a particular definition and a particular rate of growth.'*

Expectations and unemployment

In 1958 A.W. Phillips introduced the notion of the 'Phillips Curve' to economics showing that there existed a trade off between unemployment and inflation. This fitted in nicely with Keynesian analysis showing that governments could reduce unemployment by injecting demand into the economy. It seemed that if the relationship shown in the curve existed that the government could choose a preferred combination of unemployment and inflation.

However, within a few years this relationship had started to break down and by the 1970s unemployment and inflation were rising together.

Friedman tackled the relationship between these two key economic variables in his Nobel lecture of 1976, 'Inflation and Unemployment'. Friedman claimed that there is a particular unemployment rate, referred to as the natural rate of unemployment, that is consistent with constant inflation. This natural rate recognises that at any one time there will be a number of people moving between jobs, and it is pointless to try and reduce unemployment below the natural rate. If the government tries to buy

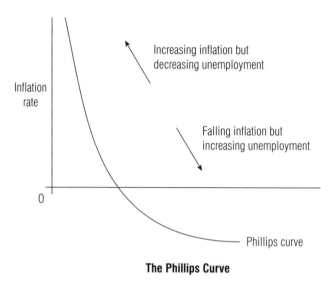

The Phillips Curve

unemployment by increasing inflation, this will only lead to increasing levels of inflation, which eventually become unsustainable.

People negotiating over wage are less concerned with the money wage rate than with the real wage rate (which takes account of changes in inflation). Wage bargaining therefore takes into account expected inflation. For example, if people expect inflation to be 10 per cent, they will want real wages to rise by 10 per cent. Thus, as inflation increases, the Phillips curve shifts upwards (an expectations augmented curve), so that there isn't a stable trade off between inflation and unemployment.

The theory of the expectations augmented Phillips curve (which was supported by empirical research) added further weight to Friedman's view that the government should use monetary policy to control inflation.

Free exchange rates

With his emphasis on free markets Friedman has always supported freedom for exchange rates in international financial markets. Friedman's observation of post-war events with its regular crises as exchange rates were pegged against each other led him to favour a more orderly set of relationships. Friedman favours a system of freely adjusting rates, enabling the market to determine the exchange rates of currencies against each other. He states that one of the most important arguments in favour of such a system is that it enables the monetary authorities to concentrate on their monetary policy without fear of its effects on the exchange rate.

Reducing taxes

Friedman argues against the wastefulness and inefficiency of taxes. He believes that the government can only second guess how to help citizens. If I have some money in my pocket I have a good idea of how I can spend that money to meet my needs and desires. Should the government take some of that money in taxes then it will be far less effective in spending that money to second guess my needs and desires.

Negative income taxes

As an opponent of the waste of state administration and control Friedman has always favoured simplifying tax and benefit systems. He was the author of the notion of a negative income tax. He proposed that income tax levels should be reduced to zero as the lower income brackets are approached and then for those on the lowest incomes, individuals and families should receive incomes (a negative income tax) the amount increasing the poorer they are. This approach guaranteed an income to the poorest members of society without the expense of setting out a dual income tax and state benefit system.

Educational vouchers

In the field of education Friedman argued the case for a voucher system enabling students to attend schools that they and their families chose, rather than being allotted places.

Conclusion

Monetarism and Friedman go hand in hand. Friedman's work in 'positive economics' was based on a detailed study of the evidence in order to better inform policy-making. His ideas helped to inform a complete reappraisal of economic thinking, which after the Second World War had been lodged within what was rapidly becoming a new orthodoxy based on Keynesian ideas. Friedman plied his economic tools of the trade to show that free markets (in his view) provide the best solutions compatible with economic and political freedom. At the same time he showed that by creating a set of rules for expansion in the money supply it is possible to create a well-ordered economy in which rational economic decisions can be made.

 Further Reading

BACKHOUSE, R.E. (2002) *The Penguin history of economics*. Penguin.

BREIT, W. AND RANSOM, R.L. (1982) *The academic scribblers*. The Dryden Press, ch. 14.

BUTLER, E. (1985) *Milton Friedman: A guide to his economic thought*. Gower Publishing.

CANTERBERY, E. (2001) *A brief history of economics*. World Scientific, ch. 12.

FRIEDMAN, M. (1953) *Essays in positive economics*, University of Chicago.

FRIEDMAN, M. (1962) *Capitalism and freedom*. University of Chicago (with new preface in 1982).

FRIEDMAN, M. AND FRIEDMAN, R. (1980) *Free to choose*. University of Chicago and Penguin Books.

FRIEDMAN, M. AND SCHWARTZ, A.J. (1963) *A monetary history of the United States, 1867–1960*. Princeton.

FRIEDMAN, M. AND STIGLER, P. (1946) *Roofs or ceilings? The current housing problem*. Great Barrington.

KEYNES, J.N. (1891) *The scope and method of political economy.* Cambridge University Press.

SILK, L. (1976) *The economists*. Basic Books.

Margaret Thatcher

(1925–)

Margaret Thatcher has dominated Conservative philosophy or ideology since the 1970s. With the election of the first Thatcher Government in 1979, the New Right philosophy of minimal state involvement and private market solutions to solving social problems became politically acceptable. It is commonly assumed that Mrs Thatcher broke the post-war consensus established by the Labour Government of Attlee (1945–51). The 'post-war consensus' was based upon the redistribution of income via the tax and benefits systems, the establishment of healthcare and education free at the point of issue as central elements in a comprehensive welfare state.

When Margaret Thatcher became Prime Minister on 4 May 1979 she described herself not as the first woman to hold the office, but as the first scientist. On the doorstep of 10 Downing Street she made her first statement as Prime Minister, using a quote from St Francis of Assisi: *'Where there is discord may we bring harmony, where there is error may we bring truth, where there is doubt may we bring faith, and where there is despair may we bring hope.'*

This was the first of many interesting and thought-provoking sound bites from a politician who was to give her name to a political doctrine – *Thatcherism* – and who was to break the mould of British politics. Anybody who lived through the Thatcher years will have their favourite quotes, mine include: *'No one would remember the Good Samaritan if he'd only had good intentions. He had money as well.'*

In response to Jacques Delors' plan to expand the political nature of the European Union: *'No! No! No!'*

And the less famous statement on meritocracy: *'Let our children grow tall, and some taller than others if they have it in them to do so.'*

Methodology

Mrs Thatcher had a number of distinct ideas on how information for the process of policy formation should be collected. Unlike the Labour prime ministers before her, Thatcher never appointed a Royal Commission to investigate and advise on policy; in addition, on becoming prime minister, she abolished the Central Policy Review Staff (the *think tank*). Mrs Thatcher took advice from academics that she felt had some sympathy with her political stance and used the grassroots of the party as a sounding board to test the popularity of new policy. Every month there is some form of conference that the party holds; these include such groups as Conservative Trade Unionists, the Conservative Women's conference, Young Conservatives etc. Under Thatcher, ministers were encouraged to attend these conferences and outline plans for new policy at the earliest possible stage. If the speech was not warmly received by the audience it would be amended and the message repeated to a different group within the party. This use of the grassroots of the party was a central element in Thatcher's statecraft. The grassroots activists were closer in touch with popular opinion than the party in parliament. This approach served the Conservative Party well until the plan for reform of local government taxation. Mrs Thatcher wanted to reform the rates, which she saw as both an unpopular and inefficient method of taxation. The government's initial plan for the reform of the rates was to phase in the Community Charge (the Poll Tax) over a number of years. The activists within the party wanted to introduce the Poll Tax without a period of phasing in. This was the first occasion in which the Thatcher government introduced a major piece of legislation that they expected to be widely accepted by the electorate because the activists wanted it, only to find that the activists were out of touch with popular opinion.

Biography

MARGARET HILDA ROBERTS WAS BORN ABOVE HER FATHER'S GROCER'S SHOP ON 13 October 1925 in Grantham, Lincolnshire. She lived above the shop with her mother Beatrice, her father Alfred and older sister Muriel. Alfred Roberts was a very strong influence on Margaret; she appears to have fully accepted her father's passion for small business, self-help, self-denial, thrift and especially balancing income and expenditure and a commitment to public life. Alfred Roberts was an active member of the local Chamber of Trade, a school governor, Justice of the Peace and local councillor, moving on to become eventually alderman and finally lord mayor. Alfred Roberts always stood as an Independent and never as a Conservative, but what Margaret Roberts took from her father was a disdain for socialism. Years after his death Margaret Thatcher was moved to tears in a television interview when she described how her father had been voted out of the office of mayor of Grantham by the Labour Group on the council. Margaret Roberts never had the same close relationship with her mother or sister, moreover, in later years whenever she was asked about her mother her answers always turned towards her father.

Margaret Roberts attended grammar school and later went on to Oxford to study chemistry. When she arrived at Oxford Margaret joined the university Conservative Association. It was here that she read Friedrich von Hayek's *The Road to Serfdom*. On graduation she worked for British Xylonite Plastics and later for Lyons Cakes. In 1949 Margaret Roberts met Dennis Thatcher and after a two-year courtship they married. From the time that Margaret arrived at Oxford she started to drift away from her roots in Grantham and visited the town less often. When she met Dennis this process of becoming a southerner became complete. In addition, she moved away from her Methodism and embraced the Church of England. Dennis was sufficiently wealthy to allow Margaret the financial freedom to read for the Bar, eventually becoming a tax lawyer. However, when Margaret was adopted for the safe Conservative seat of Finchley in 1959 she had only served for two years as a barrister and was unable to take the title of QC.

When Edward Heath won the 1970 general election Margaret Thatcher served for a time as Minister for Education. Apart from her plan to phase out school milk, which coined the phrase 'Maggie Thatcher milk snatcher' this was a fairly uneventful period in office. The process of comprehensivation of secondary school continued as it had done since 1965 under the Wilson government. However, for the Prime Minister this period in government was far from uneventful, with a threefold increase in oil price brought about by the Organisation of Petroleum Exporting Counries (OPEC), the introduction of value added tax (VAT), decimal currency, direct rule and then power sharing in Northern Ireland, Enoch Powell's *rivers of blood* speech on race, planned reorganisation of local government, reorganisation of the National Health Service (NHS), the 1970 Industrial Relations Act and the decision that Britain should join the European Economic Community (EEC). It is interesting to note that Heath's plans for the reorganisation of local government abolished the position of Alderman, which meant so much to both Alfred Roberts and his daughter. The Heath government came to power with a free market manifesto, which included: reducing the size of the state sector; reducing the state subsidy to nationalised industries; reducing direct tax; shifting the tax burden on to indirect tax – notably a new value added tax; reducing the power of trade unions and attempting to make people less reliant on the state. Heath wanted to create what was called at the time *Selsdon Man*; however, when inflation started to rise and unemployment reached one million, Heath decided to have a major change in policy – 'do a U turn'. Heath decided to revert to the Keynesian demand management techniques that most post-war governments had deployed. This was an embarrassing shift in policy for the Conservatives. In addition, Heath was becoming increasingly unpopular within the party because of his progressively more presidential, even Gaullist, style of government. Critics, both inside the party and outside, pointed to the way in which Heath would often announce new policy initiatives at press conferences in Westminster Hall.

In late 1973 the National Union of Mineworkers called a national strike over pay and conditions of service. The union tactics involved sending 'flying pickets' to power stations and other places of work, in an effort to bring the economy to a grinding halt. Heath called a 'state of emergency' and in February 1974 decided to call a general election on the issue of 'Who Rules'. For Heath the rule of law and the legitimacy of the government were being challenged by the pickets. In response to this, Harold Wilson refused to accept the Heath agenda for fighting the general election, instead Wilson raised a series of criticisms of the government's handling of the economy and announced that a Labour Government would renegotiate the terms of entry to the EEC and put the new terms to a referendum of the British people.

No single party had an overall majority in the February 1974 general election. Although the Labour Party won the highest number seats, Heath refused to concede the election defeat and attempted to form a coalition government with the Liberal Party. Over the weekend after the election there was a series of meetings between Heath and the Liberal leader Jeremy Thorpe. The talks eventually broke down and the

Queen asked Harold Wilson to form a minority government. The Conservatives abstained on the Queen's speech, which outlined the minority Labour Government's plans to end the miners' strike, suspend power sharing in Northern Ireland and repeal the 1970 Industrial Relations Act. The minority Labour Government maintained themselves in power, with the tacit support of the Ulster Unionists, until Harold Wilson called a general election in October 1974. Labour won the October 1974 general election with a majority of only three seats.

The position of Heath as leader of the Conservative Party was now seriously challenged and he decided to stand for re-election as leader of the party. The question was who would stand against Heath? For a range of reasons many of the potential leaders were unable to stand against Heath: Reginald Maudling was involved in a local government corruption scandal; Enoch Powell had left the Conservatives and joined the Ulster Unionists; Sir Keith Joseph had made a speech in Preston that suggested that poor people had too many children; and William Whitelaw believed he could not stand in the first ballot out a sense of loyalty to Heath. In March 1975 the first round of the ballot took place, Thatcher won 130 votes to Heath's 119 with a third candidate, Hugh Fraser, winning 16. When Whitelaw did enter the race in the second ballot he was unable to stop Thatcher from winning.

Once elected as Conservative Party leader Margaret Thatcher sought advice from a number of economists. The Thatcherite Conservative Party became a magnet for monetarist thinking. Although advisers came and went she never lost faith in monetarism, which she regarded as a self-evident truth. For Thatcher, Keynesian demand management could only be achieved by the state imposing itself on the lives of ordinary people. For Thatcher, such state involvement was against freedom. Major influences on Margaret Thatcher included: Sir Alan Walters, Milton Friedman, David Laidler, Michael Parkin, Brian Griffiths, Patrick Minford and others. Between the 1974 elections Sir Keith Joseph had established the Centre for Policy Studies that was a forum for the development of *New Right* ideas. In the first instance, there was an acceptance of the quantity theory of money, as advocated by Friedman and Walters according to which there should be tight control of the monetary base – by which they meant notes and coins in the hands of the public, the banks and balances at the Bank of England. In addition James Ball and Terence Burns started to develop an alternative set of principles that could form the basis for an economic policy. The Ball and Burns approach was to have a four-year medium-term financial strategy in which the money supply and the public sector borrowing requirement would be reduced at given stages. The need to reduce public borrowing was based upon the assumption that government borrowing increases interest rates by reducing the amount of financial resource available to the rest of the economy, hence discouraging investment.

Alan Walters had made his name as an economic adviser to General Pinochet in the 1970s as an architect of the 'economic miracle' in Chile after the military coup in 1973. Walters had advised Pinochet to have a programme of privatisation, with the sale of nationalised enterprises – the national telephone company; electricity generation and railways – in what became known as 'popular capitalism'. In addition, the state pension system was also privatised, trade unions were legally constrained so as to minimise their impact upon the market place, and the national health budget was reduced. There was also reform of the education system, with private companies having a greater role in the running of state schools.

By the time the 1979 general election came the key elements of the Thatcherite 'monetarist counter-revolution' were in place: control of the money supply; supply side incentives; reform of the tax system; roll back the state; trade union reform and strict control of the public sector borrowing requirement. The aim of these policies and principles was to generate an 'enterprise culture' in Britain. Apart from the sale of council houses, however, privatisation did not feature significantly in the first Thatcher government, only Thomas Cook the travel agent and the state owned public houses in Carlisle, the National Freight Corporation was sold to the employees, and a number of subsidiaries of British Steel, British Rail, a 50 per cent holding in Cable and Wireless, and Amersham International were privatised in the first term. In addition there was some partial deregulation, with the 1980 Transport Act, but this was not complete until the 1985 Transport Act. There was also some local government competitive tendering, such as school cleaning and school meals services. It was not until Mrs Thatcher's second term that we saw the privatisation of British Telecom, British Gas, British Petroleum, British Aerospace, Ferranti, Britoil, Jaguar, Sealink, the National Bus Company, Rolls Royce and British Rail Hotels.

The sale of council houses was seen by many as the attempted use of privatisation to enhance the Conservatives' own chances of re-election. In effect, by attempting to provide the conditions under which, what Ivor Crewe (1992) refers to as the 'new' working class, can emerge. This 'new' working class is a class based upon consumption, notably consumption of housing. However, mortgages hurt and mortgages with negative equity really hurt, reducing consumption and adversely affecting job mobility – a situation compounded by the financial market liberalisation during the Thatcher years, which has had the consequence of building up debt that made consumers much more vulnerable to upward movements in interest rates. Moreover, if social class is defined in terms of consumption patterns, then negative equity will produce a process of 'proletarianisation', as consumption is reduced in order to meet expanding debt demands.

From a Thatcherite perspective, the market should provide housing, either by owner occupation or via the private rented sector. Local authorities and central government should merely facilitate individual participation in the market. From 1979 until 1997 housing policy had four clear objectives:

1. to encourage owner occupation
2. a reduction in local authority provision
3. encourage the growth of the private sector
4. target resources to those with greatest need.

The 1980 Housing Act gave tenants the right to buy their houses and also made changes to the subsidy and rent systems in an effort to make owner occupation more attractive and council tenancy less attractive. The 1986 Housing and Planning Act allowed local authorities to transfer housing stock to other landlords, without the need for a ballot. The 1988 Housing Act further extended this provision by giving tenants the right to initiate the transfer process, by holding a ballot. If tenants do not vote in such a ballot, they are assumed to have voted yes. The 1988 Act also contains provision for the establishment of Housing Action Trusts, whereby council estates can be taken out of local authority control for a period of up to seven years, improved, and passed on to a landlord, which may or may not be the local authority. The 1989 Housing and Local Government Act attempted to close up any loopholes with the existing legislation. Housing subsidy and Housing Revenue Accounts of local authorities had changes made to them, so that any surpluses on account are used to pay the Housing Benefit of other council tenants. There was to be greater central control of rents, Housing Action Areas were abolished, means tests were introduced for home improvement grants, and Neighbourhood Renewal Areas were introduced. Areas of greatest need are targeted for additional resources; these areas must meet fixed criteria, be supported by a survey, and approved by the minister.

Political scientists have for some years accepted that housing has had a close relationship with political alignment, independent of the effect of social class. Even such a staunch supporter of class alignment as Peter Pulzer, was forced to admit in 'Political Representation and Elections in Britain' (1967, p. 12) that *'There is no evidence that high incomes, or the possession of consumer durables, predisposes working class people towards the right. The one exception is homeownership which, at all levels of income, makes people with manual jobs feel more middle class, and more inclined to vote Conservative than those who rent their homes.'*

Why did working-class home owners continue to support the Conservatives, rather than any other party, until 1997? Colin Rallings and Michael Thrasher (1997) in their analysis of MORI's 1992 general election survey were surprised to find that so many home owners continued to give support to the Conservatives, given that a house was no longer an inflation-proof investment. Rallings and Thrasher clearly believe that working class owner-occupiers had interests that should have determined voting to a much greater degree than they did. The MORI analysis supported what has become the orthodox view of the relationship between housing and voting, which needed to be re-examined, particularly in the light of 'negative equity' – the situation in which an individual mortgage payer owes more to the building society than they could sell their house for. If we look at the following we can trace the changes in voting intention as related to housing tenure.

Home ownership and voting

| Election | Percentage of working class home owners | | |
	Conservative	Labour	Liberal Democrat
1983	46	25	27
1987	43	32	23
1992	41	39	17
1997	35	41	17

Source: Adapted from *Sunday Times* 12 April 1992, p. 14 and *Sunday Times* 4 May 1997, p.23.

In a speech to the Royal Economic Society's 1997 Annual Conference, Andrew Henley (1997) demonstrated that negative equity peaked at 6 per cent of owner-occupiers in 1993. There are significant changes in the level of negative equity that Henley outlines. His figures are:

1991   2.6 per cent of owner-occupiers had negative equity

1992   4.7 per cent of owner-occupiers had negative equity

1993   6.0 per cent of owner-occupiers had negative equity

1994   4.6 per cent of owner-occupiers had negative equity

Source: http://www.res.org.uk/media/annconf97/henley.htm

Parliamentary constituencies with highest negative equity and percentage change in share of vote between 1987 and 1992

	Proportion of homebuyers (1988–91) who now had negative equity in 1992 and the average amount held		Percentage change in the vote 1987–92		
	%	£	Conservative	Labour	Liberal Democrat
Luton South	72	6,700	−1.4	+6.8	−6.7
Newham South	69	5,600	+4.3	+3.1	−7.2
Southend East	66	6,600	+0.8	+9.6	−12.0
Leyton	65	5,800	−6.2	+11.5	−8.5
Newham North East	61	5,200	+0.5	+5.7	−8.0
Newham North West	61	5,700	−0.2	+6.4	−6.2
Basildon	60	6,500	+1.4	+3.9	−5.3
Erith and Crayford	59	5,100	+1.3	+12.0	−13.3
Walthamstow	58	5,600	−1.4	+10.7	−10.8
Croydon North West	57	4,600	−3.5	+10.3	−10.8
Brighton Pavilion	57	4,000	−4.2	+8.6	−6.8
Peckham	57	4,300	−2.2	+7.2	−4.0
Woolwich	55	4,800	−4.6	+7.2	−1.6
Lewisham Deptford	55	4,800	−3.8	+11.6	−6.0
Brent South	55	5,600	−1.9	+5.6	−5.5
Southend West	55	6,600	+0.3	−4.7	−7.2
Southwark	54	7,600	−2.5	−8.9	+9.4
Luton North	54	6,000	−0.2	+6.1	−7.2
Dagenham	53	5,800	−2.2	+7.8	−5.6
Hove	53	4,800	−9.9	+6.2	−2.4

Notes: Net figures were: Conservative −1.8%; Labour +7.2%; Liberal Democrats −5.8%. In addition, in 1992 Labour gained three of the above seats: Walthamstow; Croydon North West and Woolwich.

Source: Best (2002), p. 257.

Butler and Kavanagh (1984, 1987) in 'The General Election of 1983' and 'The General Election of 1987', have also attempted to show that changes in housing tenure undermined Labour's position, claiming that whereas council tenants voted 49 per cent Labour and 29 per cent for the Conservatives, the figures were the reverse for the working class people who were buying or who owned their own homes (26 per cent to 47 per cent) (Butler and Kavanagh 1984, pp. 296–97). In Ivor Crewe's view these people are the 'new' working class.

The alternative view is put forward by Heath, Jowell and Curtice (1985) in the British Election Surveys (BES) of 1983 and 1987. During the 1960s there were major changes in housing tenure. Owner occupation doubled between 1951 and 1971, although this was largely because of the contraction of the private rented sector. The Conservative Government's legislation since the 1980 Act has led to a 5 per cent reduction in the size of the local authority housing stock between 1980 and 1986, as Heath et al. (1991, p. 206) point out: '*this has merely undone the expansion of the previous twenty years. The net increase in council housing over the period [1964–87] . . . is therefore effectively zero.*'

Heath et al. clearly recognise the 'association' between housing and voting. In the 1987 BES they make reference to Capderville and Dupoirier's concept of *le patrimoine* – the idea that a stake in the nation's wealth may be a major factor in determining how people vote – but they are not convinced of a causal link between housing and voting.

In the 1983 BES, Heath et al. explain that purchasers of council houses were more likely to have been Conservative voters in 1979, but the statistical significance was not great. Among the council tenants in 1979, 23 per cent had voted Conservative and 68 per cent voted Labour. However, of the former council tenants, who had bought their house between 1979 and 1983 40 per cent voted Conservative and 52 per cent voted Labour. It must be stressed, however, that purchasers were no more likely than other tenants to abandon Labour. Purchasers defected from Labour, but so did many tenants. Three-quarters of the former labour identifiers who bought their council houses continued to vote Labour in 1983, this was almost the same figure as former Labour identifiers who remained tenants, the precise figures were 76 per cent to 79 per cent. Moreover, as only 2 per cent of the 1983 sample planned to buy their council houses in future years, Heath et al. claim that any future gain for the Conservatives was likely to be limited. On the basis of the 1983 survey Heath et al. explain that they do not accept Dunleavy's assertion about housing as a sectoral cleavage, but argue that housing '*acts as a separate source for the maintenance of the class cleavage*' (Heath et al. 1985, p. 54). In the 1987 BES, Heath et al. again show that purchasers were more likely to vote Conservative. In 1979, Conservative voting was 15 percentage points higher among future purchasers; in 1983 Conservative voting was 20 percentage points higher, when some of this group had completed their purchases; in 1987, however, it was only 14 percentage points higher, when the whole group had completed their purchases. Again there was little evidence that the sale of council houses would produce many new recruits for the Conservatives. Although the Labour vote fell by 8 per cent more than it fell among tenants, only 6 per cent of the electorate were purchasers, 8 per cent of 6 per cent is only 0.5 per cent of the electorate.

In this area of voting behaviour as in a number of others, Heath, Jowell and Curtice present themselves as revisionists; they challenge the orthodox view that changes in housing tenure cause changes in voting behaviour. Heath et al. are the only researchers who have attempted a longitudinal study into the effects of housing on the electorate in 1979, 1983 and 1987 general elections.

A major objective may have been the creation of property and share-owning democracy; however, the Thatcher years also saw public disorder on a scale that had not been seen since the 1930s. There was a severe recession in 1981–82 during which there was a significant rise in unemployment and riots on the streets of many towns and cities. In 1984–85 there was a miners' strike which saw a number of violent incidents at pit gates between police and striking miners and most notably at the Orgreave coke works. In September and October 1985 there were riots in Birmingham (Hansworth) and London (Brixton and Tottenham's Broadwater Farm Estate). These riots were sparked by incidents involving the police and ethnic minorities. In Hansworth there was a stabbing after the local carnival that led to a number of people being arrested for drugs offences. In the violence that followed, two Asian residents died after their post office was fire bombed. The Brixton Riots came about after the police had shot Mrs Cherry Groce while searching her home. In Tottenham, Mrs Cynthia Jarret died of a heart attack after the police had searched her home. In the rioting that followed on the Broadwater Farm Estate PC Keith Blacklock was murdered. In response to these incidents the government introduced the 1986 Public Order Act, which introduced the new public order offences of riot, violent disorder, affray, threatening behaviour and disorderly conduct.

Key Ideas

UNDER THE LEADERSHIP OF MRS THATCHER FROM 1975 TO 1990, THE CONSERVATIVES became closely associated with 'New Right' ideas. These included:

- an emphasis on personal liberty and personal freedom
- the free market and opposition to state planning
- popular capitalism – notably privatisation and home ownership
- the promotion of the normal heterosexual family
- reduction of public spending
- giving people incentives to work by lowering both taxes and benefits
- making people less dependent upon the welfare state.

For New Right thinkers the welfare state removed freedom and responsibility, reduced incentives, produced waste, promoted social grievances and removed individual freedom. In other words, the welfare state produced a dangerous underclass.

Conservative Party leaders who followed Thatcher, notably John Major, did not abandon the Thatcherite politics totally, but moved towards improving standards of service provision in the public sector, with the citizens' charter.

At the level of rhetoric, Thatcherism was seen as conviction politics, as enterprise culture pushing back the 'Nanny State', as giving unions back to their members. Many on the left, notably sociologists Stuart Hall (1983) came to view Thatcherism as 'Authoritarian Populism' where Thatcher recreated common sense in the minds of the working class by the use of 'hegemonic messages'.

Dennis Kavanagh in his book *Thatcher and British Politics: The End of Consensus?* (1990) provides perhaps the clearest statement on Thatcherism as a major break with the post-war consensus. For Kavanagh, Thatcherism contained both style and policy. At the level of style, Thatcherism was based upon the distinct personality of Mrs Thatcher herself. At the level of policy, Thatcherism stressed control of the money supply to control inflation; the reduction of the public sector or privatisation; freeing the labour market through reform; and the restoration of the government's authority.

In a similar fashion, Philip Norton (Horsman and Marshall, 1994) suggested three propositions about Mrs Thatcher:

- she changed the nature of the political debate in Britain
- she imposed her will upon government policy and dominated Cabinet
- institutions that were seen as obstacles were abolished or reformed.

S.E. Finer (1987) explained that all post-war governments accepted the triangle of public corporations, social services and full employment. However, the Thatcher governments had a very different vision of politics and the role of government:

- Keynesian deficit financing was out
- physical controls and/or subsidies to ailing industries were out
- in came money supply economics and financial management of the economy
- unions were cold-shouldered
- public expenditure was restrained
- nationalised industries were told to make profits
- privatisation
- exchange controls were abolished
- the maximum possible scope was given to market forces.

Finer (1987, p. 129) explains: *'nothing – neither the rising unemployment that had stricken Macmillan and Heath with panic, or waves of strikes such as had paralysed former governments – simply nothing was allowed to stand in the way of these policies.'*

In many respects this was because, from a Thatcherite perspective, unemployment was blamed upon the unemployed themselves; they had priced themselves out of the jobs by demanding higher wages.

In a similar fashion to Kavanagh and Finer, other writers argued that Thatcher brought about a major change in values, attitudes and beliefs. Stephen Haseler, for example, in his *The Battle for Britain: Thatcher and the New Liberal Tories* (1989) argued that Thatcherism was a reaction to the dominant paternalist stance of the major political parties in Britain from 1945 onwards. We could add that Mrs Thatcher attempted to turn the political into the personal. 'Don't spend more than you earn' became economic policy; 'Don't trust foreigners' became foreign policy. Is this the hallmark of a postmodern politics?

The New Right under Thatcher was in favour of a return to 'Victorian values', a throw-back to Margaret Roberts' Grantham days under the paternalistic eye of Alderman Roberts. A return to 'Victorian values' came to mean privatisation of the welfare state. Instead of having 'collective' or state provision there was more private insurance, for health and pensions; more contracting out of school and hospital cleaning and hospital services; the introduction of a voucher system for nursery education; and the replacing of student grants by student loans. The idea behind these moves was to make people less dependent upon the state and more independent. Like pluralists, the New Right believes that the state should be both 'rule maker' and 'umpire'. In other words the state should police things like the market, looking for market imperfections such as large companies fixing prices etc.

According to Julian Le Grand (1986) the welfare state includes:

- A social security system that shifts cash from taxpayers to people on benefit.
- A number of 'benefits in kind', these are provided 'free' by the state because they are considered 'good' for society and include: healthcare; education; and a range of 'personal social services' such as the services of social workers, home helps, meals on wheels etc.

- There is also a range of price subsidies designed to reduce the cost to consumers of certain goods that were thought to be 'socially desirable'. These did include rent subsidies, housing improvement grants and public transport subsidies.

Before the success of the New Right, the state then was involved in social and economic activities in three ways; by providing direct provision, subsidy and regulation.

Privatisation, which the New Right clearly believes in (the reduction in state involvement), was also of three types:

- Reduction of state provision: for example, the sale of council houses.
- Reduction of state subsidy: for example, increases in charges for school trips; charges for NHS services and the replacement of student grants with loans and the introduction of tuition fees for university students.
- Reduction of state regulation: for example, the deregulation of the bus services.

According to New Right thinkers these changes are in the interests of efficiency.

Vic George and Paul Wilding (1982) give a very full and clear outline of the New Right philosophy. They argue that New Right thinkers such as Hayek, Friedman and Powell, believe in what was once known as liberalism in the nineteenth century. The New Right are opposed to state intervention, which they term 'collectivism', and also believe in freedom or liberty, individualism and inequality.

Freedom or liberty is seen in negative terms. A person is free if they are not under coercion. In other words, if people are not forcing you to do something that you do not want to do then you are free.

In addition, these New Right thinkers believe that all people are irrational and unreliable. However, if they make mistakes then it only affects a small group of people; in contrast, if the head of a government, who is also a person and also irrational and unreliable, were to make a big planning decision which went wrong, then millions of people would suffer.

The New Right also believes in inequality. Inequality is good because it provides people with incentives to better themselves. In contrast, the state can only bring about equality by coercion or force, by taking money away from people in the form of taxes which people are unwilling to pay. In addition, state intervention is socially disruptive, because according to Enoch Powell (1966), the welfare state turns 'wants' into 'rights'. I might want healthcare, I might want my children to be educated, and I might want social security. However, if the state cannot afford to provide these things then I will feel that my 'rights' have been ignored and I might turn to violence or crime to get what I believe is mine as of right.

In addition, from a New Right perspective, state services are wasteful of resources. Because state services are usually provided free of charge to the person using them, people consume as much as they possibly can. Moreover, because state services have to be paid for out of taxes then there is always a lack of concern over individual freedom.

Under the leadership of John Major, William Hague and Ian Duncan-Smith, the Thatcherite project was not abandoned. However, the Conservative leaders that followed Thatcher gave much greater emphasis to finding value for money in the public services by imposing bureaucratic Quality Assurance Systems. In addition, John Major introduced the notion of Charter Rights (such as the Further Education Charter that explains all the rights that a student can expect from their FE College) in all areas of public service.

There are, however, question marks against the monetarist credentials of the Thatcher governments. Sir Geoffrey Howe and Nigel Lawson did have great difficulty controlling the money supply. Lawson changed the treasury definition of money from the broad M3 definition to the much narrower Mo definition. In addition, the Treasury Select Committee challenged Nigel Lawson in 1985 on the grounds that government had undergone a U-turn of monetarist policy. That the Chancellor had abandoned control of the money supply in managing the economy and instead placing a greater emphasis on the use of interest rates and greater government spending to stimulate demand. As Paul Hirst (1989, p. 23) argued: *'Mrs Thatcher threw away monetarism, the apparent core of her ideas in 1979, when it became a political liability. She did the biggest "U" turn of any modern conservative politician: proving herself to be at once more pragmatic than Stanley Baldwin and more cynical than Harold Macmillan – both hard acts to follow.'*

In other words, Mrs Thatcher was a pragmatically motivated rather than ideologically motivated prime minister.

 **Further Reading**

BEST, S. (2002) *Introduction to politics and society*. Sage.

BUTLER, D. AND KAVANAGH, D. (1984, 1987) *The British General Election of 1983*. Macmillan.

CREWE, I. (1992) Why did Labour lose (yet again)? *Politics Review*, September, 2–5.

FINER, S. E. (1987) State and nation building in Europe: the role of the military, in C. Tilley (ed.) *The formation of nation states in Europe*. Princeton University Press.

GEORGE, V. AND WILDING, P. (1982) *Ideology and the Welfare State*. Routledge.

HALL, S. (1983) *The politics of Thatcherism*. Lawrence and Wishart.

HASELER, S. (1989) The battle for Britain: Thatcher and the new liberal Tories, in M. Horsman and A. Marshall (1994) *After the nation state*. HarperCollins.

HEATH, A., JOWELL, B. AND CURTICE, C. (1985) *How Britain votes*. Pergamon.

HEATH, A., JOWELL, B. AND CURTICE, C. (1991) *Understanding political change*. Pergamon.

HENLEY, A. (1997) Housing and negative equity. Speech given to the Royal Economic Society. http://www.res.org.uk/media/annconf97/henley.htm.

HIRST, P. (1989) *Politics after Thatcherism.* Macmillan.

HORSMAN, M. AND MARSHALL, A. (1994) *After the nation state.* HarperCollins.

KAVANAGH, D. (1990) *Thatcher and British politics: the end of consensus.* Oxford University Press.

LE GRAND, J. (1986) *Privatisation and the Welfare State.* Macmillan.

POWELL, E. (1966) *Medicine and politics.* Pitman.

PULZER, P.G. (1967) *Political representation and elections in Britain.* George Allen and Unwin.

RALLINGS, C. AND THRASHER, M. (1997) Housing and voting. *Sunday Times,* 4th May, 2–3.

Kenneth Boulding
(1910–1993)

KENNETH BOULDING ANTICIPATED MANY OF THE CURRENT ISSUES AND DEBATES IN world economics particularly in relation to the environment, and the need for harmonious international relations. He studied economics at Oxford University, and then went on to teach and write for many years in the United States, but most of his key ideas and principles were shaped by his family background and religious upbringing, rather than in his training as an economist. He therefore found it relatively easy to develop new ideas going beyond the bounds of existing conventional wisdom in economics. He was a firm believer in drawing on the full range of social science thinking rather than being trapped within existing orthodox views. Boulding provides an inspiration to budding economists today because his life work shows the importance of building on personal experience and original thought as well as learning from the ideas of others.

In a biographical essay ('From Chemistry to Economics and Beyond') Boulding (1992) set out the way in which his background shaped his way of thinking: 'Perhaps the most general principle of the universe is that "everything is what it is because it got that way" or, more elegantly, "every structure is the result of past processes". What I am today, therefore, certainly goes back to my conception in Liverpool in the spring of 1909, which gave me my genetic inheritance. As far as I know, all my ancestors were fairly humble people, and I am probably the first member of my family ever to go beyond the eighth grade. I came essentially out of the Methodist working class. My father was self-educated and a working plumber who had a little business of his own in Liverpool. He was a "local" – that is, lay-preacher in the Methodist Church, and Sunday School superintendent for many years. My mother and her parents were also Methodists. Her father was a blacksmith in a little town in Somerset. By today's standards they were very poor, but they did not think of themselves as such. Life was often hard. My mother read widely, wrote some charming poetry. I had a very happy and supportive childhood living in downtown Liverpool in what might easily have been called a slum. It was really rather an exciting neighbourhood – Jewish, Irish, Belgian, and one black family.'

Methodology

BOULDING SOUGHT TO THROW LIGHT ON A RANGE OF ISSUES AND SUBJECTS, BUT WAS opposed to creating a system of thinking that could be applied in a standardised way across the field. As an economist he appreciated the power of economics as a vehicle for the study of economic problems, but argued that there were many areas of life on which economics threw little light, and believed that economists should draw on a variety of disciplines and ways of thinking. He criticised the 'imperialism of economics' – the attempt by economics to take over the other social sciences. At all times he stressed the importance of the inter-related nature of knowledge and the importance of learning from other fields of study.

At the heart of his thinking lies a belief in humanistic values, and this predisposed his thinking towards a normative view of social science, that economists have values and opinions, which colour the way we see the world. He realised that knowledge is not neat and precise, and that we can all learn more. He challenged existing ways of thinking, in particular the notion that economic growth was a good thing and that the object of society was simply to increase consumption. Boulding was of the view that we can learn from the lessons of the past, so that our decision-making can become more informed. In discussing the obsession with growth in economic writing he made the criticism that *'The spurt (of growth) from the 1930s to the 1960s bears some resemblance to human adolescence, even to the production of a slightly pimply youth culture'* (Boulding 1978).

Boulding's values led him to become a champion of pacifism – the peace movement – environmentalism, and other causes. In his paper on America's power in the world economy, 'From Abundance to Scarcity: Implications for the American Tradition (1978) (a topic which has particular relevance in the post-September 11th world) he placed heavy emphasis on the importance of values: *'Unless we "stand for" something in the world . . . that power will lose legitimacy and will eventually disappear.'*

Biography

BOULDING WAS BORN IN LIVERPOOL INTO A FAMILY THAT ALTHOUGH MATERIALLY POOR considered themselves to be spiritually rich. Although his family were Methodists, Kenneth moved over to the Quaker religion in his late teens. He had been particularly influenced by accounts of conscientious objection by Quakers in the First World War. As he found out more about the Quakers he was attracted to their ideals and ways of praising God. For example, the Quaker church is based on democratic meetings of Friends, and there is no set service. Individuals simply meet together and quietly praise God. Nobody has to say anything and there is no intermediary in the form of a Priest or Preacher. The Quakers do not believe in predestination, and emphasise the perfectability of man.

Boulding won a scholarship to the Liverpool Collegiate School, and he studied hard, focusing on mathematics and science. He won an Open Scholarship to New College, Oxford in 1928. In his first year he read natural sciences but was bored by the subject, and was fortunate enough to be allowed to transfer to reading economics the following year. At Oxford, he continued to read widely, but found that there was a fair measure of class prejudice on the part of a number of middle-class students. He preferred to mix with friends from non-conformist religious groups and together they involved themselves in social service projects in working-class communities at Oxford.

Boulding excelled at economics, and graduated with first-class honours. He was fortunate to have a paper accepted by John Maynard Keynes for publication in the *Economics Journal*, and this success filled him with confidence.

In his early days at Oxford he was a keen supporter of the Labour Party, but quickly became disillusioned with the coherence of socialist thinking after reading Karl Marx's labour theory of value, which he could see was based on poor economic thinking. He was also appalled by the tyranny and brutalism of socialist revolutions in Eastern Europe.

In 1932 Boulding won a scholarship to study in America, enabling him to study at the University of Chicago under some of the most exciting and informed American economists of the period. On his father's death he returned to take up a lecturing post in Edinburgh but was disillusioned by the old-fashioned approaches that were used there. At Chicago he had been used to debating ideas with distinguished economists and a democratic approach to learning. In contrast, at Edinburgh he was treated as a junior. However, at Edinburgh he thoroughly immersed himself in the Quaker movement, and in various pacifist organisations. In 1937 he represented Scottish Quakers at an international Quaker conference in Philadelphia and while he was there was offered a teaching job at Colgate University.

At Colgate he started to write an economics textbook in earnest. His work, *Economic Analysis*, was published in 1941, and pulled together his understanding of economic theory at the time. It was a standard text, which unfortunately missed out on the revolution in Keynesian economics. Because Boulding had studied at Oxford rather than Cambridge he missed out on the new ideas that were sweeping English economics and consequently the new wave of economic thinking. When Boulding read Keynes he had difficulty coming to grips with the subject matter arranged there. However, by the time Boulding had the opportunity to produce a second edition of the book in 1948, he had developed a much clearer idea of Keynes' work and was thus able to rewrite the work taking account of the Keynesian revolution.

By the mid-1940s Boulding was faced with a dilemma. He was deeply opposed to the Nazi movement in Germany, and felt that it needed to be crushed but this clashed with his deeply held ideal of pacificism. However, on 15 May 1940 he had a deeply spiritual experience in which he saw Christ suffering on the cross, taking on himself all the sins of the world. He realised that this meant that Christ was prepared to take on himself even the most heinous crimes of the Nazi, and this rekindled his belief in peaceful approaches to conflict resolution.

In 1941 Boulding met his future wife, Elise Marie Biørn-Hansen, a Norwegian-American who was also a Quaker. The two always worked very closely together, sharing ideas, and a belief in peace.

Boulding next took on a post working for the League of Nations in their Economics and Financial Section, in New Jersey studying the problems of European agriculture.

In 1942 the two Bouldings produced a short document 'A Call to Disarm' based on nations working together in peaceful harmony rather than violent opposition. He was told that if he published the document he would be fired. He therefore resigned and published the paper.

Boulding then moved back into teaching and soon took up a post at Ames, Iowa. Here he developed his conviction that it was pointless to seek to divorce economic theory from wider social insights. He brought out his second book, *The Economics of Peace*, in 1945 outlining ways of reconstructing the economy and society in the wake of the War.

In this work Boulding set out that *'Economic problems have no sharp edges; they shade off imperceptibly into politics, sociology, and ethics. Indeed, it is hardly an exaggeration to say that the ultimate answer to every economic problem lies in some other field.'*

In 1949 Boulding moved on to the University of Michigan on the condition that he be allowed to teach a seminar on the integration of the social sciences. However, he soon found that social scientists 'didn't want to be integrated very much', so instead he focused on others who might be more interested in integration and from this he began to take an interest in biology.

The mid-1950s was one of the most exciting for Boulding, working at the new Centre for Advanced Study in the Behavioural Sciences at Stanford where he was able to work with a small group of others in considering how the social sciences could be used for peace research. A new journal was started up – *The Journal of Conflict Resolution*.

During the 1960s Boulding's work on peace issues became prominent in the United States, and in 1965 he played a crucial role in the first 'teach-in' at the University of Michigan, which started in train a series of events leading eventually to the end of the Vietnam War. Boulding produced a stream of work on environmental and ecological issues drawing on ideas from the broad range of social sciences and human knowledge. He took up posts in the West Indies and Japan, as well as giving a series of lectures in a number of countries before settling back in the United States at Boulder, Colorado.

Boulding was highly critical of neoliberal economists like Milton Friedman because he believed that they took too narrow a view of society. In contrast Boulding identified three organisers of society – love, fear and exchange. In his view, neoliberals were too wrapped up in a study of exchange. He argued that this approach failed to take account of the vast amount of economic activity based on love (the 'integrative system') and fear (the 'threat system'). To Boulding, society involves integrative elements, for example, welfare payments such as pensions, aid to developing countries, charity donations, threat elements such as regulation, and having to pay taxes, as well as market transactions. In his view exchange is important, but it is only one part of the total social structure.

Boulding's work is essentially eclectic, drawing on a range of interests and concerns that interested him during his life. He is most widely known today for his impact on the peace movement and the development of environmental economics.

Boulding is one of the most optimistic of all economists and he summed up his view of the world in the following way: *'If my life philosophy can be summed up in a sentence, it is that I believe that there is such a thing as human betterment – a magnificent, multi-dimensional, complex structure – a cathedral of the mind – and I think human decisions should be judged by the extent to which they promote it. This involves seeing the world as a total system . . . It involves seeing economics as an important part of the total social system, but certainly no more than a third of it, for we have to deal with threat systems and integrative systems. On the whole I think the threat system, beyond a certain necessary minimum, is inimical'* (Boulding 1992).

Key works

It is difficult to select the key works of Boulding because he wrote on such a broad range of topic areas.

The Economics of Peace (1945)

Environmental Quality in a Growing Economy (1968)

Evolutionary Economics (1981)

Capital and income

In his work *The Economics of Peace* (1945), he made an important distinction between capital and income using what he referred to as the simple 'bathtub theorem'. The production of new goods is like water flowing out of the taps into the bath; consumption is water flowing out of the plug. The difference between consumption and production is the stock of water (capital) that accumulates in the bath. Wars drain the bath because of wasteful consumption.

However, the size of the bath is only finite – because individuals are only willing to hold up to a certain amount of capital. He used this approach to explain booms and slumps. When people are no longer prepared to accumulate as much capital then a slump sets in.

He argued that wars tend to offset the day when a stationary state of growth arrives. In his view it was essential to reconstruct the economy in such a way as to prevent further wars from setting in. He believed that values would need to change away from the accumulation of capital if we are to sustain peace and to safeguard the environment.

Spaceship earth

Boulding's influence is most strongly present today in the field of environmental economics. In his book *The Economics of the Coming Spaceship Earth* (1966) he drew attention to the dangers of the 'cowboy economy'. He warned against treating the planet as if we are 'lonesome cowboys', riding out across the prairie, cooking a meal of beans, lighting fires with brushwood and then moving on, leaving the ashes and debris to be blown away.

The reality is that we are not cowboys but spacemen. When we create waste, instead of blowing away, it stays in our spaceship: planet earth.

'For the sake of picturesqueness, I am tempted to call the open economy the "cowboy economy," the cowboy being symbolic of the illimitable plains and also associated with reckless, exploitative, romantic, and violent behaviour, which is characteristic of open societies. The closed economy of the future might similarly be called the "spaceman" economy, in which the earth has become a single spaceship, without unlimited reservoirs of anything, either for extraction or for pollution, and in which, therefore, man must find his place in a cyclical ecological system which is capable of continuous reproduction of material form even though it cannot escape having inputs of energy' (Boulding 1966).

Boulding's concern was that unfettered growth could create pollution, which can feed back into the wider environmental system. The 'bads' that households and firms create can eventually flow back into the formal economy, weakening the resource base and endangering society's productive capacity.

Boulding's analysis provided a key part of the initial thinking that has led to the recent concern with the economics of sustainable development.

Economic progress

Boulding provided a radical critique of the notion of economic growth. He argued that simply increasing output does not measure the quality of growth, and it is necessary to examine the impact of producing more goods on the stock of capital in society. In a paper examining economic progress ('Income or Welfare', 1949) he stated that *'We cannot simply assume that output, or output per head, is a measure of economic progress. An increase in output, statistically measured by a weighted index of physical output, may easily be accompanied by a decline in economic welfare if the increased output is necessitated by a declining durability of capital or by a declining efficiency of utilisation.'*

More succinctly, he criticised conventional economic wisdom when he wrote:

'The wise economist is loath

To give up anything for growth.'

To Boulding, economic progress had to be something greater than traditional growth, something more akin to his Quaker principles of a perfectible humanity that could learn from experience: *'to fly the great engine of change . . . that it may carry us not to destruction but to that great goal for which the world was made'* (1949).

One of the key lessons that mankind must learn is that of the relationship between man and nature. Boulding (1949) stated that *'All of nature's systems are closed loops, while economic activities are linear and assume inexhaustible resources and "sinks" in which to throw away our refuse.'* In wilful ignorance, and in violation of the core principle of capitalism, we often refuse to treat environmental resources as capital.

Economic development as an evolutionary system

Boulding drew parallels with the world of biology to show how economies can develop over time. He defined (1968) economic development as *'that part of the total social developmental process which results in an increase in per capita real income in any society or segment of society.'* He clarified his definition by stating that the concept cannot be understood, *'except as part of a total process in society'.*

He showed how this process of development is paralleled in biological evolution – starting with the evolution of elements, progressing through biological evolution with increasingly complex and improbable forms culminating in man. *'The human nervous system then takes up the evolutionary task by developing increasing knowledge and complexity of organisations. What we call economic development is only a single aspect of this cumulative process'* (Boulding 1966).

Boulding shows how the evolutionary process operates through mutation and selection, involving a distinction between the genotype which mutates and the phenotype which is selected. The genotype is propagated by a process known as 'printing', or simple reproduction of structure.

Boulding (1981) goes on to show that *'The process by which the genotype constructs the phenotype may be described as "organisation".'* He states that *'in social systems, genotypes consist of such things as maps, blueprints, ideas, books, computers, ideologies, images of the future, prophets, entrepreneurs, and so on which have the capacity of organising role structures, organisation, patterns of behaviour and artefacts.'* He provides examples of cars which are social phenotypes originating in the *'ideas, plans and blueprints in the engineer's offices and materialising in the "womb" of the factory. A church is a phenotype produced by the ideas, experiences, and "sacred histories" of its founders and members.'*

Knowledge and intellectual capital

Boulding (1981) introduces the popular modern concept of 'intellectual capital' showing how this drives modern economic growth: *'Economic development manifests itself largely in the production of commodities, that is, goods and services. It originates, however, in ideas, plans, and attitudes in the human mind. These are the genotypes in economic development. This whole process indeed can be described as a process in the growth of knowledge. What the economist calls "capital" is nothing more than human knowledge imposed on the material world. Knowledge and the growth of knowledge, therefore, is the essential key to economic development. Investment, financial systems and economic organisations and institutions are in a sense only the machinery by which a knowledge process is created and expressed.'*

The role of revolution

Boulding is wary of the role of revolution in the evolutionary process. He sees that revolution can lead to a 'stepped change' or 'acceleration' in the process of economic and societal growth. However, revolutions come at a 'cost' and the 'acceleration' is the 'return'. Revolution may come at too high a cost relative to the return. As a result he is inclined to favour 'acceleration' without 'revolution'.

Limits to mathematics and statistical techniques in economics

Boulding has always been suspicious of the role of mathematics and statistics in economics. He recalled working at number crunching of economic data in the statistics laboratory while studying at the University of Chicago using mechanical calculators. While he was working on this task with other students, his tutor – Henry Schultz, an econometrician – sympathised with the class and said 'I know this is very boring, but you are getting familiar with the data.' Commenting on this event at a much later time Boulding remarked 'Today, of course, a computer gets familiar with the data and nobody else does'.

For Boulding the abstract nature of mathematical techniques means that they are often removed from the reality of social interaction. At a seminar on the 'Application of Mathematics to the Social Sciences' in 1955, Boulding remarked that mathematics is *'further abstracted from the empirical world than ordinary language. All language involves abstraction (orderly loss of information), we can never talk about as much as we know. Mathematics is an abstraction from ordinary language, an abstraction which again involves loss of "richness" of information.'* He then went on to show how mathematics can set up a linguistic barrier between the mathematician and others – and the temptation to create 'knowledge monopolies'.

He suggests that mathematics with its precision can often be an inappropriate way of communicating ideas in the social sciences because *'knowledge is not wholly intellectual, not wholly conscious, nor wholly clear.'*

Evolutionary economics

One of Boulding's major areas of interest was that of biology. Boulding told the story of a young student coming up to him at an American Economics Association meeting and saying 'My professor warned me about you – you sold your soul to the biologists.' Boulding comments that he could have replied 'Well, I didn't sell it cheap'. He asserts that he received very good terms of trade because he learnt a lot from biologists and others. Boulding asserts that his book *Evolutionary Economics* (1981) is a plea to the economics profession to learn from anybody they can.

Conclusion

In many ways Boulding broke the boundaries of traditional economic thought. In particular he argued that economics should not be compartmentalised, that it should look outwards and share ideas. His approach does not sit comfortably with that of more conventional economists because of its greater emphasis on normative values, which was inevitable given Boulding's religious background and experience. Boulding tells us that we can't examine economic issues as if they are divorced from wider society, and that social evolution is based on many criteria that have not conventionally been taken into consideration by economists. Throughout his life Boulding liked to write poetry (taking inspiration from his mother), and his work provides us with a more spiritual dimension of human growth than we are used to when examining more conventional approaches. Boulding's life also shows the importance of being prepared to take risks, rather than to run with the crowd. It is for these qualities that Boulding will always stand out as one of the most eminent economists.

Further Reading

BOULDING, K.E. (1941) *Economic Analysis.* Harper.

BOULDING, K.E. (1945) *The economics of peace.* Prentice Hall.

BOULDING, K.E. (1948) *Economic analysis.* 1st British edn. Hamish Hamilton.

BOULDING, K.E. (1949) Income or Welfare? Review of economic studies 1949–50, in *Collected Papers*, Vol. 1. Harper, 268–269.

BOULDING, K.E. (1950) *A reconstruction of economics.* John Wiley and Sons.

BOULDING, K.E. (1966) *The economics of the coming spaceship earth.* Harper and Row.

BOULDING, K.E. (1968) *Environmental quality in a growing economy.* The John Hopkins University Press.

BOULDING, K.E. (1971) *Economics of pollution.* New York University Press.

BOULDING, K.E. (1978) *From abundance to scarcity: implications for the American tradition.* Ohio State University Press.

BOULDING, K.E. (1981) *Evolutionary economics.* Sage Publications.

BOULDING, K.E. (1992) From chemistry to economics and beyond, in E. Szenzberg (ed.), *Eminent economists, their life philosophies.* Cambridge University Press.

SILK, L. (1974) *The economists.* Basic Books.

SPIEGEL, H.W. (1971) *The growth of economic thought.* Prentice Hall.

Rachel
Carson
(1907–1964)

RACHEL CARSON STANDS OUT AS ONE OF THE MOST IMPORTANT FIGURES OF THE twentieth century in radically changing our perception of the nature and purpose of conventional economics. Her ideas and concerns are those of radical ecology, a perspective which has little in common with conventional economic thinking. The radical ecology movement challenges existing patterns of thinking in society. It not only challenges vested interests (such as the powers of the giant corporations) within the existing structure, but it also questions the structure itself, questioning our assumptions about how the business of everyday life is conducted, the nature and value of 'production', and how we use 'natural resources'.

Essentially Carson was a scientist and a writer rather than an economist. However, the nature of her work and her findings, in relation to how society uses raw materials, is primarily concerned with the territory which provides the subject matter of economics.

Rachel Carson fell in love with nature from the start of her life, and this love spilled over into a passion to enhance and protect nature. Much of her writing was primarily about the sea, but her most important book, *Silent Spring*, first published in 1962, provided a scientifically passionate exposure of the effects of the indiscriminate use of chemicals by man. In *Silent Spring* she described how pesticides and insecticides are applied almost universally to farms, forests, gardens and homes with scant regard to the consequent contamination of our environment and the widespread destruction of wildlife. In his introduction to Carson's book, Lord Shackleton wrote *'Silent Spring is not merely about poisons; it is about ecology or the relation of plants and animals to their environment and to one another. Ecologists are more and more coming to recognise that for this purpose man is an animal and indeed the most important of all animals and that however artificial his dwelling, he cannot with impunity allow the natural environment of living things from which he has so recently emerged to be destroyed. Fundamentally, therefore, Miss Carson makes a well-reasoned and persuasive case for human beings to learn to appreciate the fact that they are part of the entire living world inhabiting this planet, and that they must understand its conditions of existence and so behave that these conditions are not violated.'*

Methodology

THE STRUCTURE AND LAYOUT OF CARSON'S *SILENT SPRING* GIVES A CLEAR INDICATION of the methodology used. The book is in all (in its paperback form) only 220 pages long, but at the end it lists 40 pages of references. As a trained scientist Carson set out to support her findings and analysis with detailed evidence which she gained from a variety of sources. Like many ecologists Carson's concern for the environment stemmed from an initial concern for her own immediate environment, which then built out to a wider concern for the globe. Initially she became aware of issues relating to crop spraying in her immediate vicinity, but through her contacts across the world she could see that this was a much wider problem. In the course of her work Carson developed a network across the world of scientists, journalists, and activists who helped her document environmental abuse. Her work therefore involved the rigorous accumulation of evidence.

Carson's research involved making phone calls, studying direct evidence, and sifting through thousands of reports to build up a case against the use of poisonous chemicals.

Carson employed a young researcher, Bette Haney, to help her with her work and the method used by the two is clearly described in Linda Lear's (1997) biography of Carson: *'At the beginning of each week, the two would meet and review the bibliography Carson had prepared on index cards. The evidence of what DDT and the other chemicals did to the land and to wildlife was available in the agricultural journals Carson assigned Haney to read. Bette would read the articles and write summaries of them. If an article was particularly important, Rachel starred it and asked for specific information. Carson would call the librarians and make sure the material she wanted was available before she sent Haney in to work. Sometimes Rachel wanted to read an important article or parts of it herself, in which case Bette went to the library, pulled the material, and had it laid out for Rachel.*

Most of Haney's research was done at libraries in the Interior, the Department of Agriculture, the Food and Drug Administration, the Public Health Service, and sometimes the Library of Medicine at the National Institutes of Health. She took notes in a small five-by-eight loose leaf notebook, carefully noting the bibliographic citation at the top of each page. Carson then filed these sheets by author or subject, rearranging them later as her writing required.'

The structuring of the arguments that enabled her to present the case against pesticides and insecticides involved building up overwhelming evidence by means of painstaking research into an area that first interested her in 1938 and was finally to lead to the publication of *Silent Spring* in 1962. Finally, she felt that she had a compelling case that showed how pesticides menaced the ecological balance and were a direct threat to human health.

Prior to publication she was able to assert that *'As I look over my reference material, I am impressed by the fact that the evidence on this particular point outweighs by far, in sheer bulk and also significance, any other aspect of the problem. I have a comforting feeling that what I shall now be able to achieve is a synthesis of widely scattered facts, that have not heretofore been considered in relation to each other. It is now possible to build up, step by step, a really damning case against the use of these chemicals as they are now inflicted upon us.'*

R ACHEL CARSON WAS BORN IN SPRINGDALE, PENNSYLVANIA IN 1907 TO PARENTS OF Irish-Scottish extraction. The family were Presbyterians. Rachel built a very strong bond with her mother, Maria, who was to be the major influence in her life. The two kept in very close contact and as her mother grew older Rachel took responsibility for caring for her.

Maria had initially been a teacher but in those days it was forbidden for married women to teach and so she increasingly channelled her energies into the education of her own children. Rachel inherited from her mother a love of music, literature and nature. Rachel's biographer, Linda Lear (1997), reports that *'from the time Rachel was one year old, she and her mother spent increasing amounts of time outdoors, walking in the woods and orchards, exploring the springs and naming flowers, birds, and insects . . . From the first Rachel responded emotionally to her mother's love of nature. Her acuity of observation and her eye for detail were shaped on these childhood outings.'* Rachel herself later wrote (Lear, 1997) that she was always *'happiest with wild birds and creatures as companions,'* and it would be so all her life.

From an early age Rachel also developed a love of books and reading. The start of her literary career began with a story published in a children's magazine, when she was only 11 years old, and this was to be the first of many. Rachel was strongly influenced by her mother's aspirations and the two formed a very close bond. Initially they set their sights on Rachel becoming a writer.

However, a major problem that the family had to overcome was lack of income. While the family had settled in an attractive home, which served as a small farm with surrounding land, Rachel's father never earned much income. Fortunately, this did not deter mother and daughter, and by the time Rachel entered high school she had adopted her mother's view that intellect and a good self-image are more important than material success. This attitude was later reflected in Rachel's wider system of ideas.

At 18 Rachel started a course of study at Pennsylvania College for women. She was fortunate to win a small scholarship and the idea was that her education would be further supported by selling off small plots of the family land.

Pennsylvania College was situated in Pittsburgh, a steel town notorious for the high levels of pollution that it created and an acrid smell. This provided Rachel with a clear contrast from the nature that she loved and revered. Initially Carson was most inter-ested in the writing and literature courses and produced some good pieces of writing often involving stories about the sea.

A major turning point in Carson's life came with the appointment of Mary Scott Skinker as a biology lecturer at the college. Skinker was in the process of completing postgraduate studies at The Johns Hopkins University. Skinker was a lively and intelligent teacher who provided an excellent role model for female students at a time when there were few opportunities for women in science. Skinker was immediately impressed by Carson's depth of knowledge of natural history, coupled with her methodical research skills. It was obvious that Carson's cognitive and observational skills were suited to biology. By the spring of 1927 Carson's creative energies were focused on biology rather than composition, and through the teaching of Skinker she was able to appreciate that through the life sciences she might understand, rather than merely observe, the natural world. Through Skinker, Carson also developed a strong interest in the conservation of nature. Carson therefore took the bold step of changing her major speciality to biology.

Carson then applied to do postgraduate study in zoology at The Johns Hopkins University to focus chiefly on comparative anatomy and genetics. However, she had to postpone the start of her course because of the family's financial situation (she already owed Pennsylvania College $1,500. In her letter of application she made this clear when she set out: *'My most serious handicap in undertaking my graduate work is a financial one. My undergraduate work has been a heavy strain, and my expenses next year will constitute a grave problem.'* She was therefore lucky to receive a full tuition scholarship for the first year of her course based on her undoubted ability.

Her next major breakthrough was in winning a place at the Marine Biological Laboratory at Woods Hole which was also the home for the US Fish Commission where she was able to spend eight weeks studying in her summer holidays. It was here that Carson was to develop all the skills of a practising marine biologist. Here she had access to books and journals from all over the world, and a range of marine specimens available to her 24 hours a day. In addition she was working alongside a club of leading marine biologists, sharing ideas and building up networks that would endure for life. Carson thrived in this atmosphere and was able to build up the laboratory research techniques that she was already mastering, but this time with nature on her doorstep. She fell in love with the sea, its natural systems and the creatures that it supported. Carrying out her research work at the Marine Biological Laboratory she could study living organisms in the form of live specimens of horseshoe crabs, limpets, and other molluscs without having to tramp out long distances to search for specimens.

Returning home to visit her mother she increasingly became aware of the contradictions of modern society. The woods and fields of her native Springdale were now being squeezed between two rival energy producing plants, which were progressively polluting the Allegheny River. These plants produced power, jobs and pollution – thus both catering for the needs of man and destroying the vital life systems on which man's and nature's existence is based. As a keen observer she was struck by these contrasts. Rachel was now clear about what she wanted to do in life – that is, to work in a field dedicated to research and educating the non-scientist.

On completing her studies Rachel initially expected to focus on teaching work in order to provide the income to support her family, as with the ill health of her father she would now become the main breadwinner. However, she was fortunate to have a break enabling her to build a new career based on her twin skills of writing and biological research.

The US Bureau of Fisheries had agreed to produce a public education series of 52 short radio programmes on marine life called 'Romance Under the Waters'. The official in the Fisheries Department responsible for the programmes was desperately in need of 'someone who could take over writing the scripts – someone who knew marine biology and who also could write'. Carson had approached this official seeking a teaching post and as an alternative had been asked to try her hand at writing the series. The product was a tremendous success. Carson was able to communicate the wonders of marine life to a captive audience. She was then asked to write a general introduction to marine life. It was from that time that Carson's reputation as a writer began to take off and in subsequent years she went on to write a number of highly acclaimed and rigorously researched books mainly about marine life. She worked for the US Bureau of Fisheries engaging in a range of research projects related to marine life.

In later years Carson (Lear, 1997) was to write '*I can remember no time, even in earliest childhood, when I didn't assume I was going to be a writer. Also, I can remember no time when I wasn't interested in the out-of-doors and the whole world of nature. Those interests, I know, I inherited from my mother and have always shared with her.*'

By the late 1950s, Carson had transformed colourless government research into three brilliant, popular books about the sea, including *The Sea Around Us* (1951).

She continued to look after her mother, and nurse her through a number of serious illnesses. Carson herself went on to contract cancer, and this made her later years extremely painful. However, her love of nature made her a natural champion of nature and radical ecology.

She became interested in the role of poisons in the environment in 1938, when she first proposed the idea of writing an article on naturally occurring arsenics.

She became increasingly interested in the impact that new poisons related to crop spraying and the use of DDT were having on American agriculture and particularly on human health. Using her contacts in government she gradually began to accumulate more and more information. She developed links with others who were concerned about the impact of chemicals on nature and human health.

Initially she hoped that someone else might write a definitive work on this subject but increasingly realised that despite her failing health that the mantle had fallen to her.

Examples of evidence she collected included reports of the contamination of cow milk from pastures sprayed by DDT and the reproductive failures of various birds after ingesting poisoned insects – the thrust of her arguments was that human populations were being put at risk by the use of new chemicals.

In a world of rapidly increasing technological advance Carson increasingly appreciated the threat of new technologies. While American agro-economists were seeking techno-logical solutions that would enable American agriculture to gain an advantage over rivals, Carson warned of the dangers of expansion that was not built on an adequate research base. For example, when the US Department of Agriculture announced a new programme to spray thousands of acres of land with powerful chlorinated hydrocarbon pesticides to wage war on the fire ant that had infiltrated from Brazil, Carson warned of the potential spillover effect as these chemicals fed into the food chain and into water and air supplies.

By 1957 the pesticide problem was totally out of hand, as an attempt to prevent 'an infestation of gypsy moths' in the city of New York clearly demonstrated: *'The gypsy moth,'* Carson (Lear, 1962) wrote, *'is a forest insect certainly not an inhabitant of cities. Nor does it live in meadows, cultivated fields, gardens or marshes. Nevertheless, the planes hired by the United States Department of Agriculture and the New York Department of Agriculture and Markets showered down the prescribed DDT-in-fuel-oil with impartiality. They sprayed truck gardens and dairy farms, fish ponds and salt marshes. They sprayed the quarter-acre lots of suburbia drenching a housewife making a desperate effort to cover her garden before the roaring plane reached her, and showering insecticide over children at play and commuters at railway stations. At Setauket a fine quarter horse drank from a trough in a field which the planes had sprayed; 10 hours later it was dead.'*

This was probably the single event that most influenced Carson to embark on writing *Silent Spring* which was eventually to be published in 1962, on the basis of several years detailed research. *Silent Spring* was serialised in the *New Yorker* magazine, beginning 16 June 1962 and then published complete at the end of September. It was to be an instant bestseller, and was read by many influential people including President John F. Kennedy, who paid public tribute to her work.

Immediately after publication, the agro-chemical industry and other influential pressure groups set out to discredit her work (Lear, 1997), suggesting that *'Miss Carson wants to turn us back to the Dark Ages when plagues of locusts swept the planet.'* *Time* magazine described the case presented in *Silent Spring* as *'unfair, one-sided and hysterically over-emphatic. Many of the scary generalisations . . . are patently unsound.'*

However, Carson was not worried about the criticism because she felt the book itself and the evidence it presented would speak for itself. Today the book is still widely read and is seen as a turning point in ecological consciousness. In 1963, shortly before her death, Rachel Carson had the opportunity to address the Senate Committee on Commerce about the findings in her book (a committee specially set up by John F. Kennedy). She began: *'The problem you have chosen to explore is one that must be solved in our time. I feel strongly that a beginning must be made on it now – in this session of Congress'.*

This was to be Carson's last opportunity to voice her fears in public for in 1964 she died of cancer. However, she had played an important part in creating a movement which questions conventional economic doctrines about the appropriate pathway to growth.

Key works

Silent Spring (1962)

Overproduction

Carson suggested that in advanced agricultural and industrial economies we may already be suffering from unnecessary or overproduction. She wrote (1962): *'We are* *told that the enormous and expanding use of pesticides is necessary to maintain farm production. Yet is our real problem not one of overproduction? Our farms, despite measures to remove acreages from production and to pay farmers not to produce, have yielded such a staggering excess of crops that the American taxpayer in 1962 is paying out more than $1bn a year as the total carrying cost of the surplus food storage programme.'*

Negative spillover effects of production

Carson's work was a direct challenge to technological innovations in the agro-chemical industry that were designed to increase crop yields. Carson suggested that products were being brought onto the market to destroy pests and to increase crop yields without sufficient testing. In an early chapter of her book *Silent Spring*, called 'Elixirs of Death', she outlined the highly poisonous nature of the chemicals that were being used and charted the effects that they have on plant and animal life, citing numerous examples.

For example, she wrote (1962) that *'One of the most sinister features of DDT and related chemicals is the way they are passed on from one organism to another through all the links of the food chains. For example, fields of alfalfa are dusted with DDT; meal is later prepared from the alfalfa and fed to hens; the hens lay eggs which contain DDT.'*

Silent Spring

The most poignant image of her book relates to the impact of chemicals on life and hence bird song.

In her chapter 'And No Birds Sing', Carson wrote *'Over increasingly large areas of the United States, spring now comes unheralded by the return of the birds, and the early mornings are strangely silent where once they were filled with the beauty of bird song . . .'*

. . . A year after the federal government had launched a massive spraying programme against the fire ant, an Alabama woman wrote:

Our place has been a veritable bird sanctuary for over half a century. Last July we all remarked, "There are more birds than ever." Then suddenly, in the second week of August, they all disappeared. I was accustomed to rising early to care for my favourite mare that had a young filly. There was not a sound of the song of a bird. It was eerie, terrifying. What was man doing to our perfect and beautiful world? Finally, five months later a blue jay appeared and a wren' (Lear 1997).

The human price

One of the most telling arguments that Carson put forward related to the negative impacts of chemical poisons on humans. Carson (1962) stated *'the effect of these chemical poisons – some of great toxicity – is only beginning to be assessed in its relation to the lives and welfare, not only of the whole community of animals in the area subjected to ground and aerial sprays, but of the human population as well. There exists already, however, a large body of well documented evidence that these highly toxic poisons as presently used, represent an alarming threat to human welfare, and also to the basic balance of nature on which human survival ultimately depends.'*

Man and nature

One of the most important messages of Carson's book relates to the relationship between man and nature, and involves a clear tension between radical ecology and traditional economics. Talking about man's responsibility in a new technological age Carson (1962) wrote, *'And man seems actually likely to take into his hands – ill-prepared as he is psychologically – many of the functions of God.'*

Talking about man's relationship with nature she went on, *'We still talk in terms of conquest. We still haven't become mature enough to think of ourselves as only a tiny part of a vast and incredible universe. Man's attitude towards nature is today critically important simply because we have now acquired a fateful power to alter and destroy nature. But man is part of nature and his war against nature is inevitably a war against himself.'*

Ecology

At a meeting to discuss the work of the Nature Conservancy in Maine at which the members were worried about the disappearance of ecologically unique habitats as well as the increasing development pressures on the coastal areas, Carson set out a statement which explicitly connected the need to preserve ecological habitats for the benefits they provided to wildlife with the well-being of humankind: 'Our lives are enriched by understanding the close inter-relationship between living things and their environment.'

She expanded on the importance of ecological systems in a passage from *Silent Spring* (1962) which stated, *'For each of us, as for the robin in Michigan or the salmon in Miramichi, this is a problem of ecology, of interrelationships of interdependence. We poison the caddis flies in a stream and the salmon runs dwindle and die. We poison the gnats in a lake and the poison travels from link to link of the food chain and soon the birds of the lake margins become its victims. We spray our elms and the following springs are silent of robin song, not because we sprayed the robins directly but because the poison travelled, step by step, through the now familiar elm leaf-earthworm-robin cycle. These are matters of record, observable, part of the visible world around us. They reflect the web of life – or death – that scientists know as ecology.*

But there is also an ecology of the world within our bodies. In this unseen world minute causes produce mighty effects; the effect, moreover, is often seemingly unrelated to the cause, appearing in a part of the body remote from the area where the original injury was sustained.'

The other road

Carson (1962) argues that mankind needs to seek alternative ways forward to progress that are more in harmony with nature and which involve biological solutions rather than poisons. This is the other fork in the road which *'offers our only chance to reach a destination that assures the preservation of the earth.'*

Carson's alternatives were biological solutions, *'based on understanding of the living organisms they seek to control, and of the whole fabric of life to which these organisms belong.'* These solutions are referred to as 'biotic control'.

Conclusion

Carson's work emphasises the continuity of human life, and the importance of preserving this continuity through our relationship with nature. If we want to move forward we can only do so in conjunction with nature, because we are part of nature. We therefore need to develop a far more reverential and thoughtful approach to the whole process of development over time.

 **Further Reading**

ALLEN, G. (1978) *Life science in the twentieth century*. Cambridge University Press.

BURNSIDE, J. (2002) Reluctant crusader. *The Guardian Saturday Review*, 18 May, p. 1.

CARSON, R.L. (1951) *The sea around us*. Oxford University Press.

CARSON, R.L. (1962) *Silent spring*, 3rd edn. Penguin Books.

LEAR, L. (1997) *Rachel Carson, witness for nature*. Henry Holt.

Douglass C. North

(1920–)

DOUGLASS NORTH IS REPRESENTATIVE OF A SCHOOL OF THINKING WHICH IS USUALLY characterised as 'Institutional Economics'. Much of his early work was in economic history, and through this study he was able to develop a picture of the sorts of social structures that favoured economic growth and those that slowed it down. Using evidence from a range of periods of history and different geographical areas he identified the importance of institutions in supporting or holding back economic activity. A key implication of his work is that smooth running economies require institutional arrangements which are favourable to economic activity. In recent years the work of the institutional economists has been taken very seriously, particularly when considering the transition of economies from one type of economic system to another. For example, one of the reasons advanced to explain why neoliberal market models have been slow in taking off in Eastern Europe is because the institutions there are still grounded in a legacy of centralised state planning.

North (1990) defines institutions as *'any socially imposed constraint upon human behaviour. Institutions are the "rules of the game" for human interaction.'* The key role of institutions in society 'is to reduce uncertainty by establishing a stable (but not necessarily efficient) structure to human interaction'. North notes that institutions 'are a guide to human interaction, so that when we wish to greet friends on the street, drive an automobile, borrow money, form a business, bury our dead, or whatever, we know (or can learn easily) how to perform these tasks.' He argues that it is patently obvious that institutions vary from one society to another; for example, differences would exist if we wanted to make a transaction in Bangladesh rather than the United States. As a result institutions define and limit the set of choices of individuals. Although institutions are stable this *'in no way gainsays the fact that they are changing. From conventions, codes of conduct, and norms of behaviour to statute law, and common law, and contracts between individuals, institutions are evolving and, therefore, are continually altering the choices available to use.'* In the world as we know it these institutions are changing quite rapidly. However, institutions tend to change incrementally rather than in a discontinuous way. Although formal rules (such as laws) may change quickly, *'informal constraints embodied in customs, traditions, and codes of conduct are much more impervious to deliberate policies. These cultural constraints not only connect the past with the present and future, but provide us with a key to explaining the path of historical change.'* It is important therefore to develop an understanding of these institutions and how they impact on the choice making process. North's work therefore combines insights from economics, history, politics, sociology, biology, psychology and law.

Much of North's work involves combining the tools of economic analysis with a historical analysis of changes in society over time. His work has been particularly influential in leading neoclassical economists to take account of 'transaction costs' as well as 'production costs' in calculating total costs. Transaction costs are those involved in specifying what is being exchanged and then in making sure that the subsequent agreement sticks. In some societies transaction costs are much lower than in others because social institutions favour the keeping of bargains (without any form of bribery or other hidden costs) while in others there are a lot of costs involved in making sure that agreements materialise in practice.

Methodology

NORTH'S METHOD OF ANALYSIS IS BASED ON A COMBINATION OF THE SORT OF DEDUCTIVE approach typically used in neoclassical analysis combined with empirical evidence from historical case study. North used the term 'cliometrics' to describe the combination of historical analysis combined with economic theory.

North (1990) believes that the assumptions that neoclassical economists make about human behaviour limit their ability to arrive at meaningful economic truths. He rejects the notion of economic man making choices in a purely rational way. Instead he believes that '*individuals make choices based on subjectively derived models that diverge among individuals and the information the actors receive is so incomplete that in most cases these divergent subjective models show no tendency to converge*'.

North is therefore convinced that in interpreting human behaviour we need to examine institutional arrangements. Without this understanding economic analysis will be seriously flawed. Although a significant proportion of the choices we make are selected in a routine way, because our way of thinking about these choices has become institutionalised, there are other choices for which decision making is far more complex and unique.

North (1990) explains this in the following way: '*On the face of it, the assumptions of stable equilibrium and knowledge about alternatives (made by neo-classical economists) are quite attractive, because our lives are made up of routines in which the matter of choices appears to be regular, repetitive, and clearly evident, so that 90 per cent of our actions in a day do not require much reflection. But in fact, it is the existence of an imbedded set of institutions that has made it possible for us not to have to think about problems or to make such choices. We take them for granted, because the structure of exchange has been institutionalised in such a way as to reduce uncertainty. As soon as we move away from choices involving personal and repetitive actions to making choices involving impersonal and non-repetitive exchanges the uncertainty about outcomes increases. The more complex and unique the issues we confront, the more uncertain the outcome. We simply do not possess theories to predict effectively the outcomes, and the information we receive in such circumstances frequently does not permit us to update our models to improve them.*'

North (1990) also questions assumptions that the choices that individuals make lead to efficiency. Instead he believes that '*Institutions exist to reduce the uncertainties involved in human interaction. These uncertainties arise as a consequence of both the complexity of the problems to be solved and the problem-solving software (to use a computer analogy) possessed by the individual. There is nothing in the above statement that implies that the institutions are efficient.'*

D OUGLASS NORTH WAS BORN IN CAMBRIDGE, MASSACHUSETTS, FAMOUS FOR ITS TWIN universities. His father was a manager for an insurance company, and in the early years the family moved several times as his father's work shifted, including a period in Canada. North also studied in Lausanne, Switzerland for one year. At school North was more interested in photography than in academic study.

On completing school North went to the University of California at Berkeley. In an autobiographical note (1995) he wrote that *'While I was there my life was completely changed by becoming a convinced Marxist and engaging in a variety of student liberal activities. I was opposed to World War II, and indeed on June 22, 1941 when Hitler invaded the Soviet Union I suddenly found myself the lone supporter of peace since every-body else had, because of their communist beliefs, shifted over to become supporters of the war.'*

On graduating (having only gained mediocre grades) he joined the merchant navy. He sees this period as a turning point in his life, because it provided him with the oppor-tunity to spend three years on continuous reading at the end of which he was convinced that he should be an economist (although he was almost tempted to concen-trate on photography).

North then returned to postgraduate studies in economics at the University of California. He states that up to this time his knowledge of economics was very patchy, but when he secured his first teaching post at the University of Washington in Seattle, *'and began playing chess with Don Gordon, a brilliant young theorist, that I learned economic theory. In the three years of playing chess every day from noon to two, I may have beaten Don at chess, but he taught me economics; more important he taught me how to reason like an economist, and that skill is perhaps the most important set of tools that I have acquired'* (North 1995).

Taking on a research interest from his father's line of work North produced a disserta-tion on the history of life insurance in the United States. His early work and publica-tions focused on the relationship between insurance and investment banking.

At a meeting of the Economic History Association North met Solomon Fabricant who was the Director of Research at the National Bureau of Economic Research. Fabricant invited North to work as a research associate at the Bureau. Here he produced an important empirical paper on the study of the balance of payments of the United States from 1790 to 1860. By now North was shaping into a highly respected economic historian and produced his first book, *The Economic Growth of the United States from 1790 to 1860.*

It was at this point that North took a key step in developing what is referred to as 'cliometrics' – the application of modern statistical and economic models to interpret historical events (Clio being the muse of history). In the 1960s and 70s North concentrated on developing the field of cliometrics, which was an important course development at the University of Washington.

In 1966–67 North decided to switch his focus to concentrate on European economic history; he was fortunate enough to receive a grant to live in Geneva for a year. It was during this period in which he focused on European economic history that his thinking shifted. As he states (1995), *'I quickly became convinced that the tools of neo-classical economic theory were not up to the task of explaining the kind of fundamental societal change that had characterised European economies from medieval times onward.'*

It was in seeking new tools to explain these changes that North was to focus his attention on new institutional economics.

Institutional economists argue that, over time, patterns and behaviours become institutionalised in society. These patterns shape our thinking and thus our laws and social framework. (For example, it is often argued that racism has become institutionalised in our society – i.e. that it is an ongoing legacy from the past.)

Early institutional economists showed how institutions placed constraints on individual behaviour. For example, American society was seen as being dominated by relationships based on money and money-making. Over time these existing pathways were built upon and new generations took on current values as their own, that is, progress was path-dependent.

One of the best known early institutional economists, Thornstein Veblen (1857–1929) argued that American institutions did not necessarily lead to social benefit – in fact, the opposite: business interests were about promoting narrow self-interest at the expense of society as a whole. Veblen was not just a critic of classical economics but also of the business attitudes of his time.

In recent years, interest in institutional economics has grown, partly as a reaction to the neoclassical revival. The neoclassical economists used mathematical models to show the benefits of free trade, arguing that market models can and should be applied almost everywhere. The modelling often ignored the existing institutional framework.

For example, from the time of the October Revolution of 1917 until late 2001, it was impossible for Russian citizens to buy and sell land. Institutional economists would argue against the idea of abruptly imposing a free-market model on a society which had so little knowledge or experience of how the free market works.

Recently institutional economists have studied institutional factors such as property rights and governance structures, showing how these affect economic transactions and activities. The aim of many modern institutional economists has been to identify ways of reducing petty restrictions that push up costs, to create a more stable legal and commercial framework in markets and to improve social benefits through co-ordinated institutional activity.

In the late 1960s North became a champion of what was referred to as 'new institutional economics', and his first important works in this field were *Institutional Change and American Economic Growth* (Davis and North 1971), and *The Rise of the Western World: A New Economic History* (1973) which he wrote with Robert Thomas.

Both of these books were based on a neoclassical interpretation of economic theory combined with institutional economics. However, North identified a number of weaknesses in the neoclassical model, such as its inability to provide an effective explanation of poor economic performance in the long run. North therefore set out to investigate institutional factors resulting in poor economic performance. His work emphasised the importance of ideas, ideologies, and prejudices in influencing the choices that individuals make in all forms of decision-making. These areas were typically missed out in neoclassical theory. North set out to develop a model of political economy which would take into account the underpinning sources of institutions as well as developing an understanding of why people developed the ideas and ideologies that determined their choices. North set out his ideas in two well-researched books, *Structure and Change in Economic History* (1981), and *Institutions, Institutional Change and Economic Performance* (1990).

One of North's key themes is that only through an understanding of the role of institutions in society and in the process of social change do we get a full picture of the story that is history. He sets this out in his work *Institutions, Institutional Change and Economic Performance* (1990) in the following way: *'What difference does the explicit incorporation of institutional analysis make to the writing (and for that matter the reading) of economic history and of history in general? Writing history is constructing a coherent story of some facet of the human condition through time. Such a construction exists only in the human mind. We do not recreate the past; we construct stories about the past. But to be good history, the story must give a consistent, logical account and be constrained by the available evidence and the available theory. A brief answer to the question is that incorporating institutions into history allows us to tell a much better story than we otherwise could. The precliometric economic history actually was built around institutions, and in the hands of its most accomplished practitioners it managed to provide us with a picture of continuity and institutional change, that is, with an evolutionary story. But because it was built on bits and pieces of theory and statistics that had no overall structure, it did not lend itself to generalisations or analysis extending beyond the essentially ad hoc character of individual stories. The cliometric contribution was the application of a systematic body of theory – neoclassical theory – to history and the application of sophisticated, quantitative techniques to the specification and testing of historical models.'*

In 1993 Douglass C. North won the Nobel Prize for economics. The citation read 'for having renewed research in economic history by applying economic theory and quantitative methods in order to explain economic and institutional change.'

North continues to play a central role in new institutional economics.

Key works

Structure and Change in Economic History (1981)

Institutions, Institutional Change and Economic Performance (1990)

Institutions

North (1990) defines institutions as *'the rules of the game in a society or, more formally, as the humanly devised constraints that shape human interaction.'* Importantly, in relation to the economic sphere he says that institutions *'structure incentives in human exchange, whether political, social, or economic.'*

Institutional change plays a major part in shaping the evolution of society over time.

Institutions and economic performance

North is particularly interested in the way that institutions affect economic performance, particularly poor economic performance over time. In his book *Structure and Change* (1981), he abandoned the idea that institutions are efficient and set out to *'explain why inefficient rules would tend to exist and be perpetuated'*. North was interested in political processes that would lead to inefficient institutions.

Key institutions in a capitalist society

North identifies the key institutions of a capitalist society as comprising the market, the firm and supply (or relational) contracting.

The dynamic economy

North is critical of economic theory which assumes that society and the economy is static, and remains in the same state from one period to the next. As an economic historian he is all too aware that as time moves on the economy is subject to dynamic change. Economic theory therefore needs to keep abreast of changes in the real world, rather than working on the basis that a set of assumptions can continue to be applied.

He writes that *'If I say the world is ergodic, I mean that it has a stable underlying structure, such that we can develop theory that can be applied time after time, consistently. It is very important to understand that the world with which we are concerned is continually changing, is continually novel. This does not mean that there are not ergodic aspects of the world. But we cannot develop theory that can be used over and over again and over time. For an enormous number of issues that are important to us, the world is one of novelty and change, it does not repeat itself'* (North 1990).

And again, speaking about the modern phenomena of globalisation he states: *'The systems in which we are interested reside in a world of continuous change, in many dimensions – not only in terms of physical change but also change in the social structure and behaviour of human beings. Furthermore, to make our lives even more difficult, all the theory we have in economics, at least all of the theory that is well developed is static theory. However, all of the important issues with which we are interested here concern a dynamic world, one of continuous change'* (North 1995).

Transformation costs and transaction costs

North (1995) makes an important distinction between what he refers to as 'transformation costs' which are the traditional economists costs involved in transforming raw materials to finished products; and 'transaction costs' – which are *'the costs of specifying what is being exchanged and enforcing the subsequent agreement'*.

He notes that a weakness in traditional economic thinking is that transaction costs are ignored, yet they can make up a significant component of total costs. If these transaction costs can be reduced within an economy this will lead to a much more efficient system.

North sees property rights as an important means of reducing transaction costs because they provide a system of ownership, enforcement and adjudicating disputes that encourages increased transactions (because of lower costs), leading to greater specialisation within society.

The two elements of transaction costs are enforcement costs and specification costs.

Enforcement costs relate to either (1) informal constraints and norms which tend to restrict exchange to a small group of participants in the exchange process – these costs tend to be low; or (2) formal legally enforced rights which are applicable to lots of individuals and organisations involved in economic exchange relationships. If there is a well-organised and firm set of enforcement relationships (both formal and informal), then this element of transaction costs will be low. For example, contrast a market economy where there are well-established regulations and laws about contracts and trading, and a well-established sense of fair play between buyers and sellers, and another market situation in which there is widespread corruption, bribery, suspicion and double dealing between traders and little legal enforcement. Clearly the first situation will involve lower transaction costs because individuals can enter into contracts without having to pay backhanders and fairly certain that their contracts will be met.

'When we compare the cost of transacting in a Third World country with that in an advanced industrial economy, the costs per exchange in the former are much greater – sometimes no exchange occurs because costs are so high. The institutional structure in the Third World lacks the formal structure (and enforcement) that underpins efficient markets. However, frequently there will exist in Third World countries informal sectors (in effect underground economies) that attempt to provide a structure for exchange. Such structure comes at high costs, however, because the lack of formal property right safeguards restricts activity to personalised exchange systems that can provide self-enforcing types of contracts' (North 1990).

Specification costs are more difficult to pin down – involving costs of measuring what is being exchanged. Specification costs can be reduced by lowering the cost of measuring what is being exchanged, for example by creating rigorous independent standards for measuring the quality of goods that are exchanged. If buyers and sellers can easily check that goods being exchanged are of a particular quality then this takes away the cost of detailed measuring. For example, when the government or industries create independent quality standards, such as British Standards, then these can be used as accepted specifications. This is particularly important in a world in which changes in technology affect quality standards on a regular basis. Firms invest in new technology, for example in metal production, if they yield improved profits from doing so. In an ideal world buyers will be able to identify these improvements in quality. If it is easy and cheap to show that quality has improved then this will provide an important cost reduction for both buyers and sellers.

Creating efficient institutions

North uses a range of case examples to support his assertion that institutions determine the performance of economies. He then goes on to ask the question 'what creates effective institutions?' He argues that informal constraints and the transaction costs inherent in political processes make an important contribution. Informal constraints include 'effective traditions of hard work, honesty and integrity' which lower the costs of transacting and make possible complex productive exchange.

Because in the modern world information costs are low and ideas are easily spread, it becomes increasingly likely that economic actors will be inclined to adapt these traditions because it becomes increasingly apparent that they lower costs. Politicians are increasingly likely to implement reforms involving these institutional changes because of the increased availability of information that these changes enable economies to grow more rapidly.

North (1990) cites the example of post-Communist Eastern European societies as ones in which appropriate institutional changes can lead to improved economic performance. He states '*Clearly the existence of relatively productive institutions somewhere in the world and low-cost information about the resultant performance characteristics of those institutions is a powerful incentive to change for poorly performing economies. That appears to be the case in the striking changes in Eastern European societies in 1989*'.

The role of the state

Enforcement is required to ensure that contracts that are made in society are kept. There are three levels of enforcement of contracts and other social obligations:

- First party enforcement means there is self-enforcement: I generally abide by the standards set in society because I would be ashamed to give offence.
- Second party enforcement is by retaliation: I avoid harming someone else's interest because they may retaliate.
- Third party enforcement is wider and includes the threat of public loss of face, and more importantly enforcement by law officers and the law courts.

In cases where contract compliance is not self-enforcing there is a need for a third party to carry out the enforcement. This is typically the role of the state. However, there is a problem in making sure that the enforcers do not act in their own interest rather than impartially enforcing the contract. Such enforcement involves clarifying the terms of the contract and acting as adjudicator as to whether the terms have been violated. Clearly the state or other enforcement agency will require resources to carry out this function. There is a danger that the claims of the enforcer may become inflated, adding to costs within the economy. North (1990) states the dilemma of having an over inflated state – '*You cannot live without a State and you cannot live with a State!*'

North shows that in market terms, the larger the economy, the greater the need for governmental and intergovernmental enforcement. Hence the role of institutions like the World Trade Organisation, the World Bank, and the International Monetary Fund.

In North's view, one of the major reasons we do not have a truly global economy is that this would require a global government. There would have to be enforcement mechanisms that could be applied internationally (which would involve giving greater powers than exist at present to inter-governmental bodies such as the United Nations).

Conclusion

Institutional economics provides an important extra dimension in enabling us to understand how economies function, and how economic decisions are made. Douglass North has combined economic theory with economic history to give us a better picture of how change takes place over time, and gives us a more incisive approach to developing an understanding of why some societies are more effective at managing productive change. His work poses as many questions as answers but succeeds in forcing us to take a context-based view of economic development, as well as giving us a much better understanding of the nature of costs in the economy.

 **Further Reading**

DAVIS, L.E. AND NORTH, D.C. (1971) *Institutional change and American economic growth.* Cambridge University Press.

DUGGER, W. (1995) Douglass C. North's new institutionalism. *Journal of Economic Issues,* 29 (2), 453–466.

NORTH, D.C. (1961) *The economic growth of the United States from 1790 to 1860.* Prentice Hall.

NORTH, D. (1981) *Structure and change in economic history.* Norton.

NORTH, D. (1990) *Institutions, institutional change and economic performance.* Cambridge University Press.

NORTH, D. (1995) Douglass C. North (autobiographical sketch), in W. Breit and R. Spencer (eds.) *Lives of the laureates: thirteen Nobel economists.* MIT Press.

NORTH, D. AND THOMAS, R. (1973) *The rise of the western world: a new economic history.* Cambridge University Press.

VANDENBERG, P. (2002) North's institutionalism and the prospect of combining theoretical approaches. *Cambridge Journal of Economics,* 26, 217–235.

David Pearce

(1941–)

D AVID PEARCE IS CURRENTLY PROFESSOR IN ENVIRONMENTAL ECONOMICS AT University College London. His work in the field of environmental economics came to play a prominent part in starting to shape public policy on the environment from the 1980s onwards. Today he continues to research into and to refine methods for valuing the environment, providing advice and carrying out research on environmental valuation in several countries. Another key element of his work involves identifying and explaining ways in which the market can place more value on the environment, for example through the imposition of taxes on activities that are harmful to the environment.

A major problem for ecology as a science and our environment is that many economic decisions do not take account of the value of nature. When we consume a good we usually ignore the environmental costs that are incurred in our buying decision. The purchaser of a litre of petrol is concerned with how cheaply they can purchase that litre. Rarely do they take into consideration the environmental damage, or damage to children's health caused by driving. The reality is that we don't pay the full price of the damage that we cause – we pay a fraction of this cost. The government is reluctant to make us pay the full cost because they are frightened of losing votes (as witnessed by the speed with which governments across Europe caved in to the fuel blockades in September 2000).

The idea that economic activity can have wider implications for society than the immediate activity itself was articulated by Arthur C. Pigou (1877–1959). Pigou was the Cambridge economist who was the successor of Alfred Marshall and the teacher of John Maynard Keynes. Pigou showed that social costs exceeded private costs in a number of situations; for example, the factory whose operation imposed costs upon a neighbourhood in the form of pollution, and the off-licence whose customers might need the attention of a larger police force. Pigou alerts us to the fact that in identifying situations that maximise welfare for the whole community (or on a larger scale to all global citizens) we need to take into account social costs and benefits rather than just private ones. Where the marginal net benefits (marginal social benefits – marginal private benefits) of a given activity are greater than marginal net costs (marginal social costs – marginal private costs) there is a strong case for subsidising that activity. In the reverse case where marginal net costs are higher than marginal net benefits there is a strong case for taxing the activity up to the point where mnc = mnb.

It is possible that many people don't recognise the link between having more consumer goods and having fewer environmental 'goods'.

At the heart of the tension between economic growth and environmental sustainability lies the problem of the over-use and lack of foresight that we frequently experience in the use of scarce resources.

The classic representation of this problem was set out in an article by G. Hardin (1997) ('The Tragedy of the Commons') in the mid 1970s. Hardin used the example of a piece of common land for which villagers have open access. The land is able to provide for the needs of herdsmen who graze their lands on the commons. However, there comes a point at which eventually there are too many people using the land and everyone suffers. One more person uses the land, and beyond this point the land can provide for no-one. This is a situation with which we are increasingly becoming familiar in modern society – for example, in the depletion of fish stocks (e.g. cod) in common fishing grounds.

In recent years serious attempts have been made by economists to build environmental considerations into the market mechanism. Some of the best written work in this field has appeared in a series of books or Blueprints starting with Blueprint 1 – 'Blueprint for a green economy' produced by a team of researchers working with David Pearce – which has had a major influence on UK and international environmental policy. While Blueprint 1 concentrated on the UK economy, Blueprint 2 applied the ideas to world environment problems.

Pearce and his co-writers have set out that a major policy objective should be to create sustainable development, before it is too late. However, Pearce recognises the difficulty in achieving sustainable development because 'sustainability' is such a value driven term – it can mean almost anything you want it to mean.

One of the best-known definitions of sustainable development was that set out by the World Commission on the Environment (1987) – it involves '. . . *development that meets the needs of the present generation without compromising the ability of future generations to meet their own needs.*'

This is all very well but it does not set out a clear agenda as to how sustainability will be achieved. Pearce's work goes some way to providing a set of techniques for moving towards sustainability.

Development is generally seen as something that is positive. It means being better off tomorrow than we are today. But what exactly is development? Measures such as GNP (Gross National Product) indicate the living standard of people measured in terms of quantities of goods that can be purchased in a given time period, but there is a significant difference between the terms 'standard of living' and the 'quality of life'.

Pearce suggests that sustainable development involves enhancing both the standard of living and the quality of life. The value of the environment is an important part of this quality of life.

Pearce and his team therefore suggests that in moving forward we need to consider:

- the environment
- the future and
- equity, fairness.

Pearce uses the term 'futurity' to refer to the principle of taking a long-term view of things. If one generation leaves the next with less wealth than it inherited then it has made the future worse off.

Pearce's work is primarily concerned with placing a value on environmental assets, and identifying ways of making sure that fairer prices are paid for the environment through such means as environmental taxes.

Pearce's work has been invaluable because it has informed a variety of policy tools and techniques which can be applied to place more value on the environment. Pearce has additionally been instrumental in creating networks of environmental economists who share their ideas and thus act as a pressure group for change.

While a number of the practical implications of environmental valuation are controversial, valuation and environmental pricing techniques have helped to inform public policy and provide decision-makers with evidence and results enabling them to make decisions that have favoured the environment.

Methodology

THE MOST IMPORTANT TECHNIQUE THAT PEARCE USES IS NOT A NEW ONE (IT HAS BEEN around for 30 years or more), but it is one that is increasingly being improved over time. It is the most widely used approach and involves interviewing and using questionnaires in a form of market research. In basically the same way that you would use market research to find out whether people are in favour of a potentially new type of chocolate bar – showing them what it looks like, providing them details about it, etc. – you use essentially the same approach to ask people about how much value they would place on an environmental asset (e.g. by showing them pictures and other information about the environmental asset and questioning the research subjects about the values they would place on the environmental resource).

One approach to this research is to ask the subjects of a questionnaire how much they would be willing to pay for the preservation of the asset, or by asking them to rate alternatives for conservation.

This survey approach is a powerful technique because:

1. It provides you with information where no or little information was previously available, and

2. It enables you to outline values that reflect a whole range of motives for putting a value on the environment. There are hundreds of different motives for valuing the environment – people's concern for their children, for animals, for planet earth, for the future. Questioning techniques enable you to get at these motives.

Of course, the problem of using this technique is that effective survey techniques cost about £30,000 (2002 prices) to construct, deliver and analyse. More extensive surveys are a lot more expensive. This is why there has not been enough work carried out in this area although it is an approach that Pearce encourages his graduate students to get involved in as part of their dissertations.

Pearce describes himself as an unreconstructed utilitarian, which means he has no difficulty with approaches like cost–benefit analysis. He states that while this perspective provides the intellectual foundation, in the real world over 90 per cent of decisions are made without calculating the gains and losses. He goes on to say that: *'The word "cost" often does not appear in policy assessments (e.g. risk appraisals). So while there is nothing sophisticated in what I do, it still comes as a surprise to policy makers. I also have a deep sense of the right of individuals to determine policy, however poorly informed or irrational we may be. I dislike "experts" and illiberal elites who tell others what they should want. My belief is consistent with the demise of the human race from self-destruction, but that's better than the 1984 scenario implicit in so much environmental "thought". Sadly, environment is pervaded by this kind of thing and by political correctness so I have to admit that the driving force behind some of what I do is to kick out at these illiberal tendencies. That has landed me in trouble several times, but so it goes again.'*

D AVID PEARCE WAS BORN IN HARROW. A MAJOR FORMATIVE INFLUENCE DURING HIS schooldays at Harrow Weald County Grammar School was his history and economics teacher Merlyn Rees (now Lord Merlyn Rees). Rees encouraged Pearce to appreciate learning, and to question everything, and to have a strong social conscience. At the time Rees was the Labour candidate for Harrow East, and was later to become an influential Labour Minister (following Hugh Gaitskell into his seat in Leeds). Many of the students that Rees taught at Harrow Weald (including Pearce) came from homes where there were no books or culture of learning. Rees managed to persuade Pearce's mother (by some subterfuge) to let Pearce stay on at school, and he succeeded in winning a place at Oxford University to read politics, philosophy and economics. He enjoyed philosophy the most, and was particularly interested in the idea of 'existentialism' taught by Mary Warnock (Baroness Warnock). After graduating from Oxford he went on to the London School of Economics to do a PhD in economic history. He then took up his first teaching post in the new economics department at Lancaster University. He met his wife there, and they moved down to Southampton in 1967. They both shared a love of nature and animals (his wedding present to his wife was two Siamese cats).

David Pearce first became interested in environmental economics in the 1960s after becoming fascinated by literature from the United States which for the first time was making clear connections between 'economic growth' and 'ecological degradation'. Concerned academics in the United States, including Kenneth Boulding, were pointing to a clear connection between the management of economic systems and the levels of environmental degradation. It was during this period that Pearce began to carry out his first studies in the field of environmental economics. He carried out research into areas like the Morecambe Bay Barrage (which was never built) which had an environmental overtone. He first published an article about the environment in the late 1960s and was instrumental in creating a society of environmental economists made up of UK academics – at the time it had six members. Today, the European Environmental Economics Association has thousands of members. The early 1970s saw the 'first environmental revolution': the Club of Rome published their influential book *The Limits to Growth*, using computer modelling to show that there were a number of changes taking place – rising population, use of non-renewable resources, creation of pollution etc. – which were pushing us over the precipice of the limits to growth. Pearce and a number of UK academics established a cross-university ESRC-funded environmental study group.

In 1974 he moved to Leicester to run a research group, with much of the work being on waste and recycling. In 1977 he moved to Aberdeen, the incentive being a professorship, but there were natural links between oil, gas and the environment, and from then on all of his work related to these issues. He travelled extensively, working for various governments and the World Bank, carrying out research and giving guidance on policy-making in the Far East, Central America, the Carribean, and Africa.

In 1983 he moved to University College London and it was here that he was to carry out his most important work, researching and championing the series of books – Blueprints – for a green economy. Pearce spent three years as personal advisor to the Conservative Ministers for the Environment, Chris Patten and later Michael Heseltine.

Pearce states that (2002) '*Patten had an interest in environment. Heseltine had none and, in any event, did not seek advice. They were totally hectic years, racing round London, trying to teach and do research but spending most of my time getting the message across. The message was mine and to be fair to the politicians they rarely interfered: I was a free agent so long as I did not go "off message" too much. I'm glad I did it, but I would never do it again, even if I could. I lost count of the TV, radio, newspaper interviews but at the end of the day I was like a parrot, repeating the message in 20 different ways. I guess if there was an achievement it was to have changed the language in government so that obscure phrases took on real meaning*: polluter pays, environmental taxes, tradable permits, resource accounting, etc.'

The irony was that although David Pearce had probably done more than anyone to develop approaches to thinking and then taking practical steps for the environment, he never even got a 'thank you' from the Thatcher or the Major governments. It was left to the Labour government to nominate him for an OBE in 2000 for services to sustainable development (Pearce has been critical of both the Conservatives' and new Labour's commitment to environmental responsibility). Pearce (2002) argues that '*The bottom line is that no government has shown environmental commitment – they do not believe it generates votes and perhaps the public has given them no reason to doubt their view.*' Pearce believes that academics have failed to effectively champion the cause of the environment because they are too wrapped up in being academics, and that within the economic profession there is an ignorance of institutions and real world policy.

Pearce sets out that his interest in the environment is based on his own values and beliefs as well as the clear evidence that current growth patterns are unsustainable. He likes animals and nature and believes that we should respect and seek to enhance the natural environment.

Reflecting on his work Pearce (2002) has commented that '*I would say that my work has led me to be more concerned than ever for the environment and that my work since the 1960's has made me more confirmed than ever in my belief that valuation approaches are appropriate. I believe that we still have an enormous amount of work to do in seeking to convince people of the importance of the environment. For example, in some areas of the world where grasslands are being destroyed it is important to show governments and influential decision makers how destroying grasslands has a knock-on effect – perhaps forcing people to leave these areas, creating overpopulation in the cities, leading to sanitation and other public health problems, overcrowding, unemployment and other undesirable social effects.'*

Key works

Blueprint for a Green Economy (with A. Markandya and E. Barbier, 1989)

Blueprint 2: Greening the World Economy (1991)

Blueprint 3: Measuring Sustainable Development (1993)

Blueprint for a Sustainable Economy (with E. Barbier, 2000)

Sustainability

Pearce's work is primarily concerned with identifying objectives for sustainability and a set of techniques for valuing the environment in order to make informed judgements. Typically the environment has been exploited in an unsustainable way, because it has been treated as a free resource in economic decision-making. However, it cannot continue to be treated in this way because (a) it is wrong in itself to abuse nature in this way; (b) we are posing a threat to our own survival as a species by harming the environment.

We therefore need to find ways of valuing the environment so that we can achieve sustainable development. Of course, it is inevitable that mankind may continue to trade off bits of nature, for artificial resources. However, it is important that in making these trade-offs that the trader is clear about the true costs involved. The role of the environmental economist is to alert us to the real costs involved.

Opportunity cost in environmental decision making

Pearce sees opportunity cost as being one of the most fundamental of all economic concepts, particularly in relation to the environment. We live in a finite world so that trade-offs are continually being made between the use of resources for one purpose or for another. Pearce cites the example that if protestors want to see fuel taxes reduced then they will have to give up something else. It is false logic to assume that we can keep the environment intact and experience the sort of economic growth that we have become accustomed to.

Different forms of capital

Pearce argues that traditional arguments about growth have focused on man-made capital as a store of wealth – machines, factories, plant etc. The process of industrialisation focused on expanding the capital base of the nation. However, this type of growth ignores other forms of capital.

Pearce identifies other forms of capital that are involved in sustainable development. He draws a distinction between:

- Km – man-made capital, as described above.
- Kh – human capital, consisting of capital that exists within people in terms of their skills, knowledge and abilities. Human capital is improved over time by the process of education and training.
- Kn – natural capital, which consists of environmental resources: clean rivers and oceans, animal and plant life, ecological systems. This resource base can be protected by conservation and improved by removing pollution and other impairments to nature.
- Ks – social capital, which is made up of the relationships that develop over time between members of a community such as close family bonds, good citizenship, caring for others etc.

The problem is that we have tended to concentrate on Km at the expense of other forms of capital. Pearce argues that to think sustainably we need to consider all of the four forms of capital and seek to improve them simultaneously.

The constant or rising capital rule

Pearce (2002) argues that to achieve sustainability we need to consider the issue of futurity and to make sure that we pass on to the next generation at least as much capital as we have inherited. He writes: *'The condition for sustainable development is that each generation should leave the next generation a stock of capital assets no less than the stock it has. That rule ensures that the next generation has the capacity to generate the same, or more, well-being than the previous generation. It may make a mess of it, of course, but at least the first generation has fulfilled its obligation by adopting this rule. This is the so-called constant capital rule (it should be constant or rising capital rule, but this is a bit unwieldy).'*

Weak and strong sustainability

Pearce alerts us to the issue of a difference between weak and strong sustainability. A weak sustainability position would allow a trade-off between the different types of capital, provided the total of capital ($Km + Kh + Kn + Ks$) is not reduced. In contrast, a strong sustainability view would insist that none of these types of capital could be reduced over time. The view that is most commonly associated with strong sustainability is that of strong environmental sustainability, that is, that Kn should not be eroded over time.

Pearce argues that currently there is no clear resolution of the issue of strong or weak sustainability. Some people argue that man has already taken too weak a view and that the environment is being degraded too far. In contrast, those who favour 'economic growth' point to the fact that human well-being has often come from destroying environmental assets.

Pearce (2002) is particularly concerned about the impact of population growth on sustainability. He states that when we look at the different types of capital we should do so in terms of capital per head. He points out that *'Somehow the world will have to cope with at least 50% more people in the next 100 years, and maybe 100% or more.'* This makes the constant capital criteria much harder to achieve when looked at in terms of capital per head. However, it is possible to think positively that new technologies can limit our destruction of natural capital. For example, today we use the term 'weightlessness' to describe the way in which components and products themselves are much lighter because of new materials and technologies being employed in production.

Measuring sustainability

In 1993 Pearce and Atkinson showed how to measure 'sustainability' through the notion of 'genuine savings'. This has subsequently led to the World Bank adopting the notion and issuing annual estimates of genuine saving. In essence, the process can be described in a simple way: savings must exceed depreciation on *all* assets for any one to be called sustainable. Depreciation takes place on man-made capital, environmental capital and social capital. In contrast, human capital tends to appreciate.

The rule therefore is that:

$S + A$ (human) $> D$ (man-made) $+ D$ (environmental) $+ D$ (social)

where S denotes saving; A, appreciation; and D, depreciation.

(It should be noted that attempts to measure social capital are still in their infancy).

Critical natural capital

Pearce introduces the notion of critical natural capital, which if destroyed could lead to highly damaging consequences for the planet, for example the ozone layer. In terms of trade-offs and welfare economics it is clear that no quantity of man-made capital could possibly compensate for this loss. Given this concern it would seem that even those in favour of weak sustainability would not allow any erosion in 'critical natural capital'. The problem is, however, that the market economy does not offer any safeguards or mechanisms for protecting this capital – indicating the importance of intergovernmental and governmental interference in the market place. However, it might be argued that deciding what elements of natural capital are critical is open to value judgment although it is clearly an area that scientists might be able to provide strong supporting evidence in favour of particular natural assets.

Equity

Pearce believes that another important dimension of sustainability is that of equity or fairness. He suggests that we need to tackle the issue of fairness between one generation and another (intergenerational equity) and between people living on the planet at the same time (intragenerational equity). If we fail to tackle the issue of equity we will never get agreement about how to tackle the 'tragedy of the commons'. If, for example, the United States says that because we are a developed nation we deserve to graze 100 sheep on the common land and then suggests that a developing country should not increase the number of sheep it has from one to two then this will clearly seem unjust.

Making trade-offs

While Pearce is in favour of maintaining and improving all forms of capital he realises that trade-offs sometimes have to be made. The problem is that these trade-offs are made on the basis of inappropriate valuations. For example, because the environment is not being valued at its true worth it is often being sacrificed because decision makers are not being made to pay a realistic price to use up environmental resources. Pearce is therefore in favour of valuation of environmental resources so that informed choices can be made.

Valuing the environment

Much of Pearce's work has therefore been concerned with developing ways of giving a money value to the environment. This then enables decisions to be made which do not ignore the environment. For example, if we can accurately place a value on an environmental resource, for example an area of natural beauty, then it is possible to calculate the impact of spoiling that resource, for example by building a motorway across it.

Pearce is in favour of using monetisation (i.e. placing money values) as a means of measuring environmental benefits and for measuring the cost of destroying environmental assets. He believes in monetisation because this provides a common measuring rod that people are familiar with. Money values are also readily understood by planners and other decision-makers.

Pearce (2002) argues that if we can place monetary values on the environment then these values can be used:

'1. *To reflect the strength of support for an environmental asset (e.g. by asking people how much they would be willing to pay to protect an environmental asset such as the Blue Whale, or a beauty spot).*

2. *Provided the support in monetary terms is big enough – then this presents a strong case for preserving environmental quality.*'

Pearce (2002) shows how and why values can be placed on environmental assets in the following way: *'Take the case of a "slash and burn agriculturalist" perhaps in a rainforest area. The agriculturalist knows that by burning part of the forest then he or she is able to grow cash crops for a money value. The agriculturalist may place little value on the natural resources of the forest – perhaps they might lose some natural foods growing in the forest and some other useful products, but he or she places less value on those than what they could receive from the potential cash crop. The rational decision for the agriculturalist seems to be to slash and burn and then to plant and harvest.*

However, the environmental economist will take a broader view. For example, they can see that burning the trees down will release carbon dioxide with a potentially harmful effect on the planet. The environmental economist therefore needs to show and measure the value of keeping the carbon stored in the trees. The agriculturalist can be compensated to the extent of this value for preserving the forest land. The agriculturalist can then be offered an incentive for not setting fire to the trees.

The task of environmental economics is therefore:

1. To find out what an environmental resource is worth, and

2. To provide a cash flow in this case to the farmer – providing an incentive so that he or she does not have to set fire to the forest land.'

Using survey techniques

Pearce believes that using survey techniques is the most useful way of placing values on the environment. Although this is not a new approach (having been around for 30 years or more) it is one that is being continually improved over time.

He explains (2002) that: 'It is the most widely used approach and involves interviewing and using questionnaires in a form of market research. In basically the same way that you would use market research to find out whether people are in favour of a potentially new type of chocolate bar – showing them what it looks like, providing them with details about it, etc, you use essentially the same approach to ask people about how much value they would place on an environmental asset (e.g. by showing them pictures and other information about environmental assets and questioning the research subjects about the values they would place on the environmental resource).

One approach to this research is to ask the subjects of a questionnaire how much they would be Willing to Pay for the preservation of the asset, or by asking them to rate alternatives for conservation.

This survey approach is a powerful technique because:

1. It provides you with information where no or little information was previously available, and

2. It enables you to outline values that reflect a whole range of motives for putting a value on the environment. There are hundreds of different motives for valuing the environment – people's concern for their children, for animals, for planet earth, for the future. Questioning techniques enable you to get at these motives.

Of course, the problem of using this technique is that effective survey techniques cost hundreds of thousands of pounds to construct, deliver and analyse. This is why there has not been enough work carried out in this area.

. . . Critics argue that it is more difficult to place money values on the environment than you can with putting prices on tins of corned beef or baked beans on supermarket shelves. However, it is essential to place a value on the environment if it is to be treated seriously.'

The Willingness to Pay approach lies at the heart of monetary valuation techniques. For example, by calculating how much the public would be willing to pay to preserve an area of natural beauty it becomes possible to identify the appropriate level of subsidy that governments should put into conserving the area. The government can then adjust its taxation policies to account for how much people are 'Willing to Pay' for the environment.

Paying for harm to the environment

As well as examining the benefits of preserving the environment, Pearce has also looked at ways of dealing with the costs of business and consumer activity. By calculating the negative impacts of activities such as transport, waste discharge and pollution it is possible to set taxes which penalise individuals and organisations for the harm they do to the environment. For example, the landfill tax in this country is based on the costs of having to bury waste. Because this tax has been progressively raised in this country businesses are having to look at alternative ways of doing their business, for example using less wasteful materials, using more environmentally friendly processes, creating less waste, recycling more of their wastes. In a similar way the climate levy tax proposed by Pearce and his colleagues involves placing taxes on the use of energy to discourage the use of energy in production and in domestic consumption.

Total economic value

In examining any economic activity that affects the environment, Pearce argues that we need to carry out a cost–benefit analysis. To proceed with an activity or plan, benefits should exceed costs.

Pearce (2002) identifies a number of benefits involved in any activity.

At one level there are 'user values'. An individual who walks in the Yorkshire Dales benefits directly from the use they make of this environmental asset. '*An angler, wildfowl hunger, fell walker, ornithologist, all use the natural environment and derive use from it.*'

In addition there are 'option values': although I have not recently walked in the Yorkshire Dales I may want to take up this option in the future and would feel a real sense of loss if this opportunity was taken away from me.

There is another type of environmental value referred to by Pearce as 'existence values'. This is where there is an environmental asset that I am not currently enjoying, and realise that I am never likely to enjoy, for example seeing a blue whale in its natural environment. However, I know that this species is out there enjoying nature, and I am willing to pay for it to continue to enjoy this pleasure.

In Pearce's view we therefore need to calculate all of these values, in making a total economic valuation, that is:

Total economic value = actual use value + option value + existence value

In making decisions about what we do with environmental assets we therefore need to have a full appreciation of the value of these assets. If we want to give up some of them we are better placed to do so because at least we know what they are worth.

An interdisciplinary approach to environmental economics

David Pearce and Edward Barbier (2000) argue that ecological economics will only provide meaningful findings and policy suggestions if studies are carried out in an interdisciplinary way with others who are concerned with the environment – economists, ecologists, and other scientists who can learn from each other's methods and approaches.

The study of environmental economics is of little use simply as a research exercise: *'the justification for pursuing interdisciplinary collaboration must be its policy relevance – it must pass a reality test that requires us to say what we would do that we do not already do or know about . . . For each policy option, the ideal ecological economic model should be able to trace through the various economic-environmental linkages to determine the consequences for human welfare associated with that option'* (Pearce, 2002).

Ecological and economic externalities

A key benefit of interdisciplinary collaboration is that it enables environmental economists to develop important insights into key ecological issues that have previously been overlooked. This is particularly important in developing an understanding of ecosystems which ecobiologists define as *'biological communities that interact with their non-living or abiotic environment'* (Beeby 1993). By working with ecologists to develop a fuller understanding of ecological relationships, environmental economists are better placed to understand the full nature of externalities (social costs and benefits) resulting from economic activities.

Pearce is in favour of identifying 'safe minimum standards', for example in preserving a minimum viable population of various species and the required supporting habitats. This approach serves to limit the effect of biodiversity decline, and is the best way of making sure that future generations inherit at least the same level of biodiversity as that available to current generations.

Pearce goes on to argue that it is essential to establish thresholds over which it would not be acceptable to allow biodiversity decline. He sees the principal instruments for protecting these thresholds as including market-based (e.g. taxes/subsidies) and regulatory instruments. He says that we must not rule out a major environmental catastrophe if we fail to protect these thresholds.

The precautionary principle

Pearce sees the 'precautionary principle' as being a sound basis for all environmental policy-making and shows that this has increasingly underpinned international agreements such as the Earth Summit, and EU policy. The precautionary principle asserts that there *'is a premium on a cautious and conservative approach to human interventions in the natural environment where our understanding of the likely consequences of the intervention is limited, and there are threats of serious or irreversible damage to natural systems and processes'* (Pearce, 2002). In such cases the burden of scientific evidence should rest on those who want to disrupt the environment that their actions will not pose a threat.

Conclusion

The work of Pearce and other environmental economists has been highly influential in creating an intellectual case for government policy-making in relation to the environment. It has led to increasing values being placed on environmental assets in the form of subsidies to areas of natural beauty, wilderness areas, etc. and to taxes and other disincentives being placed on the environmental costs of business and consumer activity such as the landfill tax, the climate change levy and, possibly in future, a pesticides tax. Environmental economics provides a persuasive case particularly as it talks in a language which policy-makers find easy to understand – that of monetary values.

Further Reading

ATKINSON, G. ET AL. (1997) *Measuring sustainable development*. Edward Elgar.

BEEBY, A. (1993) *Applied ecology*. Chapman and Hall.

HARDIN, G. AND BADEN, J. (1977) *Managing of the commons*. W.H. Freeman.

KEMPTON, A. (2001) An interview with Professor David Pearce. *General Studies Review*, Spring.

PEARCE, D. (1989) *Environmental policy benefits: monetary valuation*. Paris, OECD.

PEARCE, D. AND ATKINSON, G. (1993) *Blueprint 3: Measuring sustainable development*. Earthscan.

PEARCE, D. (1998) Sustainable Development, taking stock for the future. *Economic Review*, September.

PEARCE, D. (2000) *Blueprint for a sustainable economy*. Earthscan.

PEARCE, D. (2002) Interview by R. Dransfield.

PEARCE, D. (ed.) (1991) *Blueprint 2: Greening the world economy*. Earthscan.

PEARCE, D. AND BARBIER, E. (2000) *Blueprint for a sustainable economy*. Earthscan.

PEARCE, D., MARKANDYA, A. AND BARBIER, E. (1989) *Blueprint for a green economy*. Earthscan.

PEARCE, D. AND MORAN, D. (1994) *The economic value of biodiversity*. Earthscan.

SPIEGEL, H. (1971) *The growth of economic thought*. Prentice Hall, ch. 24.

WORLD COMMISSION ON ENVIRONMENT AND DEVELOPMENT. (1987) *Our Common Future*. Oxford University Press.

Amartya Sen

(1933–)

IN 1998, AMARTYA SEN WON WHAT WAS CONSIDERED BY MANY AS A LONG OVERDUE
Nobel Prize, for his contribution to the field of economics. For several years prior to
this, Sen had won straw poles among fellow economists. He has made important
contributions particularly in welfare economics, where his early interests included
social choice theory. More recently, he has focused his attention on social problems
such as poverty, famine and the role of women in the development process. His book
on the subject of *Development as Freedom* has already received the status of a 'classic'
work in economics. The wide spectrum of study undertaken demonstrates both Sen's
broad interest in social issues and his eclectic academic background. The Nobel jury
emphasised this point as they accredited the award (1998b) to *'several key contributions to the research on fundamental problems in welfare economics, ranging from
axiomatic theory of social choice to definitions of welfare and poverty indexes, to empirical studies of famine.'*

The ethical leaning found in much of Sen's work has helped to improve the public's
perception of economists and the study of economics – a field often regarded to be
bereft of morals. Indeed, Robert Solow described him as 'a conscience of our profession'.

Deirdre McClosky reiterates this in an article titled 'The Career Courage of Amartya
Sen' (2000), in which she argues that his major contribution goes beyond his technical
expertise as an economist, his real importance lies in the emphasis that he gives to
ethics in economic study. She states: *'Beginning with his little essay in the Journal of
Political Economy in 1970, "The Impossibility of a Paretian Liberal," he embarked coura-
geously on a program of reminding economists that we live in an ethical universe. We live
not in that best of all possible worlds . . . but a universe of good and evil, a universe . . .
under which human arrangements can have inefficient outcomes. People can starve in the
midst of plenty, and, Sen argued, in 1943 in his native Bengal, they did.'*

Methodology

DUE IN PART TO THE BROAD AREAS OF ECONOMICS IN WHICH SEN IS INTERESTED, HE
has no set methodology, rather he employs the method which appears to be most
appropriate for the situation in question.

One must remember that much of Sen's work has been a critique of the traditional orthodoxies in economics. Robin Hahnel (2002) sums up the strength of reasoning of his approach: 'In criticism he is meticulous and his technical virtuosity is everywhere compelling.' In the traditional sense of the term, Sen has no established methodological practice. If one is to extend the definition so that it encompasses Sen's undoubted systematic critical brilliance, a pattern to his work emerges. Sen himself admits to following a logical set of practices. When he believes that another person is mistaken it is not enough for him to be sure that he is correct in his own reasoning; instead he finds it necessary to answer the question of why the other person holds their particular view, by putting himself in the position of the other. This allows him to see things from their perspective to try to understand how a reasonable person could have thought that what they believed was correct. Until this subconsciously adversarial role has been fulfilled, Sen does not consider his work complete.

His standpoint concerning the use of mathematics in economics is neutral, a reflection of the numerous areas of the subject with which he has been involved. When discussing the usefulness of mathematics he states (2002) that he had 'found it very useful in some cases and in some forms, and in others no use at all.'

For Sen, mathematics has neither a positive or a negative status in economics, but should be used where and when it is useful. In his experience it has proved to be of great use in tackling some problems and of little or no use in others. He believes that one cannot take an a priori view as to what type or whether mathematics should be used, and that 'One has to cut the mathematical cloth according to the economic need rather than making the economic clothing fit a predetermined mathematical cloth.'

Biography

SEN STARTED HIS ACCEPTANCE SPEECH FOR THE NOBEL PRIZE (1998B) BY STATING 'I was born in a university campus and seem to have spent all my life on one campus or another.'

He was brought up in a family in which work and the role of teacher or academic was very natural. In his autobiography he maintains that while his subject of preference was not clear until his late teens, he always knew that he would be a professor. He does not regard academics to be far removed from experience in the real world. In his own words (2002): 'One does not have to be immediately practical to be practical.' He believes strongly that practical experience and wisdom involve interchange, the two processes feeding off each other. Indeed, many of the most relevant things to the real world have come from academia. The strong connection between reality and abstraction in Sen's thinking is mirrored in his work and values, much of which have been shaped by earlier experience.

During his teenage years, Sen changed his mind about his subject choice, first considering studying Sanskrit, maths and physics before deciding upon economics. An important consideration in making this decision was his interest in real world problems and their causes including poverty, hunger, and the seemingly mindless violence and rioting which he witnessed while growing up in India. While he enjoyed studying a range of subjects, he found it increasingly difficult to find time for them all. He settled on economics because it appealed to him to study a subject in which his professional training could be acquired at the same time as he was thinking about problems which moved him. He was also strongly influenced by student friends of his who were very interested in the subject. Studying economics also meant that his mathematics training would not be wasted.

Much of Sen's work is influenced heavily by experiences he had early on in his life. In his autobiography he tells the story of Kader Mia, a Muslim day labourer who was forced to take work in a predominantly Hindu area by his economic circumstances during a period of sectarian animosity between the two groups. Kader Mia was attacked and badly injured by a group of Hindus. Sen's father took the labourer to the hospital. At this early age, Sen was made aware that economic unfreedom may take other forms of freedom away from an individual. Sen also witnessed the effects of the Bengal famine in the 1940s, amid a surprisingly plentiful food supply. He also points to his growing up in India surrounded by both constant poverty and immense wealth as having a major impact on his belief system.

Sen gives credit to his background for the eclectic range of his work. He knew lots of people from different communities and religions while growing up, and was able to appreciate their diverse values and ways of living. He attempted to pool these sources together, until he felt he had assimilated some kind of 'universal logic'. His school, too, accepted students from a broad variety of backgrounds. Although it was a very anti-colonial, anti-British Raj school, it was nonetheless very international, taking students from Europe, America, Japan, China, Africa and Thailand as well as from India. In his own words 'the richness of the world was enjoyed in my school'.

In his personal life Sen has been remarkably fortunate. After initially completing a degree in India he went on to study economics at Trinity College, Cambridge and today is Master of the College. He has taught at a number of Indian universities, as well as at Harvard and Oxford. In a biographical note (1998b) he states that he chose to study at Trinity College *'after noticing in the handbook of Cambridge University, that three remarkable economists of very different political views rested there. The Marxist Maurice Dobb, and the conservative neo-classicist Dennis Robertson did joint seminars, and Trinity also had Piero Sraffa, a model of scepticism of nearly all the standard schools of thought.'*

Sen has been able to benefit from a rich diversity of personal experience in Bangladesh, India, America and Britain. In a recent lecture, given at Oxford (1998a), on the subject of reason and identity he recounted that *'Recently, when I was returning from a short trip abroad, the Immigration Officer at Heathrow, who examined my Indian passport, posed a philosophical question of some intricacy. Referring to my address, viz. Master's Lodge, Trinity College, Cambridge, he asked me whether the Master was a close friend of mine. This gave me pause since it compelled me, of course, to examine whether the binary relation of "being a friend of" can be taken to be reflexive, so that I could legitimately claim to be a friend of myself. On reflection, I came to the conclusion that I was a friend – indeed, a close friend (a view corroborated further by the fact that when I say silly things I can immediately see that, with friends like me, I don't need any enemies). Since all this took some time to resolve, the Immigration Officer wanted to know why exactly I hesitated: was there some impropriety involved in my being in Britain?'*

While 'all' of Sen's life has been spent on a university campus his biography confirms that he is greatly influenced by what is occurring in the real world. This is reflected in Sen's academic work, which acts as a form of bridge between the abstract and reality, between the 'cold rational textbook of economics and the world of moral action'.

Key works

'Rational Fools: A Critique of the Behavioural Foundations of Economic Theory' (1977)

Poverty and Famines: An Essay on Entitlement and Deprivation (1981)

'Gender and Cooperative Conflict' (1990)

On Economic Inequality (1997)

Development as Freedom (1999)

S EN BELIEVES THAT HIS MAIN CONTRIBUTION TO ECONOMICS WAS THE WORK HE DID AT Dhakar in the 1960s which gave prominence to welfare economics and helped to encourage others to take a greater interest in this field.

Social choice theory

Sen's work on social choice theory starts with a critique of traditional welfare theory. He did this by attacking the foundations upon which the whole theory is built, its assumptions, such as the notion of the 'rational economic man'. A famous example of this was his scathing criticism in 'Rational Fools' (1976), in which Sen attacked the assumption that people act purely out of self-interest. He parodies this view in the following way: *'"Where is the railway station?" He asks me. "There," I say pointing at the post office, "and would you please post this letter for me on the way?" "Yes," he says, determined to open the envelope and check whether it contains something valuable.'*

Sen (1977) argued that people can and often do act rationally by carrying out actions which do not maximise their own personal well-being, for example, when they show commitment to helping others. *'If the knowledge of torture of others makes you sick, it is a case of sympathy. If it does not make you feel personally worse off, but you think it is wrong and you are ready to do something to stop it, it is a case of commitment.'*

Traditional utilitarianism has always been concerned with the maximisation of welfare in society: 'the greatest happiness of the greatest number'. It is possible that this could be achieved by transferring resources (income, food supplies etc.) from the poor to the rich rather than the other way round. How do we know?

In the 1950s the economist and philosopher Kenneth Arrow had proposed a social-choice (or social-welfare function) based on voting mechanisms like those involved in political elections. Each voter has a preference for a political party enabling social choices to be made, in this case the election of a government. Arrow applies this approach to other social choices to examine ways in which individual members of society can make social decisions. He based his concept of social choice decision-making on a number of conditions, for example 'If everyone prefers A to B, then A should be chosen' (the Pareto principle) and 'No individual should be a dictator'. He then 'proved' that if all of a set of reasonable conditions was applied then there would be no social-welfare function that would satisfy all of them – hence 'the impossibility theorem'. As a result of Arrow's and other economists' work it appeared that welfare economics had little to offer to provide a justification for making policy changes to improve levels of social welfare. The 'impossibility theorem' suggested that there was no acceptable way to move from 'individual preferences' to 'social preferences'.

Sen, however, contested this by showing that it is possible to make at least partial comparisons in decision-making situations involving the welfare of groups in society. Partial comparisons lie between the extremes of full comparisons and no comparison.

No	Partial	Full
comparison	comparison	comparison

Sen cites the example of the satisfaction of Nero from the burning of Rome to be obviously smaller than the loss of welfare that this caused all the people that lost their lives in the fire.

Sen showed that weak forms of comparison (partial comparisons) when examined in an ordinal way (i.e. this is bigger than that) fit comfortably with Arrow's axioms (although Sen is also critical of some of the values involved in the axioms themselves).

Having shown that it is possible to make comparisons of well-being between individuals, Sen believes in the importance of finding more and more information to enable us to make better decisions about the improvement of social welfare. Sen (1998b) argues that '*quite often, rather limited levels of partial comparability will be adequate for making social decisions.*'

The approach that Sen prefers for judging improvement in individual welfare is that of '*judging individual advantage in terms of respective capabilities which a person has to live the way he or she has reason to value*'. The emphasis in this approach is on the freedoms that are made available to individuals rather than particular outcomes. Public policy should therefore concentrate on ensuring freedom to people – in this lies their advantage or disadvantage. Sen believes that using this approach provides the information for making reasoned social judgements. The more information we have about the nature and acquisition of freedom, therefore, the more we can contribute to human welfare.

In an autobiographical note Sen (1998b) states that after his early work on social choice theory his interests '*gradually shifted from the pure theory of social choice to more "practical problems"*'. However, Sen appreciates that he could not have made this step without first having confidence that the practice exercises that followed were 'foundationally secure'.

Having developed the theoretical underpinning for his work he set out (2002) to apply his reasoning to applied problems including: '*to assess poverty, to evaluate inequality,* to clarify *the nature of relative deprivation;* to develop *distribution-adjusted national income measures;* to clarify *the penalty of unemployment;* to analyse *violations of personal liberties and basic rights, and to* characterise *gender disparities and women's relative disadvantage.'*

Poverty and famines

Sen's work on famines contrasts with many conventional economic theories which insist that absolute food shortages cause famines. Instead, Sen sees famines to be the result of the functioning of the free market and the relationship between different groups within national and global economies. Arguing that famines can and often do occur in situations where adequate food is available, Sen highlights poverty inequality, and the extent of poor people's control of basic resources. He argues that government support and welfare creation alone are insufficient to avert famines and may even increase the possibility of them happening if they impact on the least well off members of society in such a way as to marginalize them and increase their vulnerability.

The famine experienced in Bengal during Sen's childhood had a profound effect upon his later work, most notably his contributions concerning famines. The 'common sense' approach to famines sees them as the consequence of natural disasters such as droughts or flooding which cause a fall in the level of agricultural production in a given region, resulting in starvation due to lack of food. Sen argues, however, that famines may occur where there has been no decline or even an increase in overall production and supply of food. During the famine in Bengal, which Sen witnessed at first hand in 1943, the area was enjoying an economic boom due to the stationing of British troops there during the Second World War. It also happened at a time when there had been no decline in food supplies. The theory behind this phenomenon was explained in Sen's 1981 book, *Poverty and Famines: An Essay on Entitlement and Deprivation.* In this work, Sen set out a new theory called the 'entitlement approach', to explain why famines occur. He started with the idea that each person has an endowment which they use to earn a bundle of commodities. The endowment commanded by each individual includes the resources they own and their labour power, while an individual's entitlement is the bundle of commodities which can be legitimately obtained using one's endowment. Sen examines the exchange relations that determine the bundle of goods an individual can obtain using their endowment in examining how a famine can occur while food production does not decline. To do this he notes how entitlements may change while endowments remain unaltered, often due to a change in the economic circumstances encountered. For example, if the price of food increases, but a person's income does not, then the quantity of food they can buy will be reduced. Sen warns of the risk of famine when economic growth disproportionately benefits one section of the population over others. He argues that the ability to exert a 'pull' on food is critical in a market economy. Where one group of people is much more affluent than another they exert a strong 'pull' on food as they are able to afford higher prices. As prices rise in response to this, groups that have not enjoyed a rise in their income are not able to exert as much 'pull' and thus can afford less food. This is what Sen witnessed in Bengal in 1943 where food prices rose to meet the increased demand from British forces in the region, while incomes among labourers, craftsmen and other groups in rural areas were unable to afford enough food. Although sufficient food was still being produced millions of people starved in a human tragedy which left an indelible mark on Sen's beliefs and work.

Sen also worked on the refinement of the way in which poverty and economic development are measured. The Sen poverty index gives greater weight to those households which are further beneath the poverty line than the Gini coefficient (a widely used statistical measuring approach). This addresses the problem encountered in standard measurement, namely that if income is transferred from households further below the poverty line to those nearer the poverty line, equality within society is seen to rise. Sen also contributed to the development of the Human Development Index (HDI) an index of development which includes a number of factors (e.g. related to health and education) in addition to the traditional 'income per capita' variable included in most previous indexes.

The role of women in development

Sen was among the first to become attuned to the essential role played by women in the process of development, when he started writing about it in the 1960s. His work, which concentrated upon inequalities in nutrition, schooling and the allocation of resources within a family, received what he found to be a surprisingly high level of criticism at the time from other social scientists. Sen (1999) argued that the effect of low levels of development in a country affect women more strongly than they affect men. He believes that the root cause of this inequality to be that of culture: *'The idea of the self sacrificing woman has been so praised, idealised and idolised that out of desperation has been created a heroism that doesn't serve the interests of women very much.'*

He demonstrated that in countries in which women were more independent and had more control over resources, more women survived for longer than in countries in which this was not the case. His work in this field reinforces his view that 'one does not have to be directly practical to be practical'. Following Sen's findings, international development policy was changed in some projects, which gave food to children rather than straight to the head of the household (to ensure that it was equally divided between the sexes in a household) and the employment of women outside the domestic environment was encouraged with the aim of increasing women's independence.

Freedom and development

Sen's work in this field built upon Paul Streeten's work, carried out in the 1970s and 80s which put forward the 'basic needs perspective'. This standpoint encouraged the provision of 'basic needs' to all in society.

Realising the limitation that this theory imposed, for example, the difficulty in determining the needs which should be considered basic and those which should not, Sen expanded it by developing what became known as the 'capability approach'. The clever twist to this approach is that goods are important, not because of the value of the good itself but the 'capability' that owning the product involves. Sen famously uses the example of a bicycle which not only bestows upon the rider the utility of owning the bike, but also gives the owner the *capability* of riding from A to B. The insightfulness of this approach rests in the fact that while the capability aspect is 'absolute', the goods required to achieve it may be relative. Robin Hahnel (2002) in his analysis of Sen's work makes this point nicely, when he states *'Clothes are important both because they protect people from the cold or heat – basic needs – and for reasons of self respect and social respect. For this reason it may require more expensive clothes for someone living in*

Beverly Hills to have the "capability of being respected" than for someone in Bangladesh'. *Development as Freedom* further extends this approach, in that an increase in people's capabilities increases their degree of freedom. Sen then links freedom as synonymous with development. In this analysis, increases in people's capabilities increase their degree of freedom and hence furthers the development process.

Sen argues (1999) that *'development requires the removal of major sources of unfreedom: poverty as well as tyranny, poor economic opportunities as well as systematic social deprivation, neglect of public facilities as well as intolerance or overactivity of repressive states'.* He believes that these development opportunities are denied to many because: *'despite unprecedented increases in overall opulence, the contemporary world denies elementary freedoms to a vast number – perhaps even the majority – of people.'* Some of this 'unfreedom' relates directly to *economic poverty*, in other cases to the *lack of public facilities and social care*. In still other cases it relates to the *denial of political and civil liberties* by authoritarian regimes.

Conclusion

Sen's years spent on a university campus have not been wasted. The work that he has done transcends the advancement that he has made to economic theory in benefiting the lives of people living in the 'real world' showing that economics is indeed a truly practical science. The great moral depth and variety of his work is a testament to his biography and his ability to see the real issues facing us, from behind the walls of the university campus.

 Further Reading

HAHNEL, R. (2002) Amartya Sen, The late twentieth century's greatest political economist? In D. Dowd (ed.), *Understanding capitalism, critical analysis.* Pluto Press.

LLOYD, P. (2001) Amartya Sen, Nobel Laureate. *General Studies Review.*

MCCLOSKEY, D. (2000) The career courage of Amartya Sen, in *How to be human, though an economist.* University of Michigan, also in *The Eastern Economic Journal,* 1999.

SEN, A. (1977) Rational fools: a critique of the behavioural foundations of economic theory. *Philosophy and Public Affairs,* Summer, 317–344.

SEN, A. (1981) *Poverty and famines: an essay on entitlement and deprivation.* Oxford University Press.

SEN, A. (1990) Gender and cooperative conflict, in I. Tinker (ed.), *Persistent inequalities.* Oxford University Press, 123–149.

SEN, A. (1997) *On economic inequality.* Clarendon Press.

SEN, A. (1998a) *Reason before identity.* Oxford University Press.

SEN, A. (1998b) *The possibility of social choice.* Reprint from Les Prix Nobel.

SEN, A. (1999) *Development as freedom.* Oxford University Press.

SEN, A. (2002) Interview by D. Dransfield.

Anthony Giddens

(1934–)

SINCE 1997 ANTHONY GIDDENS HAS BEEN THE DIRECTOR OF THE LONDON SCHOOL OF Economics, and is arguably one of the most influential academics in the world today. He popularised the phrase 'The Third Way' and has had a significant influence on the Blair Governments in Britain and on the Clinton–Gore Administrations in the USA. It is difficult to think of an academic who has had a closer link to any British Government.

While the origin of the term 'Third Way' has been used for a long time by social scientists, Giddens (1998a) has re-engineered the term to apply it to a possible agenda for social democratic parties today. He uses the term to refer to *'a framework of thinking and policy-making that seeks to adapt social democracy to a world which has changed fundamentally over the past two or three decades. It is a third way in the sense that it is an attempt to transcend both old style social democracy and neo-liberalism'*.

Although Giddens (1998a) focuses chiefly on the British situation he sees the agenda of the Third Way as having much wider implications than just the British or the Labour Party context, stating that *'I would like to think New Labour is pioneering an agenda that relates to all the changes we've been talking about. One shouldn't see this in too parochial a way – all ex-socialist parties, and parties of other political complexions too for that matter, are wrestling with these problems'*.

The Third Way provides an alternative way of organising economies, based on a belief that it is time to put an end to the 'class politics' of the past, and that it is possible to combine the market with governments' steering influence, in a democratic society in which people are committed to shared community goals.

Giddens' *The Third Way* (1998a) identifies reasons why socialism and neoliberal economics have both failed, providing an opportunity for a new type of consensus. In explaining why socialism failed to have relevance he states that: *'In hindsight, we can be fairly clear why the Soviet Union, far from surpassing the US, fell dramatically behind it, and why social democracy encountered its own crises. The economic theory of socialism was always inadequate, underestimating the capacity of capitalism to innovate, adapt and generate increasing productivity. Socialism also failed to grasp the significance of markets as informational devices, providing essential data for buyers and sellers. These inadequacies only became fully revealed with intensifying processes of globalisation and technological change from the early 1970s onwards.'*

In explaining the failure of neoliberal economics Giddens identifies a basic tension between old-fashioned Conservatism with it cautious and pragmatic view of the need for change, and modern free market philosophies which pin 'hopes for the future on unending economic growth produced by the liberation of market forces.' He argues that the permanent revolution of market change undermines traditional institutions and patterns within society, destroying the bonds that hold societies together.

Giddens has sought to create a new agenda for social democratic states based on a framework of individual responsibility for society, and the community for the individual – this is generally characterised as the Third Way.

In the new democratic state, all members of society are expected to play a part and to take responsibility for their own actions.

The aim is to create a new economic and social synthesis, avoiding the dependency culture created by the Old Left and the doctrinaire belief in market forces of the New Right. The table below shows how the Third Way lies between the social democratic state of the old left, and neoliberalism as characterised by the Thatcher and Major years (1979–97).

	Social Democracy (Old Left)	Third Way (Centre-Left)	Neoliberalism (New Right)
Political philosophy	Class politics of the left	Modernising movement of the centre	Class politics of the right
Economic philosophy	Old mixed economy	New mixed economy	Market fundamentalism
Government philosophy	State dominating society	New democratic state	Minimal state
Welfare policy	Strong welfare state	Social investment state	Welfare safety net

Giddens is a firm believer in democracy, arguing that an important precept in modern society should be 'no authority without democracy'. He believes that in a society in which tradition and custom are losing hold, that the best way to recreate authority is through democracy, so that citizens take responsibility for the societies in which they live. This concept has been very important in shaping the ideas of Tony Blair.

What Blair takes from Giddens' work is the idea that every individual is a 'human agent' – a person with the ability to make choices. Human agents also have the ability to make a difference in the world, we don't have to be pushed about by forces outside of our control and we need not be dependent. Hence, people should not be reliant upon the state, but upon their own strengths and abilities. As individual human agents we can choose to do good or evil, and we are always responsible for our own actions, although there may be unforeseen consequences of our actions. Blair also accepts the Giddens' idea of 'life politics' – a politics of individual self-realisation. Individuals should be free to lead their lives however they wish, free from discrimination, and in return they must similarly be tolerant towards others. For Giddens the modern state is a 'social investment state' which should enable the human agents to make the very best use of their skills and abilities, and ensure that potentially able people do not become excluded, but make a full and active contribution to the community. Groups that have traditionally been excluded consist of ethnic minorities, women, lesbian and gay people, the disabled, the lower working class, the over 50s and lone parents.

Hence the Blair government have introduced 'New Deals' for these people, to give them every possible opportunity to become fully included within the community. Complementing this new vision is a social investment state that enables traditionally excluded groups to become included. For example, government should invest in projects to get the long-term unemployed back to work, invest in retraining tradition-ally excluded groups etc. However, there are certain lifestyles which the state may be tolerant towards, but which it is unwilling to fund. For example, people who choose not to work for a living should be allowed to do so, however, they will not be allowed to make use of the social security system to fund their chosen lifestyle.

A reflective analysis of Giddens' ideas shows that they are highly relevant to modern economic thinking because they provide an alternative agenda for shaping institutions and relations in our contemporary 'Third Way' economy. These institutional relation-ships are clearly at odds with those previously advocated in Thatcher's Britain.

One of the central themes running through the work of Giddens, is to move away from 'dualism' which separates the individual person (human agent) on the one hand and the society or social structure on the other. Giddens seeks to bring together grand theories of how society works with micro theories of what motivates individual social action. He attempts this synthesis of theories with a concept called 'structuration', in which individuals are in a constant process of creation and recreation of social life and social structure.

Giddens' theory of structuration has been used by the Blair Government to understand the nature of the market. Markets (and other social institutions) have 'structural properties' which are formed by individual people exercising their ability to make choices. The structure of the market and changes in this structure arise from and are an outcome of human agents choosing to participate in the market place in a partic-ular fashion (for example, one choice might be to compete with each other in a harmful way, while another might be to cooperate in mutually beneficial ways). The Blair government's preferred model for individuals to structure society is on the basis of shared values and endeavours, a process known as 'communitarianism'.

Giddens has written over thirty books, was the founder of Polity Press, and as we shall now explore, he has made a significant contribution to the development of social theory. In this chapter we shall outline how Giddens' ideas developed from the end of the 1970s to the present; by the end of the chapter you should be in a position to see how the Blair Government has drawn upon a range of Giddens' abstract ideas and applied them to a range of economic and social policy areas.

Methodology

ALTHOUGH HE HAS WRITTEN OVER THIRTY BOOKS, GIDDENS HIMSELF DOES NOT GATHER empirical data, rather he uses forms of 'documentary research' – systematically drawing upon other people's writing and research. Such forms of secondary analysis are useful to the researcher in saving time, money, gaining access to groups of people who may otherwise be inaccessible, and the data is often of a higher quality than the researchers could gather themselves, for example because it is longitudinal in nature (having been gathered over many years, such as Granada Television's '7 Up' survey following a group of people at age 7, 14, 21, etc.). Giddens (1989) is very keen to argue that documentary research is not an 'also ran' among research methods: *'Documentary research, in one guise or another, is in fact one of the most widely used of all methods of gathering sociological data.'*

Nicky Gregson (1989) has argued that each study that Giddens draws upon is used to highlight a specific theoretical point that Giddens makes. For example, Paul Willis' (1977) study of the working class 'lads' subculture in a secondary modern school was used by Giddens to highlight the 'strategic conduct' of human agents in a process of structuration, which we shall discuss below.

ANTHONY GIDDENS WAS BORN IN EDMONTON IN NORTH LONDON AND AFTER HIS parents moved to Palmers Green, he went to Minchenden Grammar School in Southgate. However, Giddens has described himself as 'hardly a model pupil or star performer' – he apparently had little interest in 'school subjects' and disliked the discipline of the grammar school. Giddens' family history is typical of many young Britons growing up in the 1950s and 60s who were able to develop broader horizons and aspirations than their parents' generation. New educational and career opportunities developed in the new Keynesian era of the post-war world. Parents had higher aspirations for their children than they had had for themselves.

Giddens' father was a clerical worker for London Transport, working in the office that dealt with the refurbishment of carriages on the tube. His mother was a housewife, who stopped working when she got married, and looked after Anthony and his younger brother. Giddens' brother, who is ten years younger that Anthony, now lives in Los Angeles and makes television commercials. From 1956 until 1959 Giddens was a student at Hull University studying sociology and psychology. During his time at Hull Giddens was inspired by the teaching of Peter Worsley. Worsley's passion for sociology made a great impression on Giddens. It also appears to be the case that the sense of solidarity within East Yorkshire's fishing community had a lasting effect on Giddens; as we shall see below, there is a 'communitarian' strand within the work of Giddens which is central to Third Way politics.

Anthony Giddens was the first person in his family to attend university and graduated with a first-class honours degree. Following his time at Hull, Giddens moved on to the London School of Economics to read for an MA. Giddens' dissertation was on the issue of 'Sport and Society in Contemporary England' and his initial supervisor was David Lockwood (a sociologist whose research into changing social relations in contemporary Britain identified a tendency for increasing numbers of people to develop middle class aspirations. Lockwood showed that the old class divisions between capital and labour were being eroded).

Between 1961 and 1970 Giddens was lecturer in sociology at Leicester University. At this time the sociology department at Leicester was the largest in the country, outside of London. The department was dominated by continental social theorists, notably Norbert Elias and Ilya Neustadt. Former Leicester students of Giddens, such as Wes Sharrock, describe how he appeared to have read everything and generated great enthusiasm. Giddens has said that it was at this time that he decided to have an academic career. In 1970 Giddens left Leicester to take up a post at Cambridge University, first as a lecturer and later as a Reader (1984–86) and then as a Professor (1986–97) before he finally became Director of the LSE in 1997.

Giddens' personal history provides an interesting insight to the Third Way. He was born into a generation in which the educational ladder provided greater opportunities to children born into working class backgrounds. Success at university then provided better access to middle-class occupations, higher incomes, and more influence in society.

Based on his own experience, Giddens is committed to developing an 'inclusive society' which 'includes in' *all* members of society. As a student of sociology and politics Giddens developed important insights into the bonds that hold members of communities together, the importance of opportunity in motivating individuals to commit themselves to each other. Living through the Thatcher years he was also able to develop a critique of a model of society based on individualism and self-interest.

Key works

The Constitution of Society (1984)

Beyond Left and Right (1994)

The Third Way (1998a)

Self and social structure

According to Giddens, individual 'human agents' make choices and take actions that are influenced by their self-identity. Individuals interact with the society in which they live.

Many social scientists regard social *structure* as a durable framework, rather like the metal girders within a concrete building. It constrains our behaviour, it is beyond our control and it is out of sight. In contrast, for Giddens *structure* is always both enabling and constraining, it is shaped by social systems and gives shape to social systems. These structures are reproduced *'through the regularized conduct of knowledgeable agents'* (Giddens 1984). For example, I interact in particular ways with people at work because I have learnt over time to interact in these ways. 'Structure', according to Giddens, helps us to solve the problem of getting from one event to the next. But, as individuals we create new structures as well as being constrained by existing structures. As individuals we therefore help to shape the communities in which we live as well as being shaped by these communities.

Class structuration

Giddens points to the class structure as being representative of structures in society. As individuals we are not only shaped by the existing class structure, we can help to create and recreate the class structure over time. Parents can pass on the cultural capital of their class to their children, for example, through middle-class parents buying extra books and paying for extra classes for their children. Because some children have greater access to the sort of cultural capital that benefits them in the education system (and other parts of the social system) this gives them advantages. However, individuals do not have to passively adopt class structures, they can help to reshape them – for example, in the case of working-class parents providing greater access to educational resources for their children. The state can also alter the class structure by providing greater opportunities for everyone (e.g. through policies of inclusion).

Individualism

Giddens identifies collectivism as being one of the traditional characteristics of social democratic countries. However, since the 1970s he sees this tendency as having gone into reverse. He seeks to find explanations for this reversal pointing to the development of cultural pluralism in Western countries, and a proliferation of lifestyles as being important features of this trend. He sees this plurality as resulting in some measure from the affluence resulting from the welfare state.

Social democratic movements have found it difficult to cope with rising individualism and lifestyle diversity. In his view social democrats were not sure how much of this individualism is a product of *'self-seeking individualism portrayed in neoliberal economic theory'* (Giddens 1994).

Social democratic parties therefore need to ask questions about this new individualism such as *'What exactly is the new individualism? How does it relate to the expanding role now played by markets? Are we witnessing the rise of a "me" generation, resulting in a "me-first" society which inevitably destroys common values and public concerns?'* (Giddens 1998a).

However, Giddens' (1998a) analysis suggests that we should not be so frightened of individualism. It does not necessarily represent moral decay. He states that *'surveys show that younger generations today are sensitised to a greater range of moral concerns than previous generations were. They do not however, relate these values to tradition, or accept traditional forms of authority as legislating on questions of lifestyle.'*

He sees individualism as being a result of the retreat of tradition from our lives, and in part the result of globalisation. In addition the welfare state has helped to liberate people.

We should therefore see the current age as one of 'moral transition'. What we have to do today is to build on this new form of individualism to create solidarity within communities (rather than fragmentation). This is a challenge for the Third Way. He states (1998a) that '*we have to make our lives in a more active way than was true of previous generations, and we need more actively to accept responsibilities for the consequences of what we do and the lifestyle habits we adopt.*'

Globalisation?

Giddens identifies globalisation as one of the key processes transforming lives and relationships in the modern world. He sees globalisation (1998a) as '*not only, or even primarily, about economic interdependence, but about the transformation of time and space in our lives. Distant events, whether economic or not, affect us more directly and immediately than ever before. Conversely, decisions we take as individuals are often global in their implications. The dietary habits individuals have, for example, are consequential for food producers, who might live on the other side of the world.*' Here Giddens is returning to his theme of the two-way relationship between the individual and social structures.

He sees the communications revolution and the spread of information technology as a key process in intensifying the globalisation process. He sees the most important change as '*the expanded role of world financial markets, increasingly operating on a real-time basis.*'

Inevitably, in a globalising world some of the powers of the state are being eroded, including those of Keynesian economic management. Globalisation is changing the shape of the nation state as new economic areas and alliances are created, although local, regional and national cultures are still important.

Giddens sees globalisation as having a direct relevance to the 'new individualism' that figures large in social democratic debates. He argues that in a world in which traditional bonds are breaking down and in which individuals are increasingly mobile and treated as individuals rather than part of a group, then these individuals need to reconstitute themselves as part of society, rather than as atomised Thatcherite self-focused individuals. Although globalisation is breaking up traditional societies, we can respond to this in a responsible way, by using our individuality to build new democracies based on community values. Globalisation and the changes that it creates are a fact of life; it is the way that we respond to globalisation, that will determine the sorts of communities we build in the future.

Third Way values

Giddens (1998a) is in favour of restructuring society on a totally democratic basis – he says that '*democracy can never be partial*'. He argues that in a society where tradition and custom are losing their hold, as a result of globalisation and other forces, then the only way to restore authority is through democracy. New individualism requires that we recast authority '*on an active or participatory basis*'. He establishes what he considers to be a radical agenda for our society based on a '*new relationship between the individual and the community*' that is based on a '*redefinition of rights and obligations*' which he refers to as a new politics with the motto '*no rights without responsibilities*'.

These responsibilities are not just from the government to its citizens, but by citizens to governments: '*Unemployment benefits, for example, should carry the obligation to look actively for work, and it is up to governments to ensure that welfare systems do not discourage active search*' (Giddens 1998a).

Giddens (1998a) sets out a list of Third Way values:

- Equality
- Protection of the vulnerable
- Freedom as autonomy
- No rights without responsibilities
- No authority without democracy
- Cosmopolitan pluralism
- Philosophic conservatism.

Conclusion

Giddens' work is of particular importance to economists at the start of the twenty-first century. His views on the nature of social relationships between the individual and society have helped to shape the politics and hence economics of the Third Way. Giddens has shown that individuals help to shape social change, and that they can do this in a way that is based on social responsibility rather than individual greed. Giddens has developed a picture of participatory democracy in a world characterised by globalising forces that have broken down old systems of authority. He identifies ways in which governments can help to create the structures and incentives which encourage individuals to act in a communitarian way. The actions of individuals then help to reshape the social institutions within which economic decisions are made. He has sought to develop a new social, political and economic theory for social democracies in societies where the old structures, rules and systems of socialism and neoliberalism no longer provided effective working models for societies.

 **Further Reading**

BEST, S. (1997) Agency and structure in the writings of Anthony Giddens. *The Social Science Teacher*, 26, 250–300.

CRAIB, I. (1992) *Anthony Giddens*. Routledge.

GIDDENS, A. (1984) *The constitution of society*. Polity Press.

GIDDENS, A. (1989) *Sociology*. Polity Press.

GIDDENS, A. (1994) *Beyond left and right*. Polity Press.

GIDDENS, A. (1998a) *The Third Way*. Polity Press.

GIDDENS, A. (1998b) After the left's paralysis. *New Statesman and Society*, 1 May.

GIDDENS, A. (1998c) Risk society: the context of British politics, in J. Franklin (ed.) *The politics of the risk society*. Polity Press.

GIDDENS, A. AND PIERSON, C. (2000) *Conversations with Anthony Giddens: making sense of modernity*. Polity Press.

GREGSON, N. (1989) *The casualties of Thatcherism.* University of Newcastle-upon-Tyne.

HUTTON, W. AND GIDDENS, A. (2000) *On the edge: living with global capitalism.* Jonathan Cape.

WILLIS, P. (1977) *Learning to Labour: How working class children get working class jobs.* Saxon House.

José Bové

(1954–)

JOSÉ BOVÉ IS ONE OF THE MOST WIDELY RECOGNISED MEMBERS OF THE ANTI-globalisation protest movement in the world today. He came to the attention of the world's media when he led some of his Farmers' Confederation followers on an attack on a McDonald's under construction in the southern French town of Millau, on 11 August 1999.

Initially Bové was involved in local issues protesting against the powers of the state in France, particularly in relation to the local economy and the procurement of agricultural land for a military camp. This then developed into a fight against globalisation in the form of the American multinational McDonald's. Bové has increasingly fought the issue of globalisation on a global stage through the world's media. In 1999 he acted as a spokesperson for the anti-globalisation protest at the meeting of the World Trade Organisation in Seattle. In January 2001 he led an invasion of 1,300 Brazilian farmers of plantations run by the American biotechnology firm Monsanto. The protestors uprooted genetically modified corn and soya bean plants, burned seeds and destroyed documents in the company's offices. In June 2001 Bové demonstrated with around 100 Palestinians, Israeli pacifists and Americans in the West Bank town of Al-Khader, outside of Bethlehem to denounce Jewish settlement in the area.

In June 2002, *The Independent* newspaper reported that *'The French small farmers' leader and anti-globalisation campaigner José Bové went to prison in style yesterday.*

Amid a media caravan reminiscent of a slow-motion Tour de France, he drove the first tractor in a procession from his farm near Millau in the southern hills of the Massif Central to a jail near Montpellier, 60 miles away.

At the end of a seven-hour journey, punctuated with political demonstrations and media declarations, Bové gave himself up to the prison authorities. He has to serve a much delayed three-month sentence for organising the destruction by 200 sheep farmers using sledge-hammers and crowbars of a half-built McDonald's restaurant in Millau three years ago.'

Bové is representative of a number of other individuals from across the world who have found that their concern for local issues has developed much wider significance when they have realised that their predicament is shared by countless millions of others across the globe. Bové has always been involved in the politics of the left, and with agriculture-related issues. Today he is a global campaigner for the rights of the individual against the corporation, for the small farmer against big business and state coercion.

B OVÉ'S THINKING AND ACTIVISM IS BASED ON AN ANALYSIS OF SOCIAL RELATIONS within the economy that he is part of. Initially his thinking was focused on the issue of conscientious objection to the French military and to the growing power of technology in shaping society. His ongoing critique of capitalism is based on his life experience of working in a local agricultural community that is threatened by the development of the power of the state, the power of multinational corporations, the logic of modern technology, and global capitalism. His approach is to focus on issues of concern to local communities and then to examine these in relation to wider global forces. By taking direct action he is able to focus on the powers of the ordinary people in challenging the forces of technology and global capitalism. The heart of his approach is to identify popular issues and to expose the contradictions in the relationship between human and technological development.

He explains how social awareness develops in the following way: *'These days, in our post-industrial society, social awareness against alienation is more likely to come from thinking things through than from experience of more traditional overt exploitation'* (Bové and Dufour 2002).

J OSÉ BOVÉ WAS BORN IN BORDEAUX. BOTH OF HIS PARENTS WERE AGRICULTURAL researchers, working on diseases in fruit trees. The family moved around quite a lot during his early years, including time spent in Berkeley in the United States.

Bové had only just started secondary school at the time of the 1968 protest movements by students and trade unionists in France. He was aware of the atmosphere of turbulence and pressure for social change but did not get involved in radical politics until he was 17. Initially his chief concern was with opposition to military service – 'for the rights of conscientious objectors and deserters.' He was involved in a support group, for individuals who wanted to avoid military service and for soldiers who appeared in front of military tribunals.

After completing his baccalaureate he decided to get more involved in work with other conscientious objectors although he did spend some time studying at Bordeaux University. At university he was influenced by the ideas of Social Sciences Professor Jacques Ellul, who explained that technology had a logic of its own and that the state and the economy are both servants of technology rather than its master. During his formative years he was captivated by the writing of anarchist writers including Bakunin, Kropotkin and Proudhon, as well as by the tales of anarchists living in Bordeaux who had fought against the fascists in the Spanish civil war. He was also influenced by the civil rights movement and non-violent approaches to civil disturbance as exemplified by the life and work of Martin Luther King, and César Chávez – the Mexican farm worker who had organised groups of Latino grape pickers in California – as well as the example set by Gandhi in South Africa and India.

In the early 1970s Bové met Alice Monier, a politics undergraduate who shared the same radical ideals, and the two worked closely in partnership for the next 30 years.

At this time a number of small farmers on the Larzac plateau in France had contacted Bové's anti-military group seeking support in fighting against the expansion of the military base in the area from 3,000 to 17,000 hectares. An international support network was established, made up of resistance groups in Germany, Britain and elsewhere and over 200 such committees in France. The French military had managed to secure permission to develop their Larzac camp which would involve the eviction of local farmers from their traditional lands. At Easter 1972 a mass protest was arranged congregating at Rodez in support of 103 farmers threatened with eviction.

The military had managed to secure a legal injunction preventing any new building in the area designated as a military base. The protestors therefore decided to build a traditional stone barn right in the centre of the military zone as a symbol of rural values and resistance. Thousands of volunteers were involved in the construction of the barn over a two-year period.

The protest movement in the early 70s involved a broad alliance of groups that were disaffected with the way society was being dominated by large organisations including 'angry farmers, strikers from the occupied Lip watch factory, conscientious objectors, protesting prisoners, feminists, local militants and a good section of the far left, including the radical wing of the French Socialist Party' (Bové, 2002). Involvement in this movement helped to further radicalise Bové and Monier and showed them how organised protest could have an impact which went well beyond the local area. It also provided a base for the fermentation of a new radical anti-globalisation agenda based on the traditional values of the Larzac plateau.

In 1974 Bové was conscripted to the army and refused the right to be designated as a conscientious objector. He therefore went into hiding while trying to avoid prison, and spent a year hiding out on a farm, developing a better understanding of sustainable farming methods.

During this period Bové began to learn traditional farming methods – how to milk ewes, how to make cheese, and other important skills. The Larzac group then decided that the next stage would be to squat on land which made up the military base. José, Alice and others were encouraged to squat on farmland at Montredon on the military base belonging to a farmer in the neighbouring valley; they were offered 100 ewes and provided with a tractor bought with the help of the Larzac committee.

In the following years Bové was involved in a series of resistance actions against the military leading to a number of short prison sentences. The Larzac resistance movement was built on an alliance between local farmers and outside activists who came into the region and worked on communal farms, particularly specialising in raising ewes for their milk which goes into Roquefort cheese.

In the early 80s the Mitterand (socialist) government was elected in France which cancelled the extension to the military camp – 6,300 hectares of land became available which was not bought back by its previous owners. A legal agreement was therefore made with the government to buy the land for an agricultural collective. Bové describes the 1980s as a period of consolidation for those involved in the Larzac movement: 'On the Larzac plateau, after our victory against the army in 81, we started organising for self-management of the land, bringing in young people to farm, taking up the question of Roquefort and intensive farming, fighting for the rights of small producers, building up the trade-union networks that eventually came together in the Confédération Paysanne' (Bové and Dufour 2002).

Bové has continued to be involved in high-profile activities, such as organising the ploughing of the park beneath the Eiffel Tower to protest against European Union farm policies. In 1995, he was part of the crew of the Greenpeace ship *Rainbow Warrior* protesting against France's resumption of nuclear tests in the South Pacific. In 1998 he was arrested and convicted for destroying a consignment of genetically modified maize.

However, his 'finest hour' came with the dismantling by Bové and the Confédération Paysanne of the McDonald's at Millau in response to the tariff placed on French cheese (including Roquefort) by the United States because the French had refused to allow hormone treated beef to be imported from the USA. For Bové it was a form of natural justice to strike back at McDonald's as a symbol of *malbouffe* (bad food).

Bové (2001) described the protest in the following way: 'We wanted to do this protest in broad daylight, with a large group of people, a non-violent action, but symbolically very strong, and up front with the authorities. We were careful to explain ahead of time to the police that our objective was to dismantle the McDonald's. They informed their superiors and the police chief. Then an officer from the police department called us to say that he was going to ask the manager at McDonalds for a sign of some kind so we could destroy that, that it be more symbolic. We told him: "Are you kidding? That's nuts. We're going to dismantle the doors and windows." . . . The protest went along and everybody, including the kids, helped dismantle the interior of the building; partitions, some doors, electrical outlets, and sheet metal on the roof that was nailed down but which came up easily, because it was part of a kit, decorative stuff. It was really a light weight piece of construction the whole place . . . Everything was put into two tractor wagons, while some people repainted the roof of the restaurant . . . we took off in a parade to police headquarters in Millau . . . We unloaded the wagons in front of the police station.'

After the action, McDonald's filed a complaint and Bové and four others were placed in jail. During the period of imprisonment the campaign received letters of support and money from all over the world, including the United States.

Bové saw the protest as being essentially part of an anti-globalisation movement and was at pains to state that attacking McDonald's should not be seen as anti-American. He sees the struggle as being against *'free trade global capitalism'*.

Bové next appeared at Seattle as part of a mass protest against the World Trade Organisation, and in the following year in Brazil and Mexico as part of a Zapatista protest against global capitalism. In the following April he protested in Quebec City at the Summit of the Americas Conference that was seeking to unify some of the largest countries in the world into a giant free trade zone. He continues to campaign against globalisation.

Key works

The World Is Not For Sale – Farmers Against Junk Food (with François Dufour, 2002)

Organisation of the Confédération Paysanne

Bové's ideas are closely tied up with his actions. In 1987 he established the Confédération Paysanne, a group made up of small peasant farmers in France. This group feel that they are exploited in a European system which favours large agricultural combines and multinational agro-chemical companies. Multinationals that dominate agricultural production focus on an intensive mass-production farming system which is capital intensive. The small producer is squeezed on all sides – by the banks, companies who buy agricultural produce, and the firms who supply the farmers with fertilisers, seeds and equipment. The emphasis in agriculture is on producing high volumes of crops for export onto global markets. In such a market place the smaller farmer has little influence, and is unable to compete fairly. The Confédération Paysanne is committed to the development of forms of sustainable agriculture 'which respect the need for environmental protection, for healthy food, for labour rights'. It is not limited just to farmers using organic methods. As well as acting as a pressure group the Confédération is a political force with over 40,000 members and a growing influence in agricultural politics in France.

Technology stripping meaning from life

Bové values life as represented in the culture of the individual and the community. He sees this as a culture based on sharing and personal values. He sees traditional bonds between people as being represented by families enjoying meals together. This, in his view, is becoming less and less common, as the pressures of modern life lead to the consumption of junk food, and convenience food, as individuals become atomised and spend more time simply watching television removed from each other. He argues (2002) that the traditional mealtime which involved conviviality and sharing is disappearing. *'This change is due to the pressures of contemporary culture at work and during leisure time. It's also a symptom of the vacuity of much of modern life. Similar points can be made about birth and death. Death is no longer confronted, and the dying are no longer welcome at home but are sent to nursing homes or hospices. In fact, our deaths like our food, have become standardised. It's the same with medical intervention at birth. Technology is stripping meaning from all of life's activities.'*

The primacy of politics

Bové sees neoliberal economics as being one of the root causes of problems in the world today with its emphasis on free trade, and capitalist growth models.

He argues that the real issues facing global citizens today relate to 'health, education, culture, food'. Today these things are in danger as simply being seen as commodities.

He gives the example of medicines that could be used to eradicate certain diseases in Africa. However, these medicines are not supplied (or not in sufficient quantities) because they are too expensive on the open market, particularly in the case of proprietary drugs. He states (2001) that *'Waves of opposition to this commodification can be felt from all corners of the world, calling for a return to the primacy of politics over capitalist economics.'* He sees the free market as one that fails to understand and meet the needs of ordinary people.

Popular protest

José Bové believes that pressure for change should come from the life experience of views of ordinary people rather than through sets of neatly constructed ideological theories. In *The World is Not For Sale* (2002) he states that *'There are no preconceived ideas. Those days have gone – thank goodness – when popular movements were slotted into theoretical constructs. Seattle showed the opposite. People came together not with any worked-out theory, but to take action. From wherever they came they brought their experiences and points of view, often finding common ground. For far too long, theories and analyses have been shuffled around, promising change. People today have lost confidence in these theories. Seattle revealed the existence of an informal worldwide network. There were no red flags in Seattle, no portraits of Che, no ideas of socialism in one country; that's all finished.'*

The World is Not For Sale

At a meeting in Millau on 30 June 2000, Bové told a mass audience of supporters that: *'If, today, we are able to say no to being seen as a commodity, it's all because of you.'* He went on to send a message to the French President (Chirac) that his Farmers' Confederation *'will not accept the selling of citizens' rights to the multinationals or the WTO. We are here to resist, to construct, to reclaim power at the base, and not let ourselves be manipulated by the world's powerful people.'*

Bové believes that free trade in agriculture has helped to destroy the power of small farmers and made them subservient to giant capitalist agribusinesses who are shaping the worlds' food production to meet their own requirements. In 1986 food and agriculture were brought into the General Agreement on Tariffs and Trade process, bringing these industries into the control of neoliberal regimes. Countries could no longer choose their own food policies. Signatories to the agreement had to lower tariffs and increase their imports of foodstuffs principally from the European Union and the USA (which produce over 80 per cent of the worlds' food exports). This process was extended still further through the Marrakesh Agreement in 1994 that set up the World Trade Organisation. Today individual states are only permitted to prevent the import of agricultural or food produce on health grounds.

The biggest losers from the opening up of free trade in agriculture and food according to Bové are the countries of the poor South, whose subsistence agriculture has been threatened by free trade. Bové (2001) cites the examples of South Korea and the Philippines which *'used to be self sufficient in rice production. Now they're compelled to import lower-grade rice at a cheaper price than the local crops, decimating their own paddy production. India and Pakistan are being forced to import textile fibres, which is having a devastating effect on small cotton farmers. In Brazil – a major agricultural exporter – a growing percentage of the population is suffering from actual malnutrition.*

The multinationals are taking over, denying large numbers of farming families access to the land and the possibility of feeding themselves.'

Alternative institutions for world trading

Bové would like to see an alternative framework for organising world trading relationships, involving the following ingredients:

1. The right of countries to impose their own tariffs, in order to create agriculture and food production focused on meeting local needs, and creating an appropriate balance between rural and urban areas.

2. The prevention of giant multinational food producers from 'dumping' cheap produce in the markets of poorer countries to destroy local agriculture. Bové argues that the multinationals flood local markets with cheap subsidised foodstuffs at a very low cost to drive local producers out of business. Once they have severely reduced local competition they start to raise their own prices of food products. He sees the abolition of export aid (subsidies) as the first step in creating fairer trading relations.

3. The abolition of the right of multinationals to place patents on living things which Bové calls 'bio-piracy'. He argues that patents are supposed to protect the development of new techniques rather than natural resources. He sees the multinationals' development of genetic modification as an attack on bio-diversity. Over time, for example, 140,000 types of rice have been developed across the world – the multinationals seek to replace this diversity with their own standardised GM versions of rice. He states (2002) that: *'The food companies are working on five or six strains, genetically modified for intensive, low-labour cultivation, and imposing them in areas of traditional subsistence farming. In some Asian countries – the Philippines and China are the worst cases – these half-dozen varieties now cover two-thirds of rice-growing land.*

Critique of *malbouffe*

Bové sees the spread of *malbouffe* as being representative of the spread of globalised mass production technology leading to lowering of standards, and the erosion of quality experiences based on local traditions. The nearest English translation of *malbouffe* is junkfood – although at the original protest at Millau, Bové referred to 'shit food'.

He states that *'For me the term means both the standardisation of food like McDonald's – the same taste from one end of the world to the other – and the choice of food associated with the use of hormones and GMOs, as well as the residues of pesticides and other things that can endanger health. So there's a cultural and a health aspect. Junk food also involves industrialised agriculture – that is to say, mass produced food; not necessarily in the form of products sold by McDonald's, but mass produced in the sense of industrialised pig rearing, battery chickens, and the like'* (Bové and Dufour 2002).

Bové believes that agro-business got a major boost under Margaret Thatcher with privatisation and the lack of government controls, eventually resulting in foot-and-mouth and mad cow disease. He argues that one of the major problems is the domination of agricultural research by the multinationals who have a vested interest and are mainly concerned with profits. He calls for more independence in research, for example in organic farming, and farming that is based on meeting local needs.

He sees the development of free trade areas as a major threat to sustainable agriculture because of the emphasis in these areas of producing agricultural products in bulk for the export market. For example, he is concerned that Eastern European producers will increasingly tailor their production to the requirements of the mass market, rather than concentrating on their own local markets.

At the same time the small-scale farmer in Europe and America finds it very difficult to survive because mass production drives down prices. The peasant farmer with a small flock of goats, sheep or cows, simply can't compete, and the subsidies they receive are much smaller than those going to giant agro-business combines.

Conclusion

José Bové presents a concerted attack on the powers of new technology to shape the relationships between man and nature, and the state and the individual. He is opposed to neoliberal assumptions about the nature of development and through radical politics seeks to create an alternative agenda based on identifying local needs, and through popular non-violent protest to arrive at new ways of making decisions in society. He is not opposed to globalisation but to capitalist globalisation. He is in favour of individuals from across the globe working together for a common humanity based on meeting local needs, rather than the standardisation that results from the logic of the uniformity of giant multinationals and low cost/high profits based technology.

Bové believes that a turning point for him and for many French people was the American boycott of Roquefort cheese. He says that this *'brought about a "déclic" – a wake-up call – that touched something in the French psyche as fears over BSE, GMOs and food safety were compounding longstanding uneases over the loss of French identity. Hormones versus Roquefort. You couldn't get a better contrast between local quality and globalisation. It took small farmers to get people to make the link between farming, food and international politics'* (Bové and Dufour 2002).

 Further Reading

BOVÉ, J. (2001) A farmer's international? An interview with José Bové. *New Left Review* 12, November–December.

BOVÉ, J. AND DUFOUR, F. (2002) *The world is not for sale: farmers against junk food.* Verso.

BREMNER, C. (2000) The new Asterix, French farmer now world leader against globalised, industrialised food. *The Times*, 25 October.

JEFFRIES, L. (2001) A world struggle is underway: an interview with José Bové. *Z magazine*, June.

LICHFIELD, J. (2002) José Bové goes to prison (very slowly). *The Independent*, 20 June.

Index